ROUTLEDGE LIBRARY EDITIONS:
REVOLUTION IN ENGLAND

Volume 1

A HISTORY OF POLITICAL THOUGHT IN THE ENGLISH REVOLUTION

A HISTORY OF POLITICAL THOUGHT IN THE ENGLISH REVOLUTION

PEREZ ZAGORIN

Routledge
Taylor & Francis Group

LONDON AND NEW YORK

First published in 1954 by Routledge & Kegan Paul Ltd

This edition first published in 2023
by Routledge
4 Park Square, Milton Park, Abingdon, Oxon OX14 4RN

and by Routledge
605 Third Avenue, New York, NY 10158

Routledge is an imprint of the Taylor & Francis Group, an informa business

© 1954

British Library Cataloguing in Publication Data
A catalogue record for this book is available from the British Library

ISBN: 978-1-032-47827-2 (Set)
ISBN: 978-1-032-46812-9 (Volume 1) (hbk)
ISBN: 978-1-032-46820-4 (Volume 1) (pbk)
ISBN: 978-1-003-38341-3 (Volume 1) (ebk)

DOI: 10.4324/9781003383413

Publisher's Note
The publisher has gone to great lengths to ensure the quality of this reprint but points out that some imperfections in the original copies may be apparent.

Disclaimer
The publisher has made every effort to trace copyright holders and would welcome correspondence from those they have been unable to trace.

PEREZ ZAGORIN

A HISTORY

OF

POLITICAL THOUGHT

IN

THE ENGLISH

REVOLUTION

ROUTLEDGE & KEGAN PAUL

First published in 1954
by Routledge & Kegan Paul Ltd
Broadway House, 68–74 Carter Lane
London EC4
Printed in Great Britain
by Latimer Trend & Co Ltd
Plymouth

PREFACE

IT WAS in the English revolution that modern democratic ideas began their great career. Developed amidst fierce controversy, they inspired their exponents to make unprecedented demands upon social life. In the course of the argument and struggle around these demands, the bounds of social life itself were widened. That is why England's revolution is a decisive fact in Western history.

In the following pages, we shall encounter the large range of political doctrines which played their part in the English revolution, particularly those which appeared between 1645, when the Levellers first seized upon the revolution's wider implications, and 1660, when Charles II was restored. These years form something of a unity, for it was approximately within their span that the magnificent ferment of ideas for which the age is memorable achieved definitive expression in a number of writings of permanent importance. For the first time since Richard Hooker, a body of political literature was produced which, as we can see in retrospect, at once placed its authors in the foremost rank of European political theorists. And yet, although the revolution is a period of the greatest accomplishment in political thought, this aspect of it has not been dealt with in all its fullness. Neither the special studies, nor even the more general works concerning some of the ideas of these years, have taken up all the important writers who were then active. A few of the latter remain all but unknown and are here discussed for the first time. Some of the principal conceptions and theorists, moreover, are not yet so well understood as they might be. This is true, for example, of the Leveller *Agreement of the People*, that earliest written constitution to be proposed in English history; it is certainly true of Hobbes. Indeed, concerning most of the major figures of the time, more remains to be learned if we are to gain a fuller comprehension of their work. It is this conviction, and the belief also in the desirability of having what has thus far been lacking, a general survey which would discuss analytically, and with reasonable completeness, the revolution's political thought, especially in its most splendid years, that have led me to undertake this book.

In mentioning the titles of seventeenth-century writings, I have usually given only the first part of the title, not the full one. Texts have been reproduced in their original spelling and punctuation, except where changes had to be made for the sake of intelligibility. When the day and month of a publication is stated, I have taken it either from printed evidence in the work itself, or from the MS. inscription in the copy in the Thomason Collection at the British Museum. The bookseller, George Thomason, who formed his great collection between 1640 and 1660, commonly inscribed on his books, pamphlets, and broadsides their date of acquisition; and as he most frequently obtained a writing on the day of publication or soon after, his date enables us to place the time of appearance with sufficient accuracy. In all cases, however, I have dated the year as beginning on January 1st, not, as was ordinarily reckoned in seventeenth-century England, on March 25th. For most of the seventeenth-century works mentioned, London is to be understood as the place of publication. Finally, the abbreviation, *D.N.B.*, signifies, of course, the *Dictionary of National Biography*.

It is a pleasure to acknowledge the obligations I have incurred during this study, though it will be understood, of course, that my errors are my own, none of the persons who have aided me being in any way responsible for them. President W. K. Jordan of Radcliffe College has inspired me by his scholarship, and his friendship has meant much to me. He has read my manuscript and suggested many improvements. I am grateful to the Corporation and to the Committee on General Scholarships of Harvard University which, by awarding me the Sheldon Travelling Fellowship, enabled me to do the research for this book in England. For the knowledge which they have placed at my disposal on special points, I must thank Professor Merritt Y. Hughes of the University of Wisconsin, Professor A. S. P. Woodhouse of the University of Toronto, Mr. A. F. Johnson, Assistant Keeper of the Printed Books in the British Museum, and Mr. H. N. Brailsford. Professor David Owen of the Department of History in Harvard University has shown me many kindnesses. The staffs of the Houghton and Widener Libraries at Harvard, of the Union Theological Seminary Library in New York City, of Dr. Williams's Library in London, and of the British Museum, have been uniformly helpful. I am especially appreciative of the cooperation of the librarians and attendants of the British Museum Reading Room and North Library during the year in which I worked there. My greatest obligation is to my wife, Honoré Desmond Sharrer, to whom this book is dedicated with love and respect.

Vinalhaven, Maine, July 1952.

CONTENTS

I

INTRODUCTION

THE revolutionary decades, 1640–60, are of the highest significance in the history both of English and of European political philosophy. In England, no other period of comparable brevity has borne so splendid a harvest. There appeared then all the important writings of Hobbes and Harrington, of the Levellers and Winstanley. That the two former have a place in the general history of European, as well as English, political thought, no one will deny. That the Levellers and Winstanley have such a place also, and a high one, is, I think, now being increasingly recognized. Moreover, the occasion of great and unprecedented times, when the old order was being shaken to its foundations, prompted small men, men who would have been mute in quieter days, to take pen in hand. Hobbes, no doubt, would have written a system whether he were a schoolman with Occam of a reformer with James Mill. But only in revolutionary years were men moved to rush into print who had previously brooded in silence over their Bibles and their grievances. So it is that in hundreds of pamphlets of social protest and proposals for reforms we hear the authentic voices of the small trader, the artisan, and the peasant of the mid-seventeenth century. And thus the political thought of the time comprises a double richness: there is the passionate and many-sided agitation of the little-known and unknown pamphleteers, and there is the more systematic ratiocination of the leading theorists. Together, these accomplished the preview or the consummation of ideas that had a superb role to play for a century and a half, and more, after 1660. Their achievements made English political thought the most advanced in Europe at that time. Indeed, most of the leading principles which inspired the eighteenth-century revolutions in Europe and America received their first commanding expression during the years when the Long Parliament defeated the king and Cromwell set up his power.

The political ideas which we are to consider here are democratic, radical, and royalist. To suggest a criterion for the last of these offers no difficulty. Royalist ideas are those whose main intent it was to vindicate the constitutional claims of the crown and to provide a theoretical justification for monarchy. The question of democratic and radical thought is more complicated, and also more important, for it is the theories in these categories with which we shall be largely concerned. What is meant by democratic and radical is determined by the view which is taken here concerning the nature of political philosophy. It has often been held that the problems of philosophy are eternal and unchanging, and that the history of any of its branches is merely the record of how the same problems have been dealt with down the ages. On such a view, political philosophy would have as one of its problems, for example, the relation between the state and the individual, and its history would consist partly of the treatments which this has received at the hands of particular thinkers. But further reflection, I think, will disclose the illusory character of this notion. In the case of the problem just instanced, the political theorist does not meditate on The State as such. His concern, rather, is with some historically-determined political order, which is the only state he can know. So the problems of political philosophy are not the same but different problems, and the state of Plato's meditations is not the state of Aquinas or of Hobbes. This suggests one of the principal reasons why utopian writings differ. For though a thinker may intend his utopia to be the best of all possible communities eternal reason can devise, he is, in reality, prescribing a political order which we can neither comprehend nor assess except as we know its relevance to the historically-given and, therefore, transient problems of his own time.

It is from this standpoint that the democratic and radical doctrines of the following essay are to be discriminated. I have in mind those doctrines, which, consciously or not, were in opposition either to the traditional order as it appeared before the revolution, or to traditional methods of thinking about that order. Ultimately, the results of the work done under each of these headings came to the same thing, or complemented one another: that is to say, they justified, or advocated acquiescence in, or demanded extension of the far-reaching changes which the great struggles of the 1640s brought about. Specifically, among the ideas to be looked at are those, for example, which upheld the franchise as every man's right or defended a republic as superior to monarchy; which vindicated the revolutionary governments that supplanted the rule of Charles I or founded a theory of politics on the subjective claims of the individual. In the context of seventeenth-century England, and of Europe, too, these were perturbing and essentially inimical to the inherited order of things.

Some of them were identified and denounced by seventeenth-century royalists. The most notable instance is the decree passed by the University of Oxford in July 1683 against 'certain pernicious books, and damnable doctrines, destructive to the sacred persons of princes, their state, and government, and of all human society'. Twenty-seven opinions are singled out for condemnation, among which are many of the *dramatis personae* of this study. 'Wicked kings and tyrants ought to be put to death; and if the judges and inferior magistrates will not do their office, the power of the sword devolves to the people.' 'King Charles I. was lawfully put to death, and his murderers were the blessed instruments of God's glory in their generations.' 'Self-preservation is the fundamental-law of nature, and supersedes the obligation of all others, whensoever they stand in competition with it.' 'Possession and strength give a right to govern, and success in a cause ... proclaims it to be lawful and just. To pursue it is to comply with the will of God, because it is to follow the conduct of his providence.' 'The powers of this world are usurpations upon the prerogative of Jesus Christ, and it is the duty of God's people to destroy them in order to the setting Christ upon his throne.'[1]

Something now requires to be said concerning the affiliation of these and the other ideas examined in this study to the tradition out of which they emerge. That they are innovative, in the main, I have no doubt. Yet some of them still retain striking traces of the religious presuppositions upon which political thinking was for so many centuries conducted. It would be quite misleading to ignore these traces, as has sometimes been done in an effort to exhibit the political thought of the revolution as essentially secularized.[2] But it would be equally misleading to regard the revolution's thought, particularly the denunciations of contemporary social injustice, as a mere echo of the old Christian condemnation of the acquisitive society.[3] We have to do with something more complex than either of these evaluations would allow for, a complexity which is determined by the special character of the seventeenth century itself. This century is, I think, the critical stage in the shift from the medieval to the distinctively modern way of comprehending the world.[4] In those hundred years, the declining theological-transcendental mode of thought was at last disintegrated, and the first phase of the naturalistic-immanental mode of thought consummated. It was the century of the 'new philosophy' created by Bacon, Descartes, and Hobbes, and of the new science created by Galileo and Newton. It was the age when the denun-

[1] *Concilia Magnae Britanniae et Hiberniae*, ed. D. Wilkins, 4 vols., London, 1737, IV, 610–12.

[2] Cf., e.g., D. Petegorsky, *Left-wing democracy in the English civil war*, London, 1940, and C. Hill and E. Dell, *The good old cause*, London, 1950.

[3] Cf., e.g., W. Schenk, *The concern for social justice in the Puritan revolution*, London, 1948.

[4] Cf. H. Wolfson, *The philosophy of Spinoza*, 2 vols., Cambridge, 1934, II, Ch. XXI; B. Willey, *The seventeenth century background*, London, 1934; and P. Hazard, *La crise de la conscience européenne*, Paris, 1935.

ciation of scholasticism, inaugurated earlier, reached its climax; when political economy, one of the most profane of studies' experienced its first real development; and when religious passion was giving place to that Augustan calm which held enthusiasm on sacred subjects in contempt.

This shift, however, was not accomplished smoothly. And therefore we often find in seventeenth-century writers strange combinations of discrepant beliefs, the essence of whose opposition lay in the growing disharmony between the claims of religious thought and those implied by science.[1] These two departments had become 'divided and distinguished worlds'.[2] If some minds sought for eclectic solutions to bridge the widening chasm, others succumbed, in their perplexity, to a kind of disorientation which is exposed for us in John Donne's familiar lament that the 'new philosophy' had deprived the old religious outlook of coherence and credibility.[3] Throughout the century we may see this disharmony at work, and we may see, as well, the conclusive triumph of the mechanistic philosophy toward which the science of the time pointed. Religion, accordingly, was forced to accommodate itself to this momentous fact, and to give ground.

Now in English political thought, too, the seventeenth-century disharmony was operative. Here it was exemplified by the naturalistic notions covertly inhabiting doctrines which were inspired by religion, by the tendency of these latter to become secularized, and by the germ of traditional moral teaching which gave birth to claims that were really new and without precedent. Confronted by these conflicting elements, we must not omit to give them due consideration. At the same time, we must be careful to distinguish plainly the main line of development. That this latter conforms to the movement of seventeenth-century thought as a whole, there can be no doubt. Political ideas were becoming detached from the religious associations in which they had been steeped, and were taking on a decided secular character. In this process, it is the revolution that marks the critical moment. The struggles of those two decades provided the opportunity to push doctrines to their conclusions, and the result was a transformation in the tone of political thought. This is obviously true of the work of Harrington and Hobbes, for their affiliation with the most advanced philosophic currents of their day was unambiguous and undisguised. It is no less true of the writings most immediately influenced by that strong religion which, despite all its varieties, we may here generally call Puritan. Puritanism, it has been well pointed out, has affinities with science in its impatience of traditional

[1] Cf. D. Bush, 'Two roads to truth: science and religion in the early seventeenth century,' *English literary history*, VIII, 2.
[2] The phrase is, of course, Sir Thomas Browne's (*Religio medici*, I, xxxiv).
[3] *An anatomie of the world. The first anniversary*, lines 205–14.

4

authority and in its stress on progress, utility, and reform.[1] And the more radical the political beliefs were of those men whose ultimate inspiration was Puritanism, the more these affinities tended to show themselves. Of this fact, Gerrard Winstanley is a conspicuous illustration. The ultimate ideal consequence, though it does not, of course, hold empirically for all the radicals of the period, was the bursting and the sloughing off of the religious husk in which their thought had germinated.

Our study begins with the Levellers because only with them did the ideas present in germ at the revolution's outset receive a really wide and thoroughgoing application. Prior to the Levellers' appearance, however, there were several competent writers on Parliament's side who ought briefly to be noticed because of the new positions they were maintaining.

The most important was Henry Parker, perhaps the ablest of Parliament's publicists, but one whose views were more extreme than those entertained by the majority of his party. In his *Observations upon some of his Majesties late Answers and Expresses* (1642), Parker made out a case for the sovereignty of Parliament without the king,[2] insisting that Parliament 'is neither one, nor few, it is indeed the State itself'.[3] But for the development of democratic ideas, such affirmations as these were of small significance in comparison with his declaration that political power derives from the agreements of men, that the 'Charter of nature' entitles all men to safety, and that 'there bee . . . tacite trusts and reservations in all publike commands, though of the most absolute nature, that can be supposed'.[4] It was these which assisted the growth of democratic doctrines in his own day and were of some influence on the Levellers.[5]

Another writer who went beyond the general Parliamentarian standpoint was Samuel Rutherford, a resplendent ornament among the Scottish Presbyterians. Rutherford's main ideas were not especially original,[6] but he held some notions whose effect was to redefine out of all possibility of recognition the traditional role of monarchy in England. In his chief political work, *Lex, Rex* (1644), he asserted that the king is merely the people's creation, and altogether denied any principle of legitimacy, affirming that the crown passes not by descent but by

[1] D. Bush, *op. cit.*, 89.
[2] Cf. W. K. Jordan, *Men of substance*, Chicago, 1942, Ch. V; M. Judson, *The crisis of the constitution*, New Brunswick, 1949, 429–30; J. W. Allen, *English political thought, 1603–1644*, London, 1938, 426–35. Professor Allen has needlessly complicated Parker's views.
[3] *Observations*, 34.
[4] *Ibid.*, 1, 4.
[5] Cf. M. Judson, *op. cit.*, 416–17.
[6] Cf. J. W. Allen, *op. cit.*, 424.

popular choice from one generation to the next. No nation, he said, is bound either to one royal line or to monarchy, nor can any generation bind the conscience of its posterity to any family or to kingship.[1] Rutherford declared, too, that the people's safety is the supreme law, taking precedence over all other laws.[2] Resistance to an unjust king, he said, is not resistance to a king at all, but to a tyrant.[3] He also glanced at the possibility of popular resistance to Parliament, and asserted that if Commons 'abuse their fiduciary power to the destruction of these Shires and Corporations, who put the trust on them . . . the people may . . . resist them, annul their Commissions and rescind their acts, and denude them of fiduciary power. . . '.[4] There is nothing, however, to show that Rutherford ever considered such a development capable of occurring, and, indeed, in 1644 he was unlikely to do so. Despite his pronounced aristocratic bias—he seems never to have meant by the 'people' anything but the *pars valentior*—Rutherford's ideas could be made to serve purposes he himself abhorred, and a few years later, the Levellers occasionally culled supporting passages from *Lex, Rex*.

The Levellers' coming introduces a new force. They are the first left-wing party in English history. They had their press and propaganda, their theorists and agitators, and an independent programme. In 1647, when they first began to function as a separate movement, the conflict of interests present on the parliamentary side from the outset was at last irreparably dividing it. The triumph over the king in the first civil war had removed the danger of Parliament's defeat and opened the way for a split among the victors. The coalition made up of peers and landed gentlemen, rich merchants, middle and small traders, craftsmen, as well as some copyholders and other tenants, was not a firm one at any time. To the differences based on economic interests were added others, equally important, rising from the refusal of Presbyterians to tolerate religious opinions other than their own. In the ranks of the Independents and the sects, where sprang most of the opposition to Presbyterian persecution, there had grown up deep divisions also, some men desiring political and social changes which seemed menacing and visionary to others.

It was from the middle and small people, economically speaking, among the adherents of Independency and the sects that the Leveller leaders won their supporters. To conservatives, victory over the king seemed to conclude the revolution. To the Levellers, it seemed to begin it. Many of the former were reluctant revolutionaries from the outset and took more than one look back along the furrow they felt forced to plough. The latter, in contrast, had shouted hymns and hallelujahs while they girded on their swords to defend Israel. To them, the real

---

[1] *Lex, rex*, 1–78.　　　　　　[2] *Ibid.*, 218–19.
[3] *Ibid.*, 212–13.　　　　　　[4] *Ibid.*, 152.

meaning of the war lay still unfulfilled in 1647. On one aspect of this meaning, they were in agreement with the aristocratic Independents, Cromwell and his friends. Cromwell defined liberty of conscience with less latitude than the Levellers, but while its fate remained in doubt owing to the sway of Presbyterian gentlemen over Commons, neither he nor the Levellers could rest. Yet to the latter the meaning of the war included not only liberty of conscience, but the redress of political and economic grievances. What they called grievances did not mostly seem so, however, to aristocratic Independents. Hence, by the end of 1647, despite their common advocacy of toleration, the Levellers were separated from the Cromwellians by a fundamental difference. And because the Levellers had succeeded in winning many supporters in the rank and file of the army, Cromwell's position was seriously endangered.

The Leveller movement arose mainly to prosecute a political and economic programme. For this reason, its identity did not consist so much in its broad tolerationist views as in its left-wing political ideas. For brief periods during 1647 and 1648, it was in uneasy alliance with Cromwell and his followers. But the latter were unwilling partners. They joined with the Levellers when they could not avoid it because they required a counterbalance against the Presbyterians. They broke with the Levellers as soon as they could and suppressed them in the army and out of it. Yet for a time, the Leveller movement was a considerable force. Its leaders, John Lilburne, Richard Overton, William Walwyn, and John Wildman, could number their adherents by the thousands. And in the days of their defeat, the Levellers' last *Agreement of the People* bore witness still to the wondrous hopes the English revolution had kindled in the minds and hearts of many men.

II

THE LEVELLER THEORISTS

1. JOHN LILBURNE

THE greatest party leader of the Levellers was John Lilburne. It is no exaggeration to describe him as for a time the most popular man in England. He was certainly the only man of his day who seems continuously to have enjoyed the affection of large numbers of people. Cromwell's impact on contemporaries was different: he was admired, feared, held in awe towards the end of his career, and, by some of his associates, liked. Lilburne, however, with all his contentiousness, seems to have been loved. His whole adult life until his early death at the age of forty-three was given to ceaseless struggle for the principles on whose behalf he had engaged. Almost two-thirds of his mature years were spent in the prisons to which the enmity first of the bishops, then of the Long Parliament, finally of Cromwell, consigned him. He was absolutely incorruptible, and a great-hearted and fearless agitator. He was no professional theorist, for his political ideas were evolved in the closest connection with his own experience of injustice, and were never expressed in any formal treatise. They must be sought in all his writings, where they lie embedded amidst long passages of autobiography, self-defence, and denunciation of his political opponents. Nevertheless, in their totality, they comprise a true political theory appropriate to the left-wing democrat Lilburne became.[1]

When he first began to write, it was before the revolution as a pious and enthusiastic separatist who held no considered political theory. He

[1] The fullest account of Lilburne's career is M. Gibb, *John Lilburne, the Leveller*, London, 1947. Lilburne's bibliography is complicated. The most useful aids in its establishment are: E. Peacock, 'John Lilburne: a bibliography,' *Notes and queries*, 7th Series, 1888, 122, 162, 242, 342, 423, 502; W. Haller, *The rise of Puritanism*, New York, 1938, 432–40; D. Wolfe, *Milton in the Puritan revolution*, New York, 1941, 469–81; D. Wolfe, *Leveller manifestoes of the Puritan revolution*, New York, 1944, 425–6; W. Haller and G. Davies, *The Leveller tracts, 1647–1653*, New York, 1944, *passim*. W. Haller, *Tracts on liberty in the Puritan revolution*, 3 vols., New York, 1934; Wolfe's *Leveller manifestoes*, and Haller and Davies's *Leveller tracts* reprint some of the important writings which are referred to in this and the following chapter.

8

was then a London apprentice, and for disseminating seditious literature against the bishops had been barbarously sentenced by the Court of Star Chamber to whipping, the pillory, and prison. At that time, he spoke exclusively as a martyr to the prelates' unchristian rage, and his political ideas were the commonplace ones of non-resistance such as were often found among Protestant communions a century before. The king's authority is from God, he said, and to disobey it is to disobey God. If the king should command anything against God's word, though he dare not obey, he will submit his body for punishment, 'for I doe hold it unlawfull for any of Gods people, in their greatest Oppression by the Majestrate, to rebell or take up any Temporall armes . . .'.[1]

But his views on the church were pregnant with possibilities for the redefinition of the political order. The point is of some importance. In the manner of the sectarian, he emphasized the voluntary and contractual character of church government. A true church, he said, is created by the free consent of the believers 'to enter into that . . . holy State, City, or Kingdome . . . and by the power of Christ to become a constituted or Politique Body or Corporation . . . and then by virtue of their . . . uniting & joyning themselves together each to other & so unto the Lord . . . they become a true visible Church of Jesus Christ . . . & so hath power from Christ . . . to cast out offenders . . . to chuse elect & ordaine her owne officers . . . and to reprove . . . her owne Officers. . . .'.[2]

Lilburne first applied these ideas on the polity of the sect to secular subjects when he forsook his belief in non-resistance and supported Parliament in the civil war.[3] It was not, however, until 1645 that he began to seize on their wider implications. In that year, after having risen to the rank of lieutenant-colonel in the Parliamentary army, he resigned his commission rather than take the Presbyterian-inspired Covenant which was being imposed on the officers.[4] Retired into civilian life, he was soon stimulated by several personal encounters with oppression to give shape to his radical programme. First, there was his experience of Presbyterian efforts to suppress liberty of conscience;[5] next, he was prevented by the monopoly of the Merchant Adventurers Company

---

[1] *Come out of her my people*, 1639, 14.

[2] *An answer to nine arguments*, 1645, 28. Lilburne wrote this work about 1638, as its title-page and content make clear.

[3] Lilburne accused the king of breaking his contract with the people; see *The legal fundamental liberties of the people of England*, 2nd ed., 1649, 26–7. He was influenced to support Parliament by such writings as St. John's speech against ship money, Pym's speech against Strafford, and Henry Parker's *Observations*; see *Innocency and truth justified*, 1646, *passim*.

[4] He was the only officer recorded as resigning for this reason (S. R. Gardiner, *History of the great civil war*, 4 vols., London, 1893, II, 195).

[5] *A copie of a letter written by John Lilburne . . . to Mr. William Prinne*, 1645, provides details.

from pursuing the cloth trade in which he had been apprenticed;[1] then, in the summer of 1645, Commons ordered him into custody on a charge of slandering its speaker, and when he refused to answer interrogatories against himself, his refusal was voted a breach of privilege and he was committed to Newgate.[2] Treatment of this sort was exactly calculated to teach Lilburne that Parliament was spokesman for interests that could be as tyrannous as Charles I. It caused him to become a self-constituted tribune of the people and to launch the career of agitation out of which the Leveller movement grew. And it resulted in the first announcement of those perspectives of change and reform which so disquieted the Levellers' opponents.

Immediately after his detention by Commons, he denounced the House's proceedings as a violation of rights guaranteed him by Magna Carta. Already, then, it is clear, he regarded Commons 'as the supream Power of England, who have residing in them that power that is inherent in the people . . .'. Yet its members, he insisted, 'are . . . not to act according to their own wils and pleasure, but according to the fundamentall constitutions and customes of the Land, which I conceive provides for the safety and preservation of the people . . .'.[3]

At last, after several failures to obtain his freedom, he published his pamphlet, *Englands Birth-Right Justified* (1645), perhaps the earliest statement of radical policy to appear in the revolution.[4] Here, making himself spokesman for the 'poore, and men of middle quality',[5] he not only denounced such grievances as tithes, unjust laws, monopolies, and the excise tax,[6] but also demanded a Parliament which should be under popular control. No pretended privileges, he declared, can justify Parliament in acting against law. The people never gave it such power, and the unknown privileges it claims are as dangerous as an unlimited royal prerogative.[7] Moreover, while men are members of Parliament, they should exercise no other functions, he said, 'for to me it is one of the most unjust things in the world, that the Law-makers should be the Law executors. . . '.[8] Let Parliament be dissolved and a new one summoned, he proposed, and let the people elect new members annually so

---

[1] *Innocency and truth justified*, 46–7.

[2] For details, see M. Gibb, *op. cit.*, Ch. V.

[3] *The copy of a letter from . . . John Lilburne, to a freind*, 1645, 14 (mispaged).

[4] This was published anonymously. Haller (*Tracts on liberty*, III, 257), Haller and Davies (*Leveller tracts*, 47), and Gibb (*op. cit.*, 134) accept it as Lilburne's. Wolfe (*Leveller manifestoes*, 5 n.) attributes most of it to Overton. I regard it as Lilburne's on grounds of style and thought. He seems virtually to acknowledge its authorship in his *Londons liberty in chains discovered*, 1646, 31.

[5] *Englands birth-right justified*, 45.

[6] *Ibid.*, 13, 36–7, 8–11, 44–5.

[7] *Ibid.*, 3–4.

[8] *Ibid.*, 31.

that they can call unworthy representatives to account.[1] Further, every freeman should contribute one year's service to the nation, and those elected for this purpose who lack means must have a competent allowance provided them.[2]

These demands, innovative as they were, were still further expanded by Lilburne upon his release from prison in the autumn of 1645. Continuing his agitation, he now called for the trial of the king, who must be made, he said, to expiate with his own blood the blood shed in the war.[3] He also proposed the complete reform of law and legal procedure, asking why Englishmen should be subject to the legal system introduced by the tyrant, William the Conqueror. Even Magna Carta, which he had appealed to only a short time before, is but little, he now pointed out. Though it is commonly thought to be the Englishman's inheritance, it falls far short of the Saxon laws, and is merely the best that could be wrung from a despot by force.[4] As for the House of Lords, Lilburne resolved its status in the summer of 1646, when, for refusing to testify against himself at its bar, he found himself once more in prison.[5] The peers, he straightway declared, have no right to the constitutional position which they enjoy, for they sit by the prerogative patents of kings, not by consent and election of the people. In attempting to exercise jurisdiction over him, a commoner, they have transgressed against the majesty of the House of Commons, 'the absolute supream derivative power of all the Commons of England . . .'. They may exercise no negative voice, because if the king's coronation oath requires him to pass such laws as the people choose—and this, Lilburne points out, is what Parliament had asserted in its declarations—then he can grant no power to the peers '(his meer creatures made by his will & pleasure) for them to oppose or to give a Law unto the people'.[6]

With this, Lilburne's political position was essentially complete, and its outlines fixed in a clear and definite programme. By the end of 1646, he was urging that the monarchy should be dispensed with, and supremacy recognized in a free and popularly elected Commons acknowledging its subjection to law and effecting broad reforms. Step by step, he had been led to the realization that the justice he sought would have to be general, and would require extensive changes in the political order and in legal and economic practices. Basic in the evolution of his ideas was, as I have already emphasized, his own personal experience of oppression. But it is doubtful that he could have come to project re-

---

[1] *Ibid.*, 33.
[2] *Ibid.*, Postscript.
[3] *The iust mans iustification*, 1st ed., 1646, 10.
[4] *Ibid.*, 11, 13–15.
[5] For details, see M. Gibb, *op. cit.*, Ch. VI.
[6] *An anatomy of the lords tyranny*, 1646, 3, 9, 22.

forms on so large a scale had he not by this time also acquired a far-reaching theory of the nature of government. Its immediate source lay in the radical side of the Parliamentary declarations and publicists and, beyond this, in the ideas of the sect on Church-government. But what had been in the Parliamentary writings a mere suggestion Lilburne expanded to the point where his position emerged as a distinct entity in its own right, standing, because of the extensiveness of its claims, in opposition to the very thought that had helped beget it. And what in the sects had applied to a select handful of believers, he now demanded on behalf of mankind at large. No longer would he appeal to precedent as his ultimate sanction. Henceforth, he would invoke Christian right reason itself as the justification for his radical programme. At this tribunal only would he plead.

A remarkable passage written in 1646 while he was in prison illustrates these considerations so well that it is worth printing at length. God, he said, created man in His own image, which consists principally of reason and understanding, and made him lord over the earth.

'But made him not Lord . . . over the individuals of Mankind, no further then by free consent, or agreement, by giving up their power each to other, for their better being; so that originally, he gives no Lordship . . . to any of Adams Posterity, by Will and Prerogative, to rule over his Brethren-Men; but ingraved by nature in the soule of Man, this goulden and everlasting principle, to doe to another, as he would have another do to him; but man by his transgression, falling from the perfection of reason . . . became tyrannical, and beastly . . . [then] God taking mercy of Mankind . . . and not executing the fulnesse of his wrath . . . to revenge that beastlinesse . . . that, by the fall, had now entred into the Spirits of all Mankinde, institutes a perpetuall, moral . . . Law. . . . That whosoever . . . would be so beastly . . . as to fall upon his neighbour, brother, or friend, and do unto him that, which he would not he should do to him, by taking away his life and blood from him; God ordaines and expresly saith he shall lose his life without mercy for so doing. . . . And when the fulnesse of time was come, that Christ the Restorer and Repairer of mans losse and fall, should come and preach Righteousnesse & Justice. . . He saith, it is the Law & the Prophets, that whatsoever we would that men should do unto us, that wee should do to them. . . . So that by this, it is clearly evident, that . . . Christianity . . . doth not destroy morality, civility, justice, and right reason; but rather restores it to its first perfection, beauty, splendor, and glory. . . .'[1]

[1] *Londons liberty in chains discovered*, 17–18. Cf. the similar passage in *The freemans freedome vindicated*, 1646, 11–12, where Lilburne says that all the descendants of Adam and Eve have equal rights and privileges, and that no one is to exercise power over another except by institution, donation, agreement, and consent.

These words make clear how long a journey Lilburne had come since his imprisonment as a young apprentice by the Star Chamber. Then his preoccupation had been with man as a believer. Now it was with man as a citizen. Then he had denied a right of resistance. Now he was affirming the right of all men to consent to the government under which they live. Then he had stressed man's sinfulness from which the elect were to withdraw into separate congregations. Now he was stressing man's reasonableness. Optimism breathed in all his thoughts. Despite the fall, man had not lost his native freedom. Christ had restored the pristine law of right reason as a norm for judging all the powers of the world. Man, as a rational creature, could not be bound by commands emanating from a government to which he had not consented. When a government attempts to take away the people's freedom, men are absolved from obedience, for they are not obliged 'to destroy . . . their Fundamentall naturall Liberties . . . the injoyment of which makes them to differ from bruit and savage Beasts which were never created with reason . . . that glorious Image, that God made man in. . .'.[1] Because consent alone gives scope to reason, it must follow that 'the poorest that lives, hath as true a right to give a vote . . . as the richest and greatest. . .'.[2] And it must follow, too, that an unrepresentative Parliament can have no standing,[3] and that no enactment of the past can qualify as fundamental law unless it accords with reason.[4]

These ideas lead straight on to the great conception in 1647 of an agreement of the people as the basis for a settlement of the problems raised by the revolution. By proposing the complete reform of the existing system of representation, the first Leveller *Agreement of the People* exhibited a democratic vision beyond anything yet known in English history. But even more remarkable, we shall see, was the form in which this vision was embodied. The first *Agreement* appeared in the autumn of 1647, when the army, irritated by arrears of pay and other grievances, had ceased to be controllable by Parliament, and when many regiments, under Leveller influence, had elected representatives who were voicing radical demands. Published in the name of the elected agents of five cavalry regiments, its title reads: *An Agreement Of The People For a firme and present Peace, upon grounds of common-right and freedome . . . offered to the joynt concurrence of all the free Commons of England.* As a platform of settlement, it was a statement of rights and of fundamental law declaring the powers of any future government, and a mutual covenanting of the people with one another to establish the principles thus set forth as the basis for the state's subsequent functioning. Most

[1] *The charters of London*, 1646, 36.
[2] *Ibid.*, 4.
[3] *Londons liberty in chains discovered*, 53–4.
[4] *Ibid.*, 41.

important of all, it was to obtain its validity by the subscription of individual Englishmen, not by act of Parliament, for, as Lilburne wrote: 'An Agreement of the People is not proper to come from Parliament, because it comes from thence . . . with a command . . . it ought not so to do, but to be voluntary and free. Besides, that which is done by one Parliament . . . may be undone by the next . . . but an Agreement of the People begun and ended amongst the People, can never come justly within the Parliaments cognizance to destroy. . . '.[1]

Though the conception in 1647 of such a form of settlement was, doubtless, a collective product of Leveller thinking, it would seem to owe more to Lilburne than to anyone else, and his ideas, in particular, throw light on its genesis. The *Agreement* could never have been conceived without his earlier practice in the polity of the sect and his belief in contract as the origin of government and in consent as its basis. It was these, I think, which united with his evaluation of the political situation in 1647 to be the chief factors in producing this unprecedented form of settlement.

We have seen how Lilburne's experience as a sectary had familiarized him with the covenant made between believers as the basis of the church. In 1638, it will be recalled, he described a true church, in language reminiscent of the secular order, as 'a constituted or Politique Body or Corporation' established by common consent. It was the transfer of this notion to society at large that was partly responsible for the *Agreement*'s conception.[2]

But a church in these terms may be created at any time because it is merely a grouping within society and, from the sectarian's point of view, can never be identical with society itself. How was it that in 1647, Lilburne and his friends, ignoring Parliament, proposed a covenant or agreement among all Englishmen, thus presupposing the inauguration of a new political order? The answer to this question will show that the *Agreement* goes far beyond the notion of democratic constitutionalism and the formulation of fundamental law in which its significance has commonly been discerned.[3] The first *Agreement* was a democratic con-

---

[1] *The legal fundamental liberties of the people of England*, 2nd ed., 41.

[2] The connection between the covenant-idea and democratic constitutionalism has been stressed by C. Borgeaud, *The rise of modern democracy in old and New England*, trans. B. Hill, London, 1894, Ch. III; W. Rothschild, *Der Gedanke der geschriebenen Verfassung in der englischen Revolution*, Tübingen and Leipzig, 1903, 3–4; and A. D. Lindsay, *The modern democratic state*, Oxford, 1943, 117–21. A. S. P. Woodhouse, *Puritanism and liberty*, London, 1938, Introduction, 72–6, discusses the relation between the covenant-idea and the *Agreement of the people*. The best treatment of the covenant-idea in general is by Perry Miller, *The New England mind*, New York, 1939, Chs. XIII–XIV and Appendix A.

[3] Cf., e.g., T. C. Pease, *The Leveller movement*, Washington, 1916, 199 ff.; D. Wolfe, *Leveller manifestoes*, 49, 223; and F. D. Wormuth, *The origins of modern constitutionalism*, New York, 1949, Ch. IX.

stitution, and much more. It was also the re-enactment of the great myth of the social contract, indeed, the very pact by which political society was to be created anew, and England removed from the state of nature into which Lilburne believed she had now been dissolved.

This, it is essential to realize, was literally the case in which he thought his country to be in the middle of 1647. The previous year, we recall, he had been imprisoned by the Lords. Neither his denial of their jurisdiction over him, a commoner, nor his calls for liberation to the House of Commons were of avail. In consequence, by January 1647, he was threatening an appeal from Parliament to the whole people.[1] In February, he and Richard Overton, who was also a prisoner by decree of the peers, denied that an appeal to the people would make them enemies of all magistracy. Not themselves, they declared, but the Parliamentary tyrants 'dissolve the legall frame and constitution of the civill policy and government of the Kingdome, by suffering will and lust, but not lawe to rule and governe us, and so reduce us into the originall Law of nature, for every man to preserve and defend himselfe the best he can. . . '.[2] When those whom the people have trusted with power betray their trust, those who had trusted them may withdraw all subjection and look to their safety how they can.[3]

This gives us the clue to a full understanding of the genesis of the *Agreement*. Lilburne maintained that his long failure to obtain justice, the oppressions to which he, a symbol of all commoners, was being subjected, and the government's refusal to redress grievances had dissolved the country into a state of nature. There was no longer a true magistracy. Beastly will held sway, not reason. Tyranny and no government were the same. Hence, he concluded that the law of nature is warrantable against Parliament, and urged the people to take up arms.[4] He turned for support to the army, which in defiance of Parliament, had sworn its famous *Solemn Engagement* not to disband until its own and the nation's grievances were removed.[5] Holding that the country was in a state of nature and that Parliament no longer possessed any standing, Lilburne denied that the army was subject to Parliament or that it now existed in virtue of the powers Parliament had conferred on it. It had betaken itself to 'the prime Laws of Nature',[6] he affirmed, and its actions were based on 'the principles of Saifety, flowing from Nature, Reason, and Justice, agreed on by common consent' of the soldiers as

---

[1] *The oppressed mans oppressions declared*, 1647, 37–8.
[2] *The out-cryes of oppressed commons*, 1647, 14. This work was written jointly by Lilburne and Overton.
[3] *Ibid.*, 17–18.
[4] *Rash oathes unwarrantable*, 1647, 7, 38–9, 47–8.
[5] J. Rushworth, *Historical collections*, 7 vols., London, 1659–1701, VI, 510–12.
[6] *An impeachment of high treason*, 1649, 2.

expressed in their *Solemn Engagement*.[1] The only visible authority remaining was the sword, '(for it is cleerly evident, there is now no power executed in England, but a power of force, a just and morall act done by a troop of Horse, being as good law as now I can see executed by any Iudge in England). . .'.[2]

Since Lilburne was convinced that the people had been reduced to a state of nature, the problem, as he now saw it, was greater than simply formulating a fundamental law which Parliament should enact. Parliament as an authoritative body no longer existed. The task was that of reconstituting society. He made no distinction between a pact creating society and another creating government, evidently regarding them as one and the same. What was required, then, was to make the social-political contract anew.

There can be no greater evidence of the strength inherent in the contractual idea than the proposal of a settlement in the form of an agreement of the people. It showed that to Lilburne and the Levellers, the social contract was no mere hypothetical premiss of the political order, nor, if historical, an act sealed once for all in the distant past. It was a living and literal source of a common political existence. If this existence were destroyed by tyranny, the social contract alone could re-establish it.

The *Agreement*, therefore, goes beyond the analogy to a constitution and presents us with the very terms of the social contract which must be entered into if the political order is to be resurrected. Given this, it becomes fully clear why the *Agreement* needed to be ratified by every man, and not by Parliament. It was not merely that what one Parliament enacts, another can rescind. It was also because men in a state of nature retain their natural rights entire, and can give up a portion of them only by their own consent; no one can do it in their names. And so also, the future state which the *Agreement* envisages is to act exclusively in virtue of the power the subscribers have transferred to it. The reservations—the matters over which jurisdiction is reserved from the state—are only explicable as that part of the subscribers' natural rights which they have withheld and will transfer to no earthly authority. In all these respects, the *Agreement* is the social contract. At the same time, it is also, of course, the fundamental law which we associate with the notion of constitutionalism. Lilburne had wrestled with the problem of fundamental law. Though he went in search of it to the law books, he never regarded it as merely equivalent to the enactments of the past. Only that part of the law agreeable to reason and the word of God would he call fundamental.[3] Now, however, the problem was solved at

[1] *Ionahs cry out of the whales belly*, 1647, 13.
[2] *Two letters writ by Lieut.-Col. John Lilburne . . . to Col. Henry Marten*, 1647, 6.
[3] *Londons liberty in chains discovered*, 41.

last. By laying down what the people would permit the government to do, and what not, the fundamental law was given visible and forever unmistakable definition.

Thus the Levellers' form of settlement goes to the ultimate assumptions of democratic political thought in the seventeenth century, and is one of its classic expressions: its individualism, manifest in the requirement that only the consent of the subscribing individuals can make the *Agreement* valid; its belief in the social contract, which the *Agreement* was literally intended to be; its allegiance to the principle of natural rights, the transfer of which the *Agreement* was intended to effect; and finally, its assertion of a fundamental law, the exemplification of reason, which the historic past could never quite disclose, but to which the *Agreement* at last gave palpable shape.

Lilburne had hoped that the army general council, on which the Cromwellians and the Levellers sat together in uneasy alliance, would sponsor the *Agreement of the People*. This was not to be. Cromwell and Ireton, his son-in-law, opposed the *Agreement's* resort to the law of nature, and denounced its specific proposals for reform as a menace to property.[1] Alarmed by the implications of the Leveller position, they immobilized the general council and silenced the Leveller soldiery by force.[2] Fearing that Cromwell was seeking to erect a military dictatorship, Lilburne again had recourse to Parliament at the beginning of 1648 as the only alternative to rule by martial law.[3] But to whatever strategies political developments forced them, the Levellers continued to uphold an agreement of the people as the only tenable settlement. Two later versions of their *Agreement* were far more detailed than the brief one of 1647,[4] and the elaborate list of powers and reservations in the former gives prominence to the aspect of fundamental law. The idea of social contract continued conspicuous, however, in the insistence upon individual ratification. Such a method, the Levellers asserted, was the only way to fix 'the Common-wealth upon the fairest probabilities of a lasting Peace, and contentfull establishment'.[5]

Cromwell's purge of Parliament at the end of 1648 brought about his final breach with the Levellers. Thenceforth, Lilburne remained in

[1] A. S. P. Woodhouse, *op. cit.*, 26, 57, 94, 97 *et passim*. The citation is from Professor Woodhouse's edition of the famous Putney debates of the army's general council in the late autumn of 1647, at which the *Agreement* was discussed.

[2] See the details in S. R. Gardiner, *op. cit.*, IV, Chs. LVI–LVII.

[3] *An impeachment of high treason*, 14. Lilburne was promoting a petition to Parliament and, according to his account, had to justify this course to his followers because of his previous denial of Parliament's authority. Commons, he now said, though corrupted, is the best visible authority. It should be preserved in such a way that it will not vassalize the people.

[4] See below, Ch. III.

[5] *A manifestation*, 1649, 8. This is signed by Lilburne, Overton, Walwyn, and a lesser figure, Thomas Prince.

opposition until his death in 1657. He condemned the illegality of putting Parliament under military force, and denied the lawfulness of the king's trial on the ground that the power that carried it out had no authority whatever.[1] A rightly constituted republic is superior to monarchy, he told Cromwell, but '. . . to have the name of a Commonwealth imposed upon us by the Sword, wherein we are and shall be more slaves than ever we were under kingship . . . such a Commonwealth as this I abhor . . . and therefore I had rather be under a King reasonable bounded than under you, and your new Sword Tyranny called a Common-wealth'.[2]

While in banishment in 1652 by government decree, Lilburne made acquaintance for the first time with Machiavelli and some of the classical writers.[3] The Italian theorist, whose ideas were so often used in the seventeenth century to justify reason of state, he straightway adapted to his own philosophy. Once he had employed Machiavelli's name as a reproach.[4] Now he praised him as 'one of the most judicious, & true lovers of his country of Italies liberties, and . . . the good of all mankind that ever I read of in my daies . . . who though he be commonly condemned . . . by all great state polititians . . . yet by me his books are esteemed for real usefulnesse in my streits to help me clearly to see through all the disguised deceits of my potent, politick . . . adversaries . . . '.[5] He was also deeply impressed with the classical authors, and compared England's military rulers 'with what I have read with a great deal of observation (in those most excellent and famous Roman and Greek Historians Titus Livius and Plutark) of the Triumvery of Rome' who totally subdued the people's liberties.[6]

As an incentive to the government to allow his return from banishment, Lilburne promised to put forward proposals that he said would increase his country's population, win commercial supremacy over Holland, raise the price of land, and help the 'poor Husband-men' and the 'middle sort of people'. He seems to have had in mind the settlement of lands incapable of alienation upon the soldiery and the poor, comparable with 'the Law Agraria amongst the Romans'.[7] He very probably conceived this scheme under the influence of Plutarch's lives of the Gracchi. Despite the fact that he never developed it, it was a sign of his mind's capacity for growth that amidst exile and other difficulties, his new reading in the classics should have suggested such schemes to him.

This was almost his last word. Upon his unauthorized return from

[1] *The legal fundamental liberties of the people of England*, 2nd ed., 43–7.
[2] *Strength out of weakness*, 1649, 12.
[3] *L. Colonel John Lilburne revived*, 1653, 23. He read them in translation.
[4] *The legal fundamental liberties of the people of England*, 2nd ed., 3.
[5] *The upright mans vindication*, 1653, 7.
[6] *Ibid.*, 9.
[7] *Ibid.*, 21–2.

exile, he was placed on trial for his life, and though his courageous defence won him acquittal, he was sent to the final imprisonment during which he died. His career spanned the rise and decline of the movement whose greatest leader he was. At his death in 1657, the royal restoration which doomed all hopes was near. Yet Lilburne's ideas had many a long day to live, and his objectives were espoused by a generation of radicals one hundred and fifty years later. His lode-star was the principle of popular rights and the subjection of government to reason. To the question, who shall judge of reason, he answered, '. . . Reason is demonstrable by its innate glory . . . and man being a reasonable creature, is Judge for himself. . . '. But because a man may be partial in his own case, 'Reason tels him, Commissioners chosen out and tyed to such rational Instructions as the Chusers give them, are the most proper . . . judges. . . '. Yet, he concludes, '. . . a Commission given unto them against the Rules of common Reason is Voyde In It Self. . . '.[1]

And on this last—the sovereign individual conscience judging the rationality of all commands, enfranchized to do so by the law of Christ, which is itself reason—he took his ultimate stand.

2. RICHARD OVERTON

Almost nothing is known of Richard Overton's life. From obscure antecedents, he comes before us for a few brief years during the 1640s to fade into the shadows after 1649, and into total darkness after the Restoration.[2] This is a pity, because Overton was an exceedingly able theorist about whom we should like to know more. He began his career by publishing inferior verse satires against the bishops,[3] but attracted attention only with the anonymous appearance in 1643 of his work, *Mans Mortallitie*,[4] which contended that the soul is mortal and perishes with the body to rise only at the resurrection. This book has provoked some discussion centring on whether or not Overton was a materialist whose assertion of a resurrection was merely an insincere concession to contemporary prejudice.[5] The point is of some importance, I think, as

[1] *Strength out of weakness*, 14.

[2] The few known details of Overton's life are recorded in C. H. Firth's article on him in the *D.N.B.* His bibliography is discussed by W. Haller, *Tracts on liberty*, I, Chs. XII, XVI, *passim*, and by D. Wolfe, *Milton*, 480–1, *Leveller manifestoes*, 426.

[3] See, e.g., *New Lambeth fayre*, 1642.

[4] This had an enlarged edition in 1655 which appeared under the title, *Man wholly mortal*. For proof of Overton's authorship of this work, see P. Zagorin, 'The authorship of *Mans mortallitie*', *The library*, fifth series, V, 3.

[5] D. Masson, *The life of John Milton*, 7 vols., London, 1859—94, III, 157; W. K. Jordan, *The development of religious toleration in England*, 4 vols., Cambridge, 1932–40, IV, 191–2; D. Saurat, *Milton man and thinker*, 2nd ed., London, 1944, 278–9; and A. S. P. Woodhouse, *op. cit.*, Introduction, 55, all call Overton a materialist. W. Schenk, *op. cit.*, Appendix A, denies it.

indicating the extent to which a seventeenth-century democrat united a naturalistic philosophy to his left-wing politics.

Overton's seems to have been a mind which harboured notions basically incompatible. I see no reason to doubt his belief in a resurrection. Yet he was also, it will be seen, materialistic. The coexistence of these positions, however, apparently created no serious problem for him, because from all evidences, the non-materialistic elements lacked the vitality to evoke serious tension.

The real significance of *Mans Mortallitie* lay less in its assertion that the soul perishes than in its conception of the nature of the soul.[1] He conceived of it, it is quite clear, not as a distinct entity temporarily united with body, but as the sum total of the operation of man's faculties resting indispensably on a basis entirely physical. 'Soul' for him was, in effect, nothing but a metaphor for designating man's higher powers, without any intention of regarding them as supernatural.

After defining the soul as 'the internall and externall Faculties . . . joynly considered', he goes on to urge that as 'All the Faculties of Man . . . are all, and each of them mortall . . . and if all those, with his corpulent matter compleating Man . . . be mortall; Then the invention of the Soule upon that ground vanisheth. . .'.[2] As heat, he says, is the property of fire and 'cannot be, if fire cease: nor fire be, if it cease . . . as well may we say the heat of the fire continueth after the fire is dead out, as those Faculties when their Body is dead. . .'.[3] The soul must be matter because 'that which is not material, is nothing'. And as all matter, he continues, is compounded of the four elements, 'whole man being matter created, is elemental, finite, and mortall; and so ceaseth from the time of the grave, till the time of the Resurrection'.[4]

Why he believed the soul was raised then we have no way of knowing. It is clear that his reasoning gave him no basis for admitting this without a miracle. Nor can we tell on what grounds he thought there were a heaven and hell after the resurrection, though he does say that such a doctrine is an aid to virtue.[5] But it is obvious that Overton was of an empirical turn of mind. He was familiar with the work of the great physician, Ambroise Paré,[6] and had apparently studied chemistry.[7] Interests of this sort account for his materialistic arguments. He was,

---

[1] Greater men than Overton—e.g. Milton and Sir Thomas Browne—believed the soul mortal. See G. Williamson, 'Milton and the mortalist heresy', *Studies in philology*, XXXII, 4.

[2] *Mans mortallitie*, ed. 1644, 11.

[3] *Ibid.*, 13.

[4] *Ibid.*, ed. 1655, 21–2.

[5] *Ibid.*, ed. 1644, 22, ed. 1655, Postscript.

[6] *Ibid.*, ed. 1644, 13.

[7] This is what an anonymous critic charged in *The recantation of Lieutenant Collonel John Lilburne*, 1647, 6.

without doubt, a rationalist over whom dogma had all but lost its hold.

From the first, Overton was an enemy of religious persecution. He had attacked the intolerance of the bishops, and in 1645, following his bold excursion into philosophy, he joined the fight against Presbyterian bigotry. He held views remarkably broad for his time, and far beyond those of most men, for he would have extended liberty of conscience to Jews and Roman Catholics, and lamented the latters' persecution by Protestants as much as the Protestants' persecution by them.[1] But these affirmations were unaccompanied by any large formulation of his political thought. And strange to say, his tone towards Parliament in his known pamphlets was, on the whole, mild, despite Commons' treatment of John Lilburne to a term of imprisonment in the summer and fall of 1645.[2]

Only in the next year, when Lilburne was made a prisoner by command of the peers, did Overton turn to the expression of his political ideas. First he took up his pen in Lilburne's behalf, then in his own, because in August, he was himself imprisoned by the peers for refusing to acknowledge their jurisdiction over him.[3] Now he began to state his position in writings astonishingly bold. In plain terms, he denied the Lords any standing. They are, he wrote, 'but painted properties . . . that our superstition and ignorance, their own craft and impudence, have erected: no naturall issues of lawes, but the exuberance and mushrooms of Prerogative, the Wens of just government . . . Sons of conquest they are and usurpation, not of choice and election, intruded upon us by power, not constituted by consent, not made by the people from whom all power, place, and office that is just in this kingdome ought only to arise.'[4]

He also laid down the essence of his political theory in a statement that presented nature as a norm and as the origin of right. Quite in accord with his rationalistic temper, he set aside all received arrangements, acquiescing in nothing but what nature itself holds forth. Overton's thought, as he here expressed it, was almost detached from the Christian context which was its ultimate source. Where Lilburne in a

---

[1] *The araignement of Mr. Persecution*, 1645, 23, 11–12, 28–9. This was published under the pseudonym, Martin Mar-Priest, and was acknowledged with some of his other unsigned works in *A defiance against all arbitrary usurpations*, 1646, 24, 25–6.

[2] The anonymous *England's miserie, and remedie*, 1645, which denounced Parliament's handling of Lilburne, has been ascribed without evidence partly to Overton by D. Wolfe, *Milton*, 480. I do not think it is Overton's. Its style is not his, nor is it his way to quote Livy and other classical writers.

[3] *Lords journals*, VIII, 457.

[4] *The iust man in bonds*, 1646, 1. This anonymous pamphlet has been ascribed by Haller (*Tracts on liberty*, I, 122, 126) and by Wolfe (*Leveller manifestoes*, 9 n.) to William Walwyn. I believe it is Overton's on grounds of style. Its satire is much harsher and less mellow than Walwyn's.

similar declaration had spoken of Adam, the fall, and Christ's law, Overton spoke of God and nature, and the latter as the agent of the former. His words could almost have been those of a deist.

By natural birth, he said, 'all men are equally born to like propriety, liberty and freedome, and as we are delivered of God by the hand of nature into this world, every one with a naturall, innate freedome . . . even so are we to live, every one equally alike to enjoy his Birthright and priviledge; even all whereof God by nature hath made him free'. As men are born free, the only just origin of power is in a grant from every individual, '. . . and no more may be communicated then stands for [their] better being, weale, or safety . . . and this is mans prerogative . . . he that gives more, sins against his owne flesh; and he that takes more, is a Theife and Robber to his kind; Every man by nature being a King, Priest and Prophet in his own naturall circuite . . . whereof no second may partake, but by deputation, commission, and free consent from him, whose naturall right and freedome it is'.[1]

These conceptions were linked with a definite programme in Overton's great pamphlet, *A Remonstrance Of Many Thousand Citizens . . . To their owne House of Commons* (1646), one of the most brilliant of revolutionary manifestos.[2] The imperious tones in which this work addressed the Commons had never been equalled by any monarch, but they were only such as befitted the majesty of the people in whose name Overton spoke. Ever since the Norman conquest, he said, the people have been kept bondsmen by force and craft. At last they would endure it no longer, 'and then yee,' he told the Commons, 'were chosen to work our deliverance . . . for whatever our Fore-fathers were; or whatever they did or suffered, or were enforced to yeeld unto; we are the men of the present age, and ought to be free. . . '.[3] But instead of fulfilling its proper task, the Commons still temporize with the royal tyrant and maintain his doctrines. Let the House abolish monarchial government, he demanded, along with the negative voice of the Lords, for 'Yee only are chosen by Us . . . and therefore in you onely is the Power of binding the whole Nation. . . '.[4]

The Commons have also been acting despotically in claiming unlimited privileges for their members and in aiding the Presbyterians, 'as if also ye had discovered . . . That without a . . . compulsive Presbytry in the Church, a compulsive mastership, or Aristocraticall Government

---

[1] *An arrow against all tyrants*, 1646, 3–4.
[2] This was published anonymously. T. C. Pease (*op. cit.*, 153 n.) ascribes it to Overton or Henry Marten. Wolfe (*Milton*, 480, *Leveller manifestoes*, 111) thinks Walwyn and Overton wrote it. I agree with Haller (*Tracts on liberty*, I, 111) that it is Overton's.
[3] *A remonstrance*, 4–5.
[4] *Ibid.*, 6.

over the People in the State could never long be maintained'.[1] They permit heavy grievances to continue, and unjust laws, including Magna Carta, which is itself 'but a beggarly thing, containing many markes of intollerable bondage. . . '.[2] A change must be made, Overton declared. Let the House but trust the people, and do what is just, and 'Wee will therein assist you to the last drop of our bloods . . . Forsake . . . all craftie and subtill intentions; hide not your thoughts from Us, and give us encouragement to be open-breasted unto you'; and '. . . let the imprisoned Presse at liberty, that all mens understandings may be more conveniently informed, and convinced by the equity of your Proceedings'.[3]

Overton's pamphlet was a demand for a democratic republic. His rationalistic philosophy would have no truck with tradition. It would brook only what reason found justifiable, and claimed for the present generation what Englishmen's forefathers had been tyrannically denied. His fearless language made perfectly clear that he and those supporting him would not be satisfied with half a loaf. But certainly no House of Commons like that he addressed would ever trust the people or carry out the programme he proposed.

Overton soon realized this. Imprisoned in August 1646, all his efforts to have the Commons liberate him failed. Together with his fellow-prisoner, Lilburne, he determined to appeal above the Commons to the sovereign people. Like Lilburne, he believed that their failure to obtain justice proved the country had relapsed into a state of nature.[4] Why then may they not tread in Parliament's steps by appealing to the people against the Houses as the latter did against the king?[5]

Overton's appeal came forth in July 1647 in *An Appeale From the degenerate Representative Body The Commons . . . To the Body Repre-sented The free people in general . . . and in especiall . . . to all the Officers and Souldiers*. This is his last great pamphlet. It is nothing less than a call for a new revolution. Had its demands been carried out, the events which began in 1640 would have achieved ends which not even two hundred and fifty years of subsequent English development were able to gain fully.

Overton admits that history gives no precedent for his appeal to the people. But he is warranted, he says, by right reason which, though all forms of law and government fall, endures forever, 'the fountain of all justice and mercy to the creature. . . '.[6] Among the principles of right

---

[1] *Ibid.*, 11–12.
[2] *Ibid.*, 15–16.
[3] *Ibid.*, 18–19.
[4] *The out-cryes of oppressed commons*, 14. See above, 15 n 2.
[5] *Ibid.*, 14.
[6] *An appeale*, 1–2.

reason are that men should preserve themselves, that necessity is the highest law, that equity is superior to the letter of law, and that all entrusted power, if forfeited, returns to those who had entrusted it. These justify him, he insists.[1] Henceforth, he will hold invalid any order of Parliament. By their tyranny, the Houses have lost their capacity. Their acts should be fought to the death, and the promoters of them judged and condemned as traitors to the safety of the people.[2]

To preserve themselves, the people may exercise their inherent sovereignty and depute or create persons for the removal of tyrants. If it be objected, Overton says, that by reason of the prevailing confusions, such a deputation cannot be formally effected, 'I answer, that the Body naturall must never be without a mean to save it selfe, and therefore by the foresaid permanent unalterable rule of Necessity and safety, any person or persons . . . may warrantably rise up in the . . . behalf of the people, to preserve them from imminent ruine. . .'.[3] It is the army, he declares, which now has this duty, for it is 'the only formall and visible Head that is left unto the people for protection and deliverance'.[4] He summons the soldiers' elected agents 'to preserve that power and trust reposed in . . . you by the body of the Army intire and absolute and trust no man . . . how religious soever appearing, further then hee acts apparently for the good of the Army and Kingdome. . .'.[5]

The *Appeale* closes with an appendix of proposals presented for the army's consideration. These include a free and popularly chosen Parliament with provision for the recall and punishment of unworthy members; the reform of law and the abolition of imprisonment for debt; the banning of all compulsion in religion and the removal of tithes and trade monopolies; the establishment of free schools throughout the country; organized care for the sick, poor, and aged; and the restoration of lands which lay in common for the poor's use and were wrongfully enclosed.

Such was the revolutionary programme Overton sketched out. He had appealed to the masses; he had not merely justified the right of revolution abstractly, but had urged the people and the soldiers to act outside all legal channels in defiance of every traditional authority. His appraisal of contemporary institutions had issued in demands which he

[1] *Ibid.*, 4–5, 7.
[2] *Ibid.*, 11, 17–19.
[3] *Ibid.*, 22.
[4] *Ibid.*, 27.
[5] *Ibid.*, 30. In another work, Overton warned that the great officers were seeking to undermine the authority of the soldiers' agents and abolish the system of army representation. This attempt, if successful, he said, 'will necessitate and reduce the Armie to a blinde ignorant, and implicite faith, even in that work wherein their very lives and liberties doth consist. . .'. (*Eighteene reasons propounded to the soldiers of the body of the army*, 1647, 3, 7).

believed were coined in the very mint of reason itself. And the conception of reason he employed was one almost secularized and dissociated from its roots and commitments in Christian tradition. Short of communism, Overton's was as extreme a vision as English radicalism attained to during the revolution.[1]

3. WILLIAM WALWYN

William Walwyn was the son of a country gentleman and the grandson of a bishop. He was, in addition, a member of the Merchant Adventurers Company. It would not seem, therefore, that he was good material for the Levellers. But he was also a sceptical and questioning personality, ceaselessly seeking truth, and insisting that reason should try all things. Like his colleagues, he was first an advocate of liberty of conscience, and was drawn from the toleration controversy into the Leveller movement by his desire for social justice and for a government which would be no respecter of persons.[2]

Walwyn's outstanding contribution to the revolution was in his writings on liberty of conscience, several of which are among the best pamphlets of the seventeenth century. Very early, he entered the toleration struggle, and in his remarkable *The Power of Love* (1643) called for the use of reason in the free examination of every religious opinion.[3] During the course of his argument, some characteristic tendencies in the religious development of the left-democratic movement are made clear. The dogmatic element is dissolved, and with it, the claim of any persons whatever to be specially qualified interpreters of the word of God. There is nothing essential to the religious enlightenment of men, Walwyn said, which God has not made accessible to the meanest capacity. No special learning is needed, for with the Bible in English, any man may declare its true meaning.[4] As dogma disappears, the essence of true religion is located in conduct. Only love manifested in action is

[1] Overton's writings following his *Appeale* add nothing to the formulation of his political theory. His best later work was *The hunting of the foxes from New-Market and Triploe-Heaths to Whitehall*, 1649, ascribed to him, correctly, I think, by Wolfe, *Leveller manifestoes*, 355–7. It contains a biting description of Cromwell, who 'will lay his hand on his breast, elevate his eyes, and call God to record, he will weep, howle and repent, even while he doth smite you under the first rib' (*The hunting of the foxes*, 12).

[2] The details of Walwyn's life are most fully given by W. Schenk, *op. cit.*, Ch. III. W. Haller has done most to bring Walwyn to modern attention, and to clarify his bibliography in *Tracts on liberty*, I, Appendix A. On his bibliography, see also D. Wolfe, *Milton*, 481–3.

[3] This appeared anonymously and is ascribed to Walwyn by Haller, *Tracts on liberty*, I, 123, and, with reservations, by W. K. Jordan, *Development of religious toleration*, IV, 186 n. It seems to me to be Walwyn's.

[4] *The power of love*, 7–8, 44–9.

true religion, Walwyn says. God is love, and only love can make men God-like.[1] The obligation to scrutinize all religious tenets is stressed. 'Come, feare nothing,' he exhorts, 'you are advised by the Apostle to try all things . . . 'tis your selfe must doe it, you are not to trust to the authority of any man . . . you will finde upon tryall that scarcely any opinion hath been reported truly to you.'[2] Finally, there is antinomianism and the belief in universal redemption. All men are sinners, Walwyn declares, but God's love is boundless and will redeem them. Mankind is no longer under the law, but under grace. '. . . your feares, nor sinnes, nor doûbtings cannot alter that condition . . . Christ hath purchased for you, for though the sting of death be sinne, & the strength of sin be the law, yet thankes be unto God, for he hath given us the victory through our Lord Iesus Christ'.[3] Thus men are all as privileged in God's eyes as they ought to be in the state's.

In his great pamphlet, *The Vanitie of the present Churches* (1649),[4] Walwyn, ever anti-clerical, expressed a view which justified an anonymous enemy's charge that he maintained 'the largest Independency that ever was heard of; that every man and woman shall have no dependence upon any Church . . . but be his own Minister, hearer, officer, all'.[5] Despite the claims of Presbyterians and Independents, Walwyn said, no church has the mark of a true church. Though ministers profess to deliver God's word, their doubts and wranglings prove the uncertainty of their opinions.[6] They make religion complicated so as to gain a maintenance and live in wealth and honour. Instead of aiding the poor and oppressed, they deliver sermons full of dubious notions.[7] But the one necessary religious doctrine is that Jesus is the saviour whose blood takes away all sin and who died even for his enemies. Many things in Scripture may exceed understanding, Walwyn declares, but this doctrine is plain and full of comfort.[8] The people ought therefore to break their bondage to churches. Let them study the Scriptures and perfect their knowledge in small meetings by mutual discussion, without sermons. As their knowledge grows, they will come to realize that true religion consists in doing good, and that the way to show love for mankind is to free the commonwealth from tyrants and deceivers.[9]

---

[1] *Ibid.*, 36, To every reader.
[2] *Ibid.*, To every reader.
[3] *Ibid.*, 20, 24–5.
[4] Haller (*Tracts on liberty*, I, 122) ascribes this to Walwyn. Walwyn said it expressed his opinions (*Walwyns just defence*, 1649, 23; *The fountain of slander discovered*, 1649, 21), but he is silent on its authorship. I believe it is his.
[5] *Church-levellers*, 1649, 1–2.
[6] *The vanitie of the present churches*, 4–11.
[7] *Ibid.*, 23–6.
[8] *Ibid.*, 30–3.
[9] *Ibid.*, 43–7.

Walwyn's temper was pragmatic. 'I abandon all niceties and uselesse things,' he said. '. . . my manner is . . . to enquire what is the use: and if I find it not very materiall, I abandon it. . . .'[1] He was addicted to reading Plutarch, Seneca, Lucian, and especially Montaigne,[2] and suggested that Christians should discard superfluities and realise, as even the the heathen do, that 'a life according to nature' is pleasantest.[3] According to his friend, Dr. Brooke, Walwyn did not think communism evil, but held that it might only be instituted by the unanimous assent of the people.[4]

In 1645, leaving his hitherto exclusive concern with liberty of conscience, Walwyn came to the defence of the imprisoned John Lilburne. Lilburne's claims, Walwyn said, are justified by reason itself, and do not require Magna Carta as a precedent. Besides, he told Lilburne, 'Magna Carta hath been more precious in your esteeme than it deserveth. . . '. It is not the sum of English liberty, but the record of the little that has been wrung by force from tyrants who held the nation in bondage. Only mere ignorance will call the grants of conquerors the people's birthright and find in them the meaning of freedom. Rather than patch up an old charter, what is needed is to make a new and better one.[5]

This depreciation of Magna Carta,[6] and Walwyn's demand that a new charter should be drawn up, throw light on the attitude of the left-wing thinkers to the problem of history. That problem was defined for them by the necessity to make the past justify a programme which seemed innovative, and failing this, to find other sanction than precedent. Simultaneously, two attitudes towards history were developed, each of which was put to use. First, the recent past with its tyrannous monarchy, its arrogant peerage, and its unjust laws was brushed aside, as innovations imposed on a free people by the Norman conquest, and appeal was made to a past more ancient, and therefore more hallowed, when men lived in a freedom the Normans destroyed.[7] In this way, the Levellers tried to appropriate history for their own ends. Analogously to the fall of man and his restitution, they represented English history as the fall of liberty and its possible restoration in their own day. Second, be-

[1] *A whisper in the eare of Mr Thomas Edwards*, 1646, 10 (mispaged).

[2] *Walwyns just defence*, 9–12.

[3] *The power of love*, 3–6. Haller, *Tracts on liberty*, I, 40, has pointed out that this passage suggests the influence of Montaigne's essay on cannibals, *Essais*, I, 30.

[4] *The crafts-mens craft*, 1649, 9.

[5] *Englands lamentable slaverie*, 1645, 3–5. Pease (*op. cit.*, 116 n.) and Haller (*Tracts on liberty*, I, 125) ascribe this anonymous work to Walwyn. It bears every mark of his style.

[6] Lilburne and Overton similarly depreciated it in 1646; see above, 11, 23.

[7] The origins of this interpretation of the English past have never been adequately studied. They definitely antedate 1640, for something not unlike the Leveller view of the Norman conquest is to be found, e.g., in Samuel Daniel's *The collection of the history of England*, 1612–18, in the latter's account of the reign of William I.

cause they were aware that the past could not always be used to support their demands, they appealed to reason. This is what inspires the affirmation of Overton that '. . . whatever our Fore-fathers were . . . we are the men of the present age, and ought to be free . . .'[1] and Lilburne's refusal to accept previous legal enactments as fundamental law unless they are consonant with reason.[2] But their appeal to reason as an ultimate basis of judgment constituted, it is evident, a rejection of history. For lacking any conception of the present, both as the past's product and its negation, they had necessarily to dismiss history as an irrational departure from the norm of justice, and to desert it for a higher principle.

It may be regarded as a general rule of the development of democratic and radical thought throughout this period and for long afterwards, that it tended to eschew history in favour of reason. A Parliamentary writer such as Henry Parker exhibited the same tendency as the Levellers when he took refuge in the rational principle of *salus populi* in defiance of all traditional arrangements. The Levellers carried this much further. Their literal acceptance of the state of nature is a remarkable illustration of this. For what did the stress on the state of nature signify, if not a reading away of all the determinate historical conditions under which men lived, with all their corporate privileges, customary rights, and traditional ties? All that remained was man as a rational creature and what he could claim in virtue of being a man—a claim more compelling than any sanctioned by immemorial custom.

The invocation of reason by the radicals left the royalists in possession of history. Reckoned by precedents, history was on their side, and most royalist writers countered the arguments of their opponents by taking their stand on the historic constitution.[3] Even Sir Robert Filmer's patriarchal theory was, if anything, an exaltation of history, a mythical history, to be sure, but real enough to him and some of his contemporaries. By upholding father-right, and tracing the right of kings back to the first fathers, to Adam and to Noah, he was appealing to the ties of tradition and the patriarchal family organization that reinforced them.[4]

The Levellers' appeal to reason was still, on the whole, to the right reason of the Christian tradition, synonymous with the law of Christ. Owing to this, their social criticism, despite all its sharpness, did not range with entire freedom, and left religion itself exempt from scrutiny. If Leveller rationalism was moved to denounce the churches, it did so only in the name of a higher religious principle. If it attacked the

[1] See above, 22.
[2] See above, 16.
[3] J. W. Allen, *op. cit.*, 485–508.
[4] Sir Robert Filmer, *Patriarcha and other political writings*, ed. P. Laslett, Oxford, 1949, Introduction, 20–33; and see below, Ch. XIV.

beneficed clergy, it had not yet learned to treat the promise of heaven as a calculated clerical manoeuvre by which men's attention was diverted from their earthly oppressors. If it declared dogma irrelevant to salvation, it had not yet diluted the Christian God into an impersonal but beneficent nature. Moreover, it did not yet question that salvation was achieved through the sacrifice of Jesus Christ. All the same, the Leveller notion of reason was deeply tinged with secular elements, and looked forward to the Enlightenment when Eternal Reason, autonomous and untrammeled, would hail every aspect of life to judgment at its bar and reduce to rubble the sanctuaries which the past had regarded with awe. This development is fully plotted in the ideas of Overton and Walwyn, less so in those of Lilburne; for the two former, as we have seen, were of a more sceptical turn of mind than their great colleague.

In common with the other Leveller leaders, Walwyn's aim was the supremacy of a democratic House of Commons. Under the present Commons, he pointed out, oppression is as great as it was under the king, and all the quarrel between Presbyterians and Independents 'is but this, namely, whose slaves the people shall be'.[1] Unless the House sets a time for its dissolution, he warned, and enacts reforms, it will be repudiated by the people, for 'the just freedom and happiness of a Nation [is] above all Constitutions . . .'.[2]

Perhaps Walwyn's profoundest political belief was in the method of discussion as the indispensable basis for free government. There is nothing, he declared, 'that maintains love unity and friendship in families: Societies, Citties, Countries, Authorities, Nations; so much as a condescension to the giving, and hearing, and debating of reason'.[3] It is a striking tribute to the breadth of the Leveller movement that it could attract this urbane and questioning mind. And it is a greater tribute to the man himself that, though he loved nothing so much as a good book and a discoursing friend, he could yet leave the quiet of his meditations to press for the freedom in which he believed amidst the alarums and strife of political life.

---

[1] *The bloody proiect*, 1648, 12, 14. This pamphlet is signed 'W P Gent', and was ascribed to Walwyn in John Canne's anonymously published pamphlet, *The discoverer*, 1649, Part I, 17, Part II, 54. Haller first denied Walwyn's authorship (*Tracts on liberty*, I, 126), but apparently changed his mind in Haller and Davies, *Leveller tracts*, 135. I regard it as Walwyn's.

[2] *Ibid.*, 14, 12–13.

[3] *The fountain of slander discovered*, 18–19. We know little of Walwyn's activities after 1649. In 1651, he put forth an unimportant tract, *Juries justified*, and eight years later his name was suggested by James Harrington (*Works*, London, 1771, 586) as one of a committee to discuss a scheme for a republic.

4. JOHN WILDMAN AND OTHER LEVELLER WRITERS

Of the four Leveller leaders, John Wildman was least important as a theorist. He wrote less than Lilburne, Overton, and Walwyn, and added practically nothing on the theoretical level that we do not find in their works. But he did play an outstanding part in the movement, and was an effective pamphleteer. In the 1650s, however, he left the Leveller camp and enlisted among Cromwell's republican opponents, where we shall meet him again.[1]

Wildman's most important Leveller writing was *The Case Of The Armie Truly Stated* (1647)[2] which gave a burning voice to the army radicalism that the Levellers had brought into being, and from which some of the specific demands in the first *Agreement* were taken.[3] Denouncing the Commons' failure to redress the soldiers' and the nation's grievances, Wildman called for the purging of the Houses, and for the enactment of a law paramount that would secure biennial Parliaments elected by all men over twenty-one years of age. '. . . all obstructions,' he said, 'to the freedome and equallitie of the peoples choice of their Representors, either by Patents, Charters, or usurpations, by pretended customes [must] be removed. . . .'[4]

Shortly after *The Case Of The Armie* appeared, Wildman cautioned the soldiers to beware of the treachery of their officers. Do not be frightened 'by the word Anarchy', he warned, 'unto a love of Monarchy, which is but the gilded name for Tyranny'. Those who fight for freedom are always 'slap't in the mouthes with these most malignant reproaches, O, yee are for Anarchy, yee are against all Government. . . .'[5] He advised the soldiers to repudiate Cromwell and create new officers.[6] He assailed the Cromwellians' platform of settlement, *The Heads Of The Proposals*, which had appeared in July 1647, as a restoration of the power of the king and his creatures, the peers, with no effective safeguards for the people's freedom. The only way to achieve a solid peace, he said, is by granting that all power comes from the people, that no power can exist except by the people's consent, and that the Commons alone are the

[1] Wildman's life is fully told by M. Ashley, *John Wildman plotter and postmaster*, London, 1947.

[2] This was signed by the representatives of five regiments, but may be ascribed to Wildman because of Ireton's uncontradicted implication at the Putney debates (A. S. P. Woodhouse, *op. cit.*, 92, 80) that he wrote it. C. H. Firth, *The Clarke papers*, 4 vols., London, 1891–1901, I, xlvii, 354 n., and Ashley, *op. cit.*, 15, accept it as his.

[3] See the first *Agreement*, Postscript.

[4] *The case of the armie truly stated*, 1–2, 6, 14–16.

[5] *A cal to all the souldiers of the armie*, 1647, 6. C. H. Firth ('John Wildman', *D.N.B.*), Haller and Davies (*Leveller tracts*, 64), and Ashley (*op. cit.*, 39) are correct, I believe, in accepting this as Wildman's.

[6] *Ibid.*, Part II, 6–7.

people's representative, not to be overtopped by any other authority.[1]

Like the other Leveller leaders, Wildman's principal requirement was the recognition of the right of all, including the poorest, to have a voice. Like them, too, he desired the redress of grievances, the effect of which would have been to cut seriously into the interests of many powerful groups: the common lawyers, members of the great trading companies, and the beneficed clergy, besides the crowd of jobbers and committee-men who were making profits out of government business. But in the writings of none of the Leveller chiefs was there an outspoken hatred for the rich as such, nor a distinct and considered concern with the problems of the agricultural population.

These themes, neglected in the works of the leaders, are to be found in the writings of some of the minor Leveller figures. A brilliant instance is Laurence Clarkson's *A General Charge Or Impeachment of High-Treason* (1647).[2] Clarkson was a sectarian preacher who ran the whole gamut of religious experience possible in his time, beginning with Anglicanism and ending as a ranter, an antinomian, and a materialist who asserted that the world was uncreated and eternal.[3] His pamphlet was a denunciation of the rich and their domination of Parliament, and takes the form of a discourse delivered by Experienced Reason in behalf of Justice-Equity. How could you expect a Parliament of rich men to free you, Experienced Reason asks the people:

'for who are the oppressors, but the Nobility and Gentry; and who are oppressed, is not the Yeoman, the Farmer, the Tradesman, and the Labourer? then consider, have you not chosen oppressors to redeeme you from oppression? . . . it is naturally imbred in the major part of the Nobility and Gentry . . . to judge the poore but fooles, and themselves wise, and therefore when you the Communalty calleth a Parliament, they are confident such must be chosen, that are the noblest and richest . . . but . . . reason affirmeth . . . these are not your equals, neither are these sensible of the burthen that lyeth upon you; for indeed . . . your slavery is their liberty, your poverty is their prosperity. . . .'

Nor do the rich desire peace, Clarkson says, for 'peace is their ruine . . . by warre they are inriched . . . peace is their war, peace is their poverty . . . .'.[4]

These remarkable statements come much closer to the ideas of the

---

[1] *Putney proiects*, 1647, *passim*. This is signed with the obvious pseudonym, John Lawmind.

[2] This is signed L.C. and is acknowledged by Clarkson in his *The lost sheep found*, 1660, 24.

[3] Clarkson is briefly noticed in the *D.N.B.* as Laurence Claxton. His autobiographical tract, *The lost sheep found*, ought to be reprinted. It is one of the most illuminating documents extant for understanding the sectarian's religious quest.

[4] *A general charge*, 11, 14.

communist, Gerrard Winstanley, than to those of John Lilburne.[1] But Clarkson's solution to the poor's oppression was not communism, but the familiar one of a popularly elected Parliament.[2]

Other writings sounded a note similar to Clarkson's. One author pointed to a 'confederacy amongst the rich and mighty to impoverish and so to enslave all the plaine and meane people. . .'. By force and fraud, the rich have gained 'most of the land of this distressed and enslaved nation into [their] clawes . . . yea, and inclosed our commons in most counties'. They have raised the rent of lands and of shops in London, and have beggared many. Thus they have perverted 'the end of Gods Creation, who in all Nations, hath most wisely . . . provided a sufficiency of necessaries . . . unto every . . . individuall person . . . and which if withheld, is in his sight no lesse then robbery and injustice . . .'.[3]

Some pamphleteers demanded the abolition of all manorial tenures. John Jubbes, an army officer under Leveller influence,[4] proposed the destruction of '. . . all inslaving tenures upon Record by Oaths of Fealty, Villanage, Homage, Fines at will of the Lords', though with compensation to landlords.[5] Another writer asked whether 'the oppressive prerogative of Lords of Manors . . . and a Free-state can consist together'.[6]

But the most remarkable protest against agrarian exploitation which the Leveller movement produced was the anonymous *Light shining in Buckingham-shire* (1648), and its sequel, *More light shining in Buckingham-shire* (1649).[7] These expressed the peasant's demand to own his land, and his hatred of enclosures. Like Overton and Lilburne, their author declared that God created man with reason, so that none was to be lord over his fellows, all being born free and with an equal share in the creation. Then man fell, and a few mercenary ones enslaved their brethren and enclosed the earth.[8] In England, kingship has been the source of all injustice, beginning with the Norman conquest. All land-tenure is by the king's authority, and rich men, lawyers, and noblemen 'cry for a King, because the poor should not claim his right that is his by Gods gift'.[9]

[1] Clarkson knew Winstanley, but said he disapproved of his ideas, *The lost sheep found*, 27.

[2] *A general charge*, 12.

[3] *Englands troublers troubled*, 1648, 2, 5, 10.

[4] See Schenk, *op. cit.*, Appendix B.

[5] *An apology unto the honorable . . . officers . . . by Lieut. Col. John Jubbes*, 1649, 13–14.

[6] J. W., *A mite to the treasury*, 1653, 14.

[7] G. P. Gooch, *English democratic ideas in the seventeenth century*, London, 1927, 187, and E. Bernstein, *Cromwell and communism*, trans. E. Stenning, London, 1930, 132, attributed these to Gerrard Winstanley. I agree with Petegorsky, *op. cit.*, 138 n., that he was not their author.

[8] *Light shining*, 2.

[9] *Ibid.*, 3–5.

'. . . is it not fit for all to eat alike, have alike, and enjoy alike privileges and freedoms? . . . weep and howl, ye Rich men . . . God will visit you for all your oppressions; You live on other mens labours . . . extorting extreme rents and taxes. . . . But now what will you do: For the people will no longer be enslaved by you, for the knowledge of the Lord shall enlighten them.'[1]

'For a man to inclose all Lands . . . from his kind,' the author said, 'is utterly unnatural, wicked and treacherous; for if man shall eat bread by his sweat, then, he must needs have ground to sow corn; therefore to inclose all grounds from him, is to starve him. . . .'[2] Though the king has been expelled, unless manor lords and other unjust privileges are removed, the nation remains enslaved.[3]

As we might expect, the Leveller movement had its anti-imperialist side, and gave rise to attacks against the English attempt to subjugate Ireland. One anonymous author asked why the English should fight to impose tyranny upon another people. '. . . is it your ambition to reduce the Irish to the happiness of Tythes upon trebble damages, to Excise, Customs and Monopolies in Trades? or to fill their prisons with poor disabled prisoners, to fill their Land with swarms of beggars; to enrich their Parliament-men and impoverish their people?'[4] A newspaper reported that such dangerous questions as the following were being disseminated in the army to undermine the Irish expedition:[5]

'Whether it be not the duty of every honest man to divert what he can the intended expedition. . . . Whether those who pretend for freedome (as the English now) shall not make themselves altogether inexcusable, in intrenching upon others freedoms, and whether it be not a character of a true Patriot to endeavour the just freedome of all as well as his owne. Whether . . . the Irish are not to be justified in all that they have done . . . to preserve and deliver themselves from the cruelty and usurpation of the English. . . . Whether it be not Englands duty to repent the Oppressions and usurpations over the Irish nation, by their Kings and Fore-fathers.'[6]

Such attacks as these on the rich, on manorial lords, and on the Irish war were significant elements in Leveller thinking. They show how

---

[1] *Ibid.*, 7.
[2] *More light shining*, 10.
[3] *Ibid.*, 13–14.
[4] *The English souldiers standard to repaire to*, 1649, 9–10.
[5] It is just possible that Walwyn was behind these. The queries have his touch. His enemies accused him of justifying the Irish rebellion, *Walwins wiles*, 1649, 25.
[6] *The moderate intelligencer*, 2nd–9th May, 10th—17th May 1649. I owe these references to the kindness of Mr. H. N. Brailsford.

many-sided the movement was, and how extensive was the protest which it stimulated. They were of less importance, however, than the demand for political reform. This was the Levellers' alpha and omega, bulking largest not only in the writings of their theorists, but also, as we shall immediately see, in their party programme.

III

THE LEVELLER PARTY PROGRAMME

IN THE separate writings of the Leveller leaders, there had been formulated a conception of the social order which insisted that institutions justify themselves before the bar of reason. Whatever the past had been, the present must be shaped so as to allow every man's rational nature scope for expression. Only thus could the law of Christ and true religion be fulfilled. By the middle of 1647 there existed a movement of men who accepted this theory as the expression of their deepest, but hitherto inchoate, feelings. By means of it, local suffering elevated itself to a height from which it could gain a view of its relationship to the social order that had produced it. For the first time, a mass-movement gathered from the victims of miscellaneous oppressions did not stop with demands for partial and isolated changes, but went on to call for a programme of comprehensive reform. A sufferer from monopolies could find in the writings of the Leveller leaders the basis for perceiving the connection between his own problems and those of many other separate men. He could find, too, that his adversaries were not only in the great trading companies, but in Parliament. And he would discover that his demand for a free trade had better foundation then precedent, being grounded in his right as a man. Thus the theory of the Leveller leaders became a force rallying soldiers and civilians to the banner Lilburne and his fellows had raised. Hob-nailed boots and clouted shoes demanded a reckoning. '. . . suffer us,' they cried, 'to free ourselves, and the whole commonalty of the Kingdome from . . . an intolerable burden and slavery; to shake and tumble downe that mountain of dishonour and oppression, that this Kingdome for so long time hath groaned under. . . .'[1]

From 1647 onward, these demands for a general justice were being given a local habitation and a name in official party statements. Beginning with a petition in the spring of 1647 which the Commons commanded to be burnt as insolent and seditious,[2] the Leveller programme

---

[1] *An alarum to the headquarters*, 1647, 4.

[2] *To the right honourable and supreme authority of this nation, the Commons . . . the humble petition of many thousands; Commons journals*, V, 179. This petition is reprinted in Lilburne's *Rash oaths unwarrantable*, 29–35. Thomason's copy is dated 19th September 1648.

evolved through two versions of *The Agreement of the People* and other petitions,[1] to culminate in a third and final version of the *Agreement* in 1649.[2] This last *Agreement*, issued by Lilburne, Overton, Walwyn, and a lesser Leveller figure, Thomas Prince, from captivity in the Tower, was the Levellers' finest legacy, and their conclusive word on the problems of their distracted country. It summed up the experience gained during intense political struggles, crystallized the chief aspirations of those parts of the community for which they spoke, and presented their maturest conception of what was necessary for the achievement of a peace based on the people's freedom. A study of it will illuminate the Leveller plan of settlement in detail at its highest point, and make clear what its social bearings were.

The third *Agreement* begins with a preamble in which the people declare their intention of ascertaining their government. Then follow a a series of articles laying down the powers and duties of the future representative. Supreme authority is to reside in a Representative of 400 persons, to which all men, twenty-one years and over, not servants or in receipt of alms, may elect and be elected. Those who have aided the royalist cause are disabled from this privilege for ten years. Members are to be paid a salary, and each constituency is to be represented in proportion to its population. While men are officers in the armed forces or treasurers of public moneys, they may not be members of the Representative; nor may lawyers who are members practise during their term of office. No man may be elected a member twice in succession. Elections are to be held annually, and no Representative is to sit for more than a year or less than four months. In adjournments, a committee of members elected by the Representative, and acting under its published instructions, is to manage affairs. The power of the Representative is to extend, without the concurrence of any persons, to the conservation of peace, the regulation of commerce, the preservation of the people's liberties and estates as declared in the Petition of Right of 1628, the raising of money, and to all other things conducive to freedom, the removal of grievances, and the commonwealth's prosperity.

Now comes a long list of subjects on which the Representative is

---

[1] *An agreement of the people*, 3rd November 1647; *Foundations of freedom: or an agreement of the people*, 15th December 1648. The most important Leveller petition of 1648 was *To the right honourable the Commons . . . the humble petition of thousands wel-affected persons*, 15th September 1648.

[2] *An agreement of the free people of England*, 1st May 1649. There were a number of documents known as agreements of the people published between 1647–9. Only three are Leveller. A discussion of the relation between all of these may be found in J. W. Gough, 'The agreements of the people, 1647–1649', *History*, N. S., XV, 60. Mr. Gough was unaware that what he lists as the third agreement was composed by a private person, Lieut.-Col. John Jubbes, and should be supplemented here by Wolfe, *Leveller manifestoes*, 311–12, W. Schenk, *op. cit.*, Appendix B.

denied power. It may not compel or restrain any person in matters of religion, nor impress men for military service, 'every mans Conscience being to be satisfied in the justness of that cause wherein he hazards his own life, or may destroy others'. In order to abolish the enmities created by the war, it may not, except in execution of the judgements of the last Parliament sitting before the *Agreement* takes effect,[1] question any person for his part in the wars. It may not exempt any person from the operation of the laws on the pretext of tenure, grant, charter, patent, degree, birth, residence, or parliamentary privilege. It may not have anything to do with the execution of laws, nor permit legal proceedings and the laws to be in any language but English. It may not continue laws abridging the freedom of foreign trade, and may not raise money by excise taxes or except by an equal rate levied upon real and personal estate. It may not make or continue laws imprisoning men for debt, nor may it continue the death penalty for any crime but murder. It may not continue tithes, though impropriators are to be compensated. It may not take away the liberty of each parish to elect its own ministers. It may not alter judgments in trials from being given by twelve jurors, dwelling in the neighbourhood, and freely elected by the people. It may prevent no one from holding office for religion except upholders of the papal or any other foreign supremacy. It may not impose officials on counties, hundreds, cities, or towns, the people of which are freely to elect their own officers annually.

There follows, finally, a list of miscellaneous provisions. Future representatives are to pay all just public debts. In order to assure the subordination of the armed forces to the civil power, each constituency shall raise its own military forces and elect its officers, reserving to the Representative, however, the naming of the general officers. Any member of the Representative, or any other person, endeavouring to destroy the *Agreement*, or to establish communism, shall incur the penalty of high treason and lesser penalties shall be incurred by persons disturbing the people's elections.

In this multiplicity of powers and reservations, the general scheme of reconstruction can be clearly seen. The popular franchise, most important of all, was clearly provided for, though it excluded servants and those living on charity, as well as women. The former classes were denied a vote because, a Leveller spokesman pointed out, they 'depend upon the will of other men and should be afraid to displease [them]',[2] and it may be imagined that in the prevailing family organization, the exclusion of women would be similarly justified by the Levellers. Supporters

---

[1] The *Agreement* provided that the sitting Parliament should dissolve in August 1649.
[2] This is Petty's explanation in the debates of the army council at Putney, A. S. P. Woodhouse, *op. cit.*, 83.

of the royal cause were deprived of political rights for ten years, but by preventing the Representative from questioning men for their part in the wars, it was hoped that the country would grow once more into unity, especially since the benefits of the *Agreement* were believed by the Levellers to affect all interests favourably. At the same time, in permitting the Parliament sitting before the *Agreement* became effective to give judgment on the chief instigators of the war, it was expected that the king and certain royalists would be punished.

The peers and the monarchy were stripped of all their privileges and powers, but neither was abolished. If we are to accept Wildman's statement in 1647,[1] the Levellers did not object to a peerage as such. So far as monarchy was concerned, there is no doubt that had not Cromwell established a military rule by the time the third *Agreement* was drawn up, it would have been done away with. Both Lilburne and Overton had expressed a desire for this,[2] and in February 1649 the former had attacked the plan of settlement of the Cromwellian group for omitting a reservation against the restoration of monarchy.[3] But Lilburne later declared, 'I had rather . . . live under a regulated and wel-bounded King . . . then under any Government with Tyrannie',[4] and the final *Agreement* did not ban monarchy because the Levellers wished to be prepared for the possibility that Cromwell might be overthrown and the king restored on condition of his acceptance of their principles.[5]

With the proposals for a popularly elected annual Parliament free from any negative voice and subject to definite rules, the Levellers gave a conclusive answer to the constitutional and political questions which they believed to be at the centre of the issues that the revolution had precipitated. Similarly, by removing all compulsion in matters of religious faith, they dealt definitively with the religious question. They laid down the principle that toleration was to extend to all professions. And, whereas in their first and second *Agreements* they had permitted Parliament at its discretion to establish a national church, provided it was voluntary, they gave the Representative no such power now. The religion of the country was to be as varied as the faiths that flourished in it, and even Catholics could practise their beliefs without disturbance.

Finally, the various grievances against which the Levellers had been protesting were to be redressed by depriving the Representative of

---

[1] At the Putney debates, *Ibid.*, 109.

[2] See above, Ch. II.

[3] *Englands new chains discovered*, First part, 1649 [3]. Lilburne referred to the officers' *Agreement of the people*, submitted by the army to the purged Parliament on 20th January 1649.

[4] *A discourse betwixt Lieutenant Colonel John Lilburne . . . and Mr. Hugh Peter*, 1649, 8.

[5] In 1652, while exiled in Holland, Lilburne was in touch with various royalists on this basis; see Gibb, *op. cit.*, 307–8.

power to continue the laws which sanctioned them. It is interesting, however, that certain demands which had been put forward earlier did not now appear. Reservations in the second Leveller *Agreement* prohibiting the rate of interest from being set higher than 6 per cent and exempting estates of less than £30 from all national taxation were omitted. So was a requirement in the second *Agreement* that a record office be erected in every county for the registration of all bills, bonds, and conveyances. These were probably oversights. Most important of all, the abolition of base tenures, which Lilburne had called for in a list of articles at the end of the second *Agreement*, was overlooked.[1]

We can best understand the Leveller programme in this, its greatest formulation, if we characterize it as a lower-middle-class utopia. Utopia it was—and no dishonour on this account to its framers—because the prevailing relationships of economic and political power offered no basis for its realization. Lower middle class we may call it because its every line expressed the aspirations of the small and middle sort of people who formed the backbone of the Leveller movement.

The *Agreement* portrayed an equalitarian order which aimed at dissociating wealth from privilege by granting the same political rights to all. Under its electoral programme, it was expected that small merchants, craftsmen, and yeomen would possess sufficient weight to balance the economic advantages of great merchants and wealthy landlords. The pronounced emphasis on decentralization and local elections was to have the result of curbing both the oligarchies of the towns and rural areas, and London's power over the rest of the country. No longer would the central government appoint the justices of the peace and the sheriffs. No longer would these and other posts be habitually occupied by the gentry and the men of substance who packed the town corporations. Thus, it was hoped, the commonalty of town and country would establish its participation in political power.

Economically, the *Agreement* secured the interests primarily of people of lesser means. The removal of excise would ease those upon whom a tax on food fell heaviest. Though foreign trade monopolies were to be taken away, nothing was said of the whole complex of regulations governing guild privileges, apprenticeships, and local trade and industry. These the Levellers had never assailed, for they were the barriers behind which small masters and craftsmen were often entrenched. Lilburne had always borne in mind the economic grievances of such men, and had pointed out, for example, how clothiers, clothworkers, and spinners were victimized by the Merchant Adventurers Company.[2] It was on behalf of these, it would seem, that the Levellers

---

[1] The Leveller petition of September 1648 had asked that enclosures of fens and commons be laid open or enclosed solely for the benefit of the poor.

[2] *Innocency and truth justified*, 50.

wished the system of regulation to function, and hence they confined their attack to foreign trade monopolies alone.

In all these respects, therefore, the Leveller programme carries the imprint of the interests of those of intermediate status in economic life. Moreover, its outlook was predominantly urban. The *Agreement's* demands, of course, called for the removal of grievances that were general, and not limited only to urban groups. But its silence on the problem of copyholds and manorial lords was more than an oversight. Despite the occasional mention of the abolition of base tenures,[1] the land question was never a critical issue in the Leveller programme, and, among agrarian elements, it reflected more the aims of the small free-holder and yeomanry than those of the poor peasantry. This was a fundamental defect. It was on the latter that much of the power of the landed gentry depended and to leave the basis of this power unaffected by reform was to contradict the equalitarian commonwealth for which the Levellers stood. Because their programme dealt so summarily with the agrarian problem, the great majority of the rural population remained indifferent to it, despite the considerable rural discontent and disturbance which occurred during the revolution.[2]

The Leveller movement was distinguished in general by its high humanitarianism and by the essential hope that it would win its way through persuading the minds of men. It expressed care for the poor, the aged, the sick, the imprisoned, the oppressed, the unemployed. What they would do for these, the Levellers believed, was only what the law of Christ and of reason evidently required. The Leveller leaders would have shunned the notion that their position expressed the outlook of any class. They believed their demands were inferences from reason, as illuminated by Christ's law, and reason was the same in one man as in a thousand. Their programme corresponded to a universal interest, they held, and only men who have become beastly or who are blind, they would have argued, could fail to see this fact. Perhaps this was why in none of their *Agreements* was any provision made for amending the rules upon which the new political order was to operate. As the Leveller commonwealth was created, so, apparently, was it to remain forever. Moreover, there can be no doubt whatever that in spite of the call of Lilburne and Overton in 1647 for the people to rise, and in spite of the mutinies of Leveller soldiers in the army, the Levellers did not regard force as a normal or a desirable method of effecting political

---

[1] See above, 39. Lilburne's position was repeated in the London Levellers' statement of 1653, *The fundamental lawes and liberties of England claimed . . . by several peaceable persons . . . commonly called Levellers*, 1653, 4.

[2] See instances in E. Lipson, *The economic history of England*, 3 vols., 1929–31, II, 406–7, and M. James, *Social problems and policy during the Puritan revolution 1640–1660*, London, 1930, 90–106.

change. They relied, they said, 'solely upon that inbred and perswasive power that is in all good and just things, to make their own way in the hearts of men, and so to procure their own Establishment'.[1] When Lilburne called for a rising, it was because he believed the country was in a state of nature. If he had really subscribed to violence as a tactic, his movement would have been far more dangerous to the Cromwellian government than it was.

The Leveller programme was the glorious hope of men who lacked all possibility of gaining power. While Lilburne led a revolution that failed, Cromwell led one that succeeded. While Lilburne strove unsuccessfully for a democratic republic, Cromwell created an oligarchic one. If Lilburne's tragedy lay in the powerlessness of his movement to achieve its ends, Cromwell's consisted in the doom of a Stuart restoration that fatally overhung him because of the narrow basis on which his power was erected. Yet with all their differences, the Levellers and Cromwell had important principles in common. Both desired liberty of conscience, though not in the same degree. They were alike also in fearing a strong central government as the source from which despotism would always arise. Many actions to which Cromwell resorted to retain power would have been left undone if his rule had been a stable one.[2] Like the men for whom the Levellers spoke, Cromwell wished to be finished forever with the tyranny he saw exemplified in the interfering government of Charles I and his ministers, Laud and Strafford. But however one limits the state's role, it will still retain positive functions which can affect either favourably or not the various interests in the community. And so while the circumscribed state of the Levellers would have enforced the equalitarian order outlined in their *Agreement*, Cromwell's discharged the task of securing the property and position of the gentry and great merchants who inherited power in revolutionary and restoration England.

The Levellers at the very birth of political democracy stated its full theoretical implications. They would tolerate no groups or orders in society with special political privileges. They required that Parliament be truly representative. And they extended the right of consent to every individual. They admitted no sovereignty anywhere, unless it was in every man's conscience. They seriously accepted the possibility of any man refusing obedience to commands incompatible with his idea of reason or justice. This may appear anarchic, but to them it was the ultimate guarantee of liberty. But they clearly believed that a representative non-sovereign Parliament, itself subject to the laws it enacted for the people, and restrained by the safeguards of the *Agreement*, would

---

[1] *A manifestation*, 7.
[2] Cf. E. Barker, *Oliver Cromwell and the English people*, Cambridge, 1937, 47–62.

erect that which every individual conscience unbiased by an irrational selfishness would be likely to accept.

Their great objective was political reform, and in the occasional Leveller pamphlets that continued to appear through the 1650s this aspiration was still being given utterance. The declaration of London Levellers in 1653 insisted that 'The people cannot be . . . Free . . . while the Supream power . . . is wrested out of their hands . . . and the prime Badge and principle of their Freedom is, Their own Election'.[1] The anonymous author of *Englands Remembrancers* (1656) advised Cromwell's millenarian opponents not to boycott the elections to Parliament announced in June 1656, because despite Cromwell's tyranny, '(unlesse there could be a personall agreement of the people) an assemblie of the peoples Deputies, is the only visible means to settle justice. . .'.

'Dear Christians, it is by the choice of your Deputies only, that the whole body politick of this nation can consult together for their preservation . . . there is no other way consistent with the laws of God, or the nature of mankind, whereby our breaches can be healed, lawfull powers and authorities created, righteousnesse and justice exercised amongst us.'[2]

The unknown Leveller who wrote *The Parliaments Plea* in October 1659 when the breakdown of all effective government seemed near, told the soldiers in the army that a durable settlement could be made only by consent of the people in Parliament, and counselled them to choose representatives and effect the army's submission to a freely elected Parliament ruling without any king or peerage, under powers prescribed in an agreement of the people.[3] And in November 1659, some inhabitants of Hampshire were still demanding an agreement of the people providing for a supreme representative body and the separation of legislative and administrative functions.[4]

The programme the Levellers announced for their own day took more than two hundred and fifty years to achieve. Like Moses, they never dwelt in Canaan. Yet the beliefs they voiced did not die, and rose from the ashes into which the hopes of revolutionary England were consumed. Long afterwards, they were taken up by new forces, by the Chartists and the trade unions, to become the battle-cry of new struggles.

[1] *The fundamental lawes and liberties of England claimed . . . by several peaceable persons . . . commonly called Levellers*, 6.
[2] *Englands remembrancers*, 4, 1–2.
[3] *The parliaments plea*, 13, 15–17, 21–2.
[4] *The weekly post*, 22nd–29th November 1659.

IV

UTOPIAN COMMUNISM

1. GERRARD WINSTANLEY

THE development of the thought of Gerrard Winstanley is a strange phenomenon in the history of English political theory. For almost eight years after the Long Parliament met, this genius, whose voice a distant posterity has listened for above the roar of his time, remained absolutely silent. Nothing of his is to be found in the discussion of the early 1640s on liberty of conscience. He contributed no writing to the Leveller agitation for reform. When at last he took his pen in hand in 1648, he put forth an unpolitical book about religion. Yet within a few months after this, Winstanley was a communist. And not four years later, after having written some works of much depth and beauty, he concluded his brief literary career with the account of a remarkable communist utopia that is impregnated with the spirit of rationalism.

The known details of Winstanley's life help little to explain his thought. In 1640, he was thirty-one years old, and carrying on a small business in London as a cloth-merchant. Three years later he became a bankrupt, ruined by the depression which the civil war occasioned, and was forced to go to live with friends in the country.[1] Sometime during these early years he was for a period a Baptist.[2] This is almost all we know of his life before he began to write.

He was, it seems clear, a man of sensitive mind and of great gifts, who yet might have remained silent had it not been his destiny to live in a revolution. The collapse of control that accompanied the end of Stuart rule permitted a marvellous proliferation of religious life and a pressing to their conclusion of tendencies at work in the various sects. The opportunity thus presented for the extremely rapid acquisition of religious experience, which in some ardent souls evoked only confusion

---

[1] D. Petegorsky, *op. cit.*, 121–4.

[2] *Truth lifting up its head above scandals*, 1649, 141. Except for *The mysterie of God*, *The breaking of the day of God*, and *The saints paradise*, all of Winstanley's writings are cited from his *Works*, ed. G. Sabine, Ithaca, 1941.

43

and uncertainty, was for Winstanley the occasion of growth. In heeding the Apostle's admonition to try all things, his powers were released. And so this communist prophet began to write, first of religion, then of politics. It is in his religious evolution, therefore, that we must seek for the source of his political theory.

Winstanley's earliest works held forth an antinomian religion of love, universal redemption, and chiliastic hope. God, he affirmed, will save all men, even the worst sinners. He will kill all evil, that is, self-love in man, and 'will dwell in the whole creation . . . and so deliver whole mankind out of . . . bondage'.[1] Men are no longer under the old law because it is 'cast out of God's hand by Jesus Christ, the Law of grace and love; and the Serpent is cast out of the whole creation in part, and shall be cast out of the whole when the Mystery of God is finished by the power of the same anointing, Jesus Christ'.[2] He was confident, too, that Christ will soon come himself. ' . . . the Winter is near past,' he exulted, 'the Summer is come, the flowers appear in the earth. . . . The time of the singing of birds is come . . . for the Lord God omnipotent . . . begins to reign in the world . . . .'[3] In the characteristic way of the sectarian, he emphasized a religion of personal experience. 'To hear that Christ was raised from death . . . is joy. But to see and feel Christ the Anointing, raised upon me; and to feel him who is the spring of life, to be opened in me, and to send forth sweet manifestations of God to my soul, this is much more joyous and full of abundance of inward refreshments.'[4] And he condemned all compulsion in religion. 'Jesus Christ,' he said, 'calls his Church out of the world, & makes them to beleeve in God by his own almighty power; but the Beast will have a whole Parish, a whole kingdome, and so the world to be his Church . . . or else she will suffer him to have no church at all.'[5] God, he was sure, would remove all usurped ecclesiastical power, and expel injustice, so that magistrates will delight in executing justice for the commonwealth's good and safety.[6]

Such ideas as these were not uncommon in his time.[7] But immediately after their expression, Winstanley entered a new phase of development. He now emerged as a pantheist, seeing God not transcendentally, but immanently within the creation, identifying God with reason and

---

[1] *The mysterie of God concerning the whole creation*, 2nd ed., 1649, 9. The 1st ed. was 1648, and according to the Address to his countrymen of Lancaster, was Winstanley's first work.

[2] *Ibid.*, 27.

[3] *The breaking of the day of God*, 2nd ed., 1649, 67–8. The 1st ed. was 1648.

[4] *Ibid.*, 71.

[5] *Ibid.*, 91.

[6] *Ibid.*, 128, 131.

[7] Cf. R. M. Jones, *Mysticism and democracy in the English commonwealth*, Cambridge, 1932.

expecting the world's restoration through the spreading of the spirit of reason in every man.[1] He has come to realize, Winstanley said, that God is not in a place of glory beyond the skies, but in the whole creation.[2] Not even Satan's power is distinct from God. It is a part of God, and is the 'power of the spirit, which is pure reason . . . that shews thee thy wickednesse . . . and fills thee with shame and torment'.[3] Reason, he affirms, is the father of all things, and governs the whole creation. It is the 'spirit that knits all creatures together in peace and sweet communion of love and meekness [and] must needs be King'.[4] Jesus 'is not a single person at a distance from you; but . . . the wisdome and power of the father, who spirits the whole creation, dwelling and ruling King of righteousnesse in your very flesh'.[5] Do not, therefore, seek for God outside the world, he admonishes, but 'know him to be the spirit and power that dwells in every man and woman; yea in every creature, according to his orbe, within the globe of the creation'.[6]

Within a short time, Winstanley enlarged on these conceptions. Neither the Father nor Jesus, he said, are confined to any particular place. They are everywhere, and in every creature.[7] God is the spirit, reason, which preserves not a part, but the whole creation.[8] Reason dwells above all in man, and enjoins him to live peaceably with his fellows. Thus, envy, covetousness, and pride are nothing but unreasonableness.[9] The origin of evil was man's revolt, when he chose to live upon the creation, and so broke the law of reason. The transgression of Adam, the first man, was an historical act, yet Adam at the same time can be seen in all who live against the spirit. There is a second man who leads mankind back to the spirit. This is Christ. Till now, the first Adam has ruled the earth. But now is the time of Christ, the second Adam, who 'will change times and customs, & fill the earth with a new law, wherein dwells righteousness and peace. . . And he shal fill the earth with himself . . . so all that live in the light and strength of pure Reason are but the sons and daughters of the second man . . .'.[10]

These first pantheistic writings mark a critical point in the complicated evolution of Winstanley's thought. By reason, he clearly meant the law

---

[1] *The saints paradise.* This work is undated, but I concur in the reasoning of Petegorsky (*op. cit.*, Appendix I) and Sabine (*op. cit.*, 91) that it was written in the summer of 1648, after *The breaking of the day of God.*

[2] *Ibid.*, 2nd ed., Address.

[3] *Ibid.*, 105.

[4] *Ibid.*, 106, 122.

[5] *Ibid.*, 116.

[6] *Ibid.*, 85.

[7] *Truth lifting up its head above scandals*, 1649, 114.

[8] *Ibid.*, 107, 104–5.

[9] *Ibid.*, 109.

[10] *Ibid.*, 120–2.

of righteousness teaching men to do as they would be done to.[1] Mankind's history consists in the absolute restoration of this law. But reason is not a force without the world. It is the immanent principle in the development of all created things. It is the spirit which inhabits all, and which Christ exemplified. It is God. Thus the created order of things and God are equated. God, as reason, can be discerned separate from the created order so far as it remains unrighteous. But righteousness is destined to triumph, and in its progress God, or reason, takes possession of the created order in which he has always been intimated. At the end, with the restoration of righteousness in the world, God and mankind are one.

Various suggestions have been made to account for Winstanley's spiritualistic pantheism. It has been said that he shows the direct influence of the great early-seventeenth-century German mystic, Jacob Boehme,[2] and that his conceptions have something in common with those of the Familists and of the mystical preachers, William Dell and John Saltmarsh.[3] All of these influences are, of course, possible, though there is no evidence for any of them. But it is a mistake, I think, to stress too much whatever similarities there may be, because Winstanley's greatness lies in just those ideas for which there was no contemporary parallel. Like may Protestant mystics, he held to a religion of personal experience, to a belief in liberty of conscience, and to a profound distrust of clerical interpretation of Scripture. But just as neither Dell nor Saltmarsh became communists convinced that reason would reign in this life, so Boehme put no very radical interpretation on the law of Christ; and his work, darkened by the esoteric symbolism of alchemy, bears the stamp of the restricted, airless atmosphere of the Germany of his time, in which the grip of the state churches pressed spiritual religion to an inwardness that nourished itself on the occult.[4]

Whatever its resemblances to certain contemporary ideas, Winstanley's philosophy, as he elaborated it, was a different one. He began, it is true, as a mystic, and the sense of inward illumination never left him. But mysticism, a great scholar has pointed out, has, in certain of its manifestations, decidedly close affinities with rationalism.[5] These arise, no doubt, when the mystic values his own experience so exclusively as to set aside all merely received teachings and interpretations,

---

[1] Cf. *The saints paradise*, 124.

[2] R. M. Jones, *Studies in mystical religion*, London, 1909, 495; M. Bailey, *Milton and Jakob Boehme*, New York, 1914, 113–14. Boehme's works were being put into English after 1644.

[3] G. Sabine, *op. cit.*, 21–35.

[4] There are many studies of Boehme. A useful treatment is H. H. Brinton, *The mystic will*, New York, 1930.

[5] E. Troeltsch, *The social teachings of the Christian churches*, trans. O. Wyon, 2 vols., London, 1931, II, 749.

and when he holds his own discoveries to be the sign of his possession of an inner light which emanates directly from the divine intelligence that rules all things. With Winstanley, these affinities are obvious in his identification of God with the immanent principle of reason pervading the world. The question is, how far will they be carried. If too far, it is doubtful that the religious-spiritualistic matrix in which they were formed can continue to survive. As a mystic, Winstanley denied the value of every external help, and conceded positive significance only to the spirit of God in man. But because he identified this spirit with reason, and located it in the world and nowhere else, he was moving to the point where to know the world would be held synonomous with knowing God. Christianity must acknowledge the presence of God in the world; but it dare not acquiesce in the belief that in the world God's presence is exhausted. Just this, I think, is what Winstanley was eventually led to. His philosophy, therefore, reproduced, even if on a far less sophisticated plane and in other terms, one of the great movements of thought that culminated in Spinoza, in which God and nature were made one.

Winstanley's rationalism, moreover, was bound up with an uncompromising affirmation that mankind's redemption would be effected in this world, not in a heaven to come, and not through Christ's vicarious sacrifice, but by the restoration of the absolute law of reason. It was this that gave his radicalism its far-reaching implications. More than any man of his time he refused to admit the permanent and unalterable fact of a fallen world, and looked to the reintroduction of the pristine good. When this unyielding quest for an absolute justice was united to a philosophy whose ultimate bearings must, I think, be regarded as naturalistic, we have a synthesis unlike anything in its day, a synthesis which essentially looks forward to the Enlightenment and beyond.

But this is to anticipate, for we have still to note Winstanley's emergence as a communist. This all-important stage was announced by him in the beginning of 1649. A few months later, he led the Diggers, a group that had grown up around his ideas, out to cultivate the common lands on St. George's Hill, Surrey. He accompanied this enterprise with a series of writings explaining the significance of communism. Following the collapse of the Digger venture because of the enmity of local landlords, he published his final work, in which he described the operation of a communist social order.

Winstanley's adoption of communism was most intimately related to all his earlier ideas on the origin of evil and the redemption of man. From the beginning, the dogmatic element had had no place in his thought. Ethics was what he had stressed exclusively, and he was looking to the imminent spread of righteousness in the world. Superficially, it may seem as if the questions to which his communist ideas provided an answer were those which any Christian must ask: What is the origin of evil? What is the role of Christ? How is the world redeemed? But in the very putting of these questions, he meant by evil, by Christ, by redemption something quite different from what they signified to orthodox Christianity in any of its great historic forms. Everything centred on conduct, and the essence of evil lay in man's unrighteousness towards his fellow creatures. It was this from which all sin grew, and it was this which any redemption must remove. Winstanley had already identified reason with justice between men, and evil with covetousness. But he had not given any substantive meaning to these ideas, nor had he shown in the large how they were exemplified. Yet his emphasis on a religion of conduct impelled him to a precise statement of the circumstances in which they were manifest. Now communism as a creation of the spirit of charity and in a wholly unpolitical form was to be seen in the New Testament in the example of the Apostles. It had also been proclaimed by some of the radical sects of the Reformation. Whether he found it here or elsewhere,[1] communism provided the solution to his problem, a communism, however, which he was to develop in a new way. He now concluded that reason and righteousness were concretely manifest in the common ownership of the earth, and that evil and covetousness had their being in private property. It was private property, therefore, which caused all mankind's sufferings, and man's redemption would be effected only by making the earth a common treasury.

These conceptions were not intended as a political programme. When he first announced them, he tells us they came to him in a trance,[2] and this is not the way political programmes are usually formulated. At the start they were simply a new substantive content of all that he had talked about before. He now showed that the origin of evil and of private property were the same. At their first entrance into the creation, men had an equal freedom from God to till the earth. Covetousness, or the triumph of the first Adam, took the form of the private appropriation of the soil.[3] Accordingly, only by the abolition of private property could evil be removed. '. . . so long as such are Rulers,' he says, 'as cals the

---

[1] Petegorsky suggested that Winstanley was led to his radical political ideas under the influence of the Leveller, William Everard, and the Leveller pamphlet, *Light shining in Buckingham-shire*, 1648 (*op. cit.*, 134–5, 138–42). But it is likely that the Everard in whose justification he wrote *Truth lifting up its head above scandals*, was not the Leveller, but another Everard, known as a mystic (see Sabine, *op. cit.*, 103 n.). Moreover, I see no evidence that Winstanley read *Light shining* before he became a communist, if he read it at all. The important argument, repeatedly mentioned in *Light shining*, that the Norman conquest brought tyranny into England, was not taken up by Winstanley in his first communist writing, *The new law of righteousness*. He first adopted it, and thereafter employed it very frequently, in *The true levellers standard advanced*.

[2] *The new law of righteousness*, 1649, 190.

[3] *Ibid.*, 182, 158.

Land theirs, upholding this particular propriety of Mine and Thine, the common-people shall never have their liberty, nor the Land ever freed from troubles, oppressions, and complainings.'[1] It is communism, he now realized, that embodies reason and righteousness. 'Did the light of Reason,' he asks, 'make the earth for some men to engrosse up into bags and barns, that others might be opprest with poverty? Did the light of Reason make this law, that if one man have not such abundance of earth as to give to others he borrowed of; that he that did lend should imprison the other, and starve his body in a close room?'[2] The rich tell the poor that to take from the rich is to offend reason's law. But the truth is the reverse. It is a breach of reason's law for the rich to have plenty and the poor to starve, because 'Reason requires that every man should live upon the increase of the earth comfortably. . . '.[3] '. . . the spiritual man, which is Christ,' Winstanley says, 'doth judge according to the light of . . . reason, that al man-kinde ought to have a . . . freedome, to live upon earth; and that there shal be no bond-man nor beggar in all his holy mountaine.'[4]

Led by his pantheistic doctrines, Winstanley completely negates the historical element in Christianity. Original sin is not due to Adam's fall, he says, and when a man sins, let him blame himself, not someone who lived six thousand years ago.[5] He doubts, too, the existence of hell. 'If there be a local place of hell as the Preachers say there is . . . time will make it manifest, but as yet none ever came from the dead to tell men on earth, and till then, men ought to speak no more then what they know. . . .'[6] Most important of all, he couples his extreme interpretation of the law of reason with an insistence that mankind is to look for its felicity in this world only. Ministers preach for gain, he declares, and make themselves serviceable to the governing power by spreading ignorance and confusion among the people.[7] It is for this reason that they tell men not to expect righteousness in earthly life. But they speak false. 'O ye hear-say Preachers,' he exhorts the clergy, 'deceive not the people any longer, by telling them that this glory shall not be known and seen, til the body is laid in the dust. I tel you . . . it must be seen by the material eyes of the flesh: And those five senses that is in man, shall partake of this glory.'[8]

The righteous society, however, Winstanley emphasizes, is not to be instituted by force, for the spirit of Christ will spread itself in all men and cause them to consent to the law of reason.[9] Yet there must assuredly be action, because it is in action alone that love is manifest, and he that professes religion and fails to 'act this universall power of Righteousnesse in labouring the earth for a common treasury, is a meer

---

[1] *Ibid.*, 159.　　[2] *Ibid.*, 177.　　[3] *Ibid.*, 181.
[4] *Ibid.*, 179.　　[5] *Ibid.*, 177.　　[6] *Ibid.*, 219.
[7] *Ibid.*, 238, 117.　　[8] *Ibid.*, 170.　　[9] *Ibid.*, 181–2.

self-lover . . . and a complementing enemy to Reason the King of Righteousness'.[1] It is the poor who must take the first step, for it is in them that the law of reason will realize itself first.[2] They must cease working for rich men and begin to work the common lands. 'Therefore you dust of the earth, that are trod under foot, you poor people, that makes both schollars and rich men your oppressours by your labours, take notice. . . If you labour the earth, and work for others that lives at ease, and follows the waies of the flesh by your labours. . . Know this, that the hand of the Lord shall break out upon every such hireling labourer, and you shal perish with the covetous rich men, that . . . hold the Creation under the bondage of the curse.'[3] As for himself, Winstanley remarks, as soon as the Lord shows him the place and the manner in which the people are to work the common lands, he will himself go forth and declare it in his action.[4] And in the spring of 1649, true to his promise, he led his little group of followers, the Diggers, in their communist experiment.

The Digger movement was not a political tactic. It was an action whose purpose was to symbolize the redemption coming within the world, and which had manifested itself already in Winstanley and his comrades.[5] Working the common lands, Winstanley said, is a 'declaring [of] freedome to the Creation, and that the earth must be set free from entanglements of Lords and Landlords, and that it shall become a common treasury to all. . .'.[6] Because their venture was a sign of the approaching restoration of mankind, the Diggers disclaimed any intention of confiscating the possessions of the rich. They wanted only the commons, they asserted,[7] and would wait, 'till the Spirit in you make you cast up your Lands and Goods'.[8]

But Winstanley's pamphlets written in justification of the Diggers are, none the less, full of acute and highly critical comments on contemporary politics. The ruling powers, he said, had promised to free England, but instead they had introduced a greater bondage. The people were oppressed by courts, justices of the peace, and committees. They were still under a prerogative power.[9] He also adopted the argument, very likely borrowed from Leveller pamphlets, that the Norman conquest had brought the people under a tyranny which weighed on them still. England, he declared,

[1] *Ibid.*, 193–4.
[2] *Ibid.*, 186.
[3] *Ibid.*, 194.
[4] *Ibid.*, 195.
[5] Cf. W. Hudson, 'Economic and social thought of Gerrard Winstanley', *Journal of modern history*, XVIII, 1, 8–9, and W. Schenk, *op. cit.*, 102.
[6] *A watch-word to the city of London and the armie*, 1649, 315–16.
[7] *An appeal to the House of Commons*, 1649, 301.
[8] *A declaration from the poor oppressed people of England*, 1649, 272.
[9] *The true levellers standard advanced*, 1649, 255–6.

had been enslaved many times, and the last yoke imposed on her was that of William the Conqueror. The best laws since that time, even Magna Carta, were but manacles, 'tying one sort of people to be slaves to another; Clergy and gentry have got their freedom, but the common people stil are . . . servants to work for them. . . '.[1] William gave his Norman soldiers power over the land as manor-lords, and manor-lords in England from that time had had only the justification of the king's will to tyrannize over the people. William also caused the laws to be written in French, and heard cases at Westminster instead of in the neighbourhood of their origin. He gave tithes to the clergy for their good services on his behalf.[2] But the people had not laid out their money and blood in the war 'that their Landlords, the Norman power, should still have its liberty . . . to rule in tyranny in his Lords, landlords, Judges, Justices, Bayliffs, and State Servants'.[3] Now that the kingly office had been abolished, manor-lords must be abolished too, because they hold their lands by the prerogative customs of monarchy.[4] England was supposed to have been made a free commonwealth; but 'if I have not freedom to live in peace, and enjoy food and rayment by my Labors freely, it is no Commonwealth at all'.[5]

In the months that followed his proclamation of communism, Winstanley's political thought became markedly deepened, and what had hitherto been isolated insights were brought together and rounded out in a theory of much penetration. Now he began to make use of the notion of property as a general principle with which to disclose the character of the contemporary order. Somewhat like James Harrington, though from a different point of view, he treated the possession of land as the critical factor in social life.[6] It is the desire to own the earth, he pointed out, which lies beneath all the great struggles and strivings of mankind.[7] This is the motive which inspires the actions of the gentry and the sermons of the clergy. The basis of all laws is the disposal of the earth.[8] Above all, the meaning of freedom lies in the unrestricted right to use the earth.[9] Though the gentry summoned the people to fight for them against the king, they did not establish a universal freedom. While

---

[1] *An appeal to the House of Commons*, 303.

[2] *Ibid.*, 311–12.

[3] *The true levellers standard advanced*, 260.

[4] *A watch-word to the city of London*, 324–5.

[5] *An humble request to the ministers*, 1650, 431.

[6] It has been suggested by H. F. Russell Smith (*Harrington and his Oceana*, Cambridge, 1914, 27–9) that Harrington was indebted to Winstanley, but there is no evidence of this.

[7] *Fire in the bush*, 1650, 493; cf. *A new-years gift for the Parliament and armie*, 1650, 373–4.

[8] *An humble request to the ministers . . . and to all lawyers . . .*, 1650, 429.

[9] *A letter to the Lord Fairfax*, 1649, 287–8.

they freed themselves from paying fines to the king and from the Court of Wards, they left the people under the slavery of manorial lords.[1] And from the beginning, wars have merely removed property from a weaker to a stronger hand, and have not abolished 'the curse of Bondage'.[2] The law pretends justice, but its purpose 'is to uphold the conquering Sword, and to preserve his son Propriety; therefore if anyone steal, this Law will hang them, and this they say is of God'. The law makes the poor work for landlords at low wages and when they refuse, they are imprisoned. If they have no dwelling and go begging, they are whipped. 'And truly most Lawes are but to enslave the Poor to the Rich and are Lawes of the great red Dragon.'[3] And then, should the poor man mourn his bondage, and ask why they who work have least and they who work not at all enjoy all, contrary to the Scriptural saying that the poor shall inherit the earth, 'Presently the tithing Priest stops his mouth with a slam and tels him that is meant of the inward satisfaction of mind which the poor shall have, though they enjoy nothing at all . . .'.[4]

From these doctrines it was but a step to the description of a commonwealth that would truly incorporate the righteousness which England's revolution had failed to achieve. Sore in heart at the antagonism and bullying which the Diggers encountered, Winstanley concluded that it was not enough for the common lands to be appropriated by the poor while the rich were left in control of their lands and of the government. Nothing short of a complete overhauling of society would provide the freedom for which he thirsted. And thus, in his final writing, *The Law Of Freedom* (1652), he presented his unheeding countrymen with a detailed plan for a communist order. This work is one of the great books of the time. It will bear comparison with Sir Thomas More's classic of the previous century. No doubt, Winstanley lacked the wide learning and the genial urbanity which make More's *Utopia* so attractive. But in his understanding of the contemporary order, in his constructive effort to devise a solution for the problems besetting his age, and in the intense ethical note which sounds in his thought, Winstanley is quite outstanding. We now see his philosophy complete the circuit along which its inner logic had impelled it. Inspired still by a deeply felt religion of conduct, he passed, nevertheless, to a substantially rationalist-materialist position. Nature he now presented as the boundary and end of human knowledge. The emancipation of man from oppression he now saw

---

[1] *An appeal to the House of Commons*, 304, 306, 308.
[2] *A new-years gift for the Parliament and armie*, 355.
[3] *Ibid.*, 388.
[4] *Ibid.*, 388–9.

could be effected only if reason were adequately embodied in all the institutions of social life.[1]

Winstanley's commonwealth has its foundation in the free enjoyment of the earth by all, for this, he emphasizes, is the basis of every other freedom, and it alone enables men to live peacefully together. Even the inward bondages of the mind—covetousness, pride, hypocrisy, envy, sorrow, fears, desperation, madness—all arise from the outward bondage under which men lie when the freedom of the earth is removed.[2] Hence, private property in the land and its products is to be abolished, as is wage-labour also.[3] Money, too, as the accompaniment of private property, will be banned, and gold and silver henceforth used exclusively for dishes and ornaments.[4] To replace the system of private property in the goods of life, communal storehouses are to be established where all products will be brought, and which will be free for the use of everyone. Here consumption goods will be stored and distributed and artisans provided with the raw materials of their crafts.[5] But every family is to live apart, and houses, furniture, and articles fetched from the storehouses are to be considered as personal property which no one may take away.[6]

The commonwealth's administration is to be carried on by organs of officials elected annually to govern towns, cities, and parishes, the counties, and, by means of a Parliament, the entire country. All men forty years of age and over are to be eligible for election, unless disqualified by uncivil living, support of monarchical power, too-great previous activity in buying and selling the commonwealth's land, or fear of speaking the truth.[7] Provisions are also made for a variety of officers to supervise trade, agriculture, and the common storehouses, to reconcile quarrels, to reform and punish offenders, and to educate, inform, and enlighten the people.[8] Parliament is to have among its duties

[1] I see not the slightest evidence for Professor Hudson's assertion (*op. cit.*, 17–20) that Winstanley's intention was to portray an interim commonwealth which would last until Christ's second coming. This is to mutilate Winstanley's whole philosophy. Communism within the world was the only redemption he expected or desired. Professor Hudson's statement (*ibid.*, 2) that except for the 'peculiarity of "digging",' Winstanley differed little from other religious radicals of the time, is very far from the mark.

[2] *The law of freedom*, 519–20.

[3] *Ibid.*, 580–1.

[4] *Ibid.*, 595. Mr. H. N. Brailsford has suggested to me that Winstanley may have derived this idea from Sir Thomas More's statement (*Utopia*, ed. J. Lumby, Cambridge, 1935, 98) that the Utopians use gold for chamber-pots and similar purposes. Petegorsky says that Winstanley had read *Utopia*, but there is no evidence of this, unless it be in such a similarity as that just mentioned.

[5] *Ibid.*, 581–4.

[6] *Ibid.*, 512.

[7] *Ibid.*, 540–3.

[8] *Ibid.*, 544–56.

the task of converting to common use all the church and crown lands, lands once owned by monastic establishments, and common and waste lands appropriated by manorial lords. In addition, it is to reform the laws and remove all grievances.[1]

No arrangements are made for religious observances. Instead, on Sundays, their day of rest, the people of each parish are to meet together, and the minister elected for that year is to read to them, first of national affairs, and then of the commonwealth's law. After this, they are to deliver discourses setting forth the history of the past with its oppressions, and the benefits of freedom. Speeches are to be made 'of all Arts and Sciences . . . Physick, Chyrurgy, Astrology, Astronomy, Navigation, Husbandry. . . .' In this way, men will learn 'the secrets of Nature and Creation, within which all true knowledge is wrapped up . . .'. Nothing is to be spoken 'by imagination', but only what is 'found out by . . . industry and observation in tryal'.[2] To know the secrets of nature, Winstanley affirms, 'is to know the works of God; and to know the works of God within the Creation, is to know God himself . . . to reach God beyond the Creation . . . is a knowledge beyond . . . the capacity of man. . . .'.[3]

Besides these Sunday discourses, schools are to be established to instruct all children in trades, arts, sciences, and languages. No one is to be raised with book-learning alone, and the emphasis is to be on experiment. For 'he that onely contemplates', Winstanley remarks, 'and talks of what he reads . . . and doth not employ his Talent in some bodily action, for the encrease of fruitfulnesse, freedom, and peace . . . is an unprofitable son'. Knowledge of husbandry, minerals, lumber, and all their products is to be imparted. Scientific investigation is to be encouraged, all who invent new things given honours, and no 'young wit' crushed in its desire to master the secrets of every art.[4]

If men were but granted the freedom of the earth and an assured livelihood, Winstanley promised, many secrets of nature would be found out. 'Kingly Bondage is the cause of the spreading of ignorance,' he declared. 'But when Commonwealths Freedom is established . . . then will knowledge cover the Earth. . . .'[5] The clergy oppose enlightenment, because they do not wish men to understand the nature of freedom. They advise against trusting reason, and promise a happiness after death, and damnation in hell to those who disagree with them. And so, 'while men are gazing up to Heaven, imagining after a happiness, or fearing a

---

[1] *Ibid.*, 556–60.
[2] *Ibid.*, 562–4. The Baconian spirit of these ideas may have prompted Petegorsky's suggestion (*op. cit.*, 122) that Winstanley had read Bacon. But there does not seem to be any evidence of this.
[3] *Ibid.*, 565.
[4] *Ibid.*, 577–80.
[5] *Ibid.*, 564.

Hell . . . their eyes are put out, that they see not what is their birth-rights, and what is to be done by them on Earth while they are living'.[1]

When he first envisaged a communist order, Winstanley saw no need for coercion and magistrates. Common ownership of the land would make them superfluous. Whipping, imprisonment, hanging, all of them fruits of private property, would pass away.[2] But his experience with the Diggers, who were driven forcibly from the land, instead of being acclaimed, must have caused him to realize the need to curb those whose behaviour menaced the welfare of their fellows. His community, there-fore, had severe penalties for offences against the common freedom. Some men are wise, laborious, and loving, he pointed out, while others are foolish and envious, and care not if their brethren perish for want. It is for these that the law exists.[3] But the purpose of law, he insisted, is the preservation of all,[4] and his penal provisions were aimed primarily at effecting reformation, except in cases punishable by death. Under the latter are included buying and selling the earth and its fruits, administer-ing law for money, and rebellion aimed at re-establishing private pro-perty.[5] Hiring labour or accepting hire, and refusal to work or learn a trade, are to be punishable by loss of freedom.[6] Those so punished are to be set at work under a Taskmaster, and to be freed after twelve months, having promised to observe the laws.[7]

After the age of forty, because they have laboured all their lives, and are now eligible for office, men are free to take their ease and not work if they wish.[8] Marriage is to be a civil ceremony. And 'every man and woman shall have the free liberty to marry whom they love, if they ob-tain the love and liking of that party whom they would marry, and neither birth nor portion shall hinder the match, for we are all of one blood, Mankind; and for portion, the Common Storehouses are every man and maids portion, as free to one as to another'.[9]

Such, in brief, are the chief features of Winstanley's communist com-monwealth. It needs no great acuteness to discern their utopian charac-ter. No provision other than the spreading of the spirit of reason and the fiat of Cromwell, to whom *The Law of Freedom* was dedicated, is made for effecting the transition to the desired order.[10] The complexity of the economic conditions under which it would have to function is ignored. Winstanley pays no heed to the rapid growth in the seventeenth century of large-scale trade and manufacture, and evidently intends that production should be carried on in individual households and small

---

[1] *Ibid.*, 569.   [2] *A letter to the Lord Fairfax*, 282–3.   [3] *Ibid.*, 535–6.
[4] *Ibid.*, 535–6.   [5] *Ibid.*, 594–5, 591.   [6] *Ibid.*, 595, 593.
[7] *Ibid.*, 597–98.   [8] *Ibid.*, 577.   [9] *Ibid.*, 599.
[10] Winstanley seems seriously to have hoped Cromwell would put his ideas into effect; cf. *The law of freedom*, 510.

shops.[1] He imagines, also, that it is possible to dispense with money, and that a professional class of lawyers will become unnecessary when buying and selling disappear.[2] But these are slight defects alongside his momentous realization that freedom requires more than a formal political equality if it is to have its full substance. In achieving this understanding, he passed beyond the categories of thought presupposed by even the most radical doctrines of his day. And it is precisely his utopian outlook which enabled him to do this. For, in a certain sense, utopianism is an essential ingredient in every standpoint that succeeds in transcending the reigning ideologies which a determinate social order begets. It is by means of this element that thought, in taking account of the problems of the moment, is made capable of so detaching itself from existing circumstances as not only to depict them in a profounder manner, but also to consider alternatives to them. This is why utopian writings occupy no small place in the history of political theory. For in them, mingled with the various illusions to which their authors are subject, there resides a power of penetration that discloses realities wholly inaccessible to mere 'common sense'. And as a result of this, these writings, in their examination of the contemporary situation, often uncover the very possibilities whose realization will be the task of subsequent social development over generations and even centuries.

It seems to me beyond denial, therefore, that by his final work, Winstanley is demonstrated to be one of the pre-eminent political thinkers of his time. His analysis of seventeenth-century England showed a wealth of understanding of the prevailing social and economic relations. He was one of the few theorists who attempted to explain the contemporary order on a high level of generality by invoking a unitary principle—the ownership of the earth. And he was the first to give a reasoned elaboration to the doctrine which upholds the eternal inseparability of political liberty and economic equality. In this, his most cherished belief, he revealed that prescience which is one of the special attributes of the utopian mind. For, in its various permutations and combinations, there is no idea which, from the nineteenth century onward, has seized the millions the world over with greater force. Nor must we overlook his astonishing views on education and enlightenment. They were entirely in tune with the tempo and outlook of the great scientific movement then proceeding. His emphasis on knowledge of nature as the only true knowledge, his belief in the importance of experiment and new inventions, and the overwhelmingly pragmatic stress he put on all learning—all these show him to have been deeply touched by the rationalistic spirit of the age.

In noting these characteristic doctrines of Winstanley, we cannot but

---

[1] *Ibid.*, 593.   [2] *Ibid.*, 512.

realize how singularly instructive a phenomenon his development is. From few other thinkers do we learn so well what strange and mighty potencies certain forms of spiritual and mystical religion contain. There were medieval mystics who, passing beyond orthodoxy, arrived at heretical pantheist views.[1] But in Winstanley, the process proceeds to its untrammelled furthest extreme. Mystic, pantheist, materialistic rationalist—this is his path. Before our eyes, moreover, he consummates the transition between two classic types of utopian outlook: from the blazing chiliastic expectancy of the religious radical who daily looks for Jesus' second coming to inaugurate a reign of righteousness, to the rationalistic communism, abounding in plans and projects, which appears as an aspect of the thought of the Enlightenment. The first is the world of the Taborites, Thomas Münzer, and the Anabaptists of Munster, the second the world of Morelly, Meslier, and Robert Owen; and Winstanley's development encompasses the course which lies between the two. This is not to say, however, that his inspiration ceased to be religious, or that he ceased subjectively to believe himself a Christian. Quite the contrary. But the religion expressed in *The Law of Freedom* was no longer Christian, despite its terminology. He had eliminated a transcendent God, an historic Christ, creed, dogma, and church, and retained naught but the ethical inspiration of the gospel. And even this he did not allow to operate, in the traditional way, as the spirit of charity and love that was to be shown despite the existence of slavery and coercion which man's fall had made inevitable. Instead, the gospel ethic was for him the imperative compelling the remodelling of institutions in the image of reason. While the early church acquiesced in the contemporary social order as incapable of reformation, and the medieval church accepted it as the first term of the harmonious duality, nature and grace,[2] Winstanley rejected it in favour of one which reason was to shape. Further, his ideal had practically nothing in common with the ascetic communism of apostolic Christianity or of the heretical medieval and Reformation sects. On the contrary, it proclaimed a rational social order of abundance, humane learning, and ease. It rested not on a sharing in the consumption of goods, but on the co-operative organization of production.

The burden of Winstanley's ideas could not have been an easy one for him, for he knew how much he had set himself in opposition to his time. In the poem which he placed at the conclusion of *The Law of Freedom*, he writes:

---

[1] Such, for example, were the Beghards and Beguins; cf. E. Underhill, 'Mediaeval mysticism,' *The Cambridge mediaeval history*, 8 vols., Cambridge, 1924–36, VII, 789–90.

[2] E. Troeltsch, *op. cit.*, I, 303.

'Truth appears in Light, Falshood rules in Power,
To see these things to be, is cause of grief each hour.
Knowledg, why didst thou come, to wound, and not to cure?
I sent not for thee, thou didst me inlure.
Where knowledge does increase, there sorrows multiply,
To see the great deceit which in the World doth lie.

While the Levellers could number their followers by the thousands, Winstanley influenced only a handful. Nor could he have found much comfort in the struggles which the Levellers waged, for he doubtless regarded their programme as an ineffectual palliative. And they, in turn, to absolve themselves of the communist label which their enemies had fixed upon them, made the endeavour to establish communism a penal offence in their final *Agreement of the People*. Thus Winstanley lived a stranger to his fellows, noticed for a moment as the eccentric publicist of an odd sect of Diggers, and then forgotten. Enveloped by silence, he nevertheless spoke the truth that was in him. The just epitome of his work is in the lines which he once wrote in vindication of the Digger movement:

'When these clay bodies are in grave, and children stand in place,
This shows we stood for truth and peace and freedom in our days.'[1]

2. *Tyranipocrit* (1649)

Such communist ideas as have been proclaimed under the preeminent influence of the Christian spirit of charity have usually been dominated by the simple notion of a sharing of goods in the apostolic manner. They have expressed a fierce indignation against the rich and an exaltation of the poor, but have lacked the elements of a genuine social theory such as Winstanley acquired. Their principal note is ethical exhortation and a conviction of the superiority of having goods in common, unaccompanied, however, by any reasoned scheme setting forth the institutions through which the oppression of private property can be removed.

An important instance of this kind of literature is the pamphlet, *Tyranipocrit, Discovered*,[2] which, apart from Winstanley's works, has the distinction of being the only communist writing produced in the

---

[1] This is from the poem on the title-page of *A watch-word to the city of London*. Sabine's edition does not reprint the poem, but it may be found in L. Berens, *The Digger movement in the days of the commonwealth*, London, 1906, 112.

[2] *Tyranipocrit* was published at Rotterdam in 1649. Excerpts from it are reprinted in *British pamphleteers*, ed. George Orwell and Reginald Reynolds, London, 1948.

English revolution. Its author is, regrettably, unknown,[1] and this seems to be the only thing he wrote. What the specific influences were which worked on him we can only guess. Some of his religious beliefs are similar to those expressed in William Walwyn's *The Power of Love*, and like Walwyn in that work, he, too, condemns the want of simplicity which causes men to seek after superfluities.[2] It was a form of religious radicalism that led him to communism, and he broached his ideas in the vocabulary of the left-democratic movement, with references to reason, nature, and the law of God. But his thought never passed the boundaries which Winstanley left so far behind.

The author of *Tyranipocrit* regarded the doctrine of predestination as wicked, and believed that all men had the grace to be saved if they would.[3] He denounced the clergy as contentious sophisters puffed up by their learning and alien to the humility requisite in all who preach the gospel.[4] It is not faith that is important in religion, he wrote in a beautiful passage, but love.

'... faith ... cannot help our neighbours, for what can it helpe mee that another man hath faith? ... but if I bee poore ... if my rich neighbour do love mee, although hee doe not beleeve as I doe, yet love will cause him to helpe mee. ... Through love all things are created, and through love all mankinde are redeemed, and through love all things are, and shall be preserved, and God is love, and when a man goeth to God with a loving heart, then Promise, Law, Prophets, Gospell, Christ, and all Doctors have done all that, for which they were ordained. ...'[5]

The author's anger is directed chiefly against the exploitation of the poor. They are, he said, victims of Tyranipocrit, that offspring of the union between the clergy's hypocrisy and the rich men's tyranny.[6] The rich feign holiness while they rob the poor. They affirm that wealth and godliness are the same thing, and prattle of reformation, though the only reformation for which they hope is one which will make them richer.[7] They steal thousands of pounds themselves, take other men's possessions by force and fraud, but decree laws which sentence a poor man to hanging if he steals thirteen-pence-ha'penny. They compel poor labourers to till the land at low wages, and value them less than their horses and dogs[8]. When the rich fall out, it is their slaves, the poor, who

---

[1] I have been unable to determine who he was. The late Professor Laski's suggestion that he was William Walwyn (*The new statesman and nation*, 25th January 1948) is unacceptable. The style does not seem to me to be Walwyn's. In 1649, Walwyn was disavowing communism (see, e.g., *A manifestation*, 4–5). Unlike Walwyn, the author was not very close to English political developments, and though he knew of the king's execution, was unaware that the House of Lords had been abolished (*Tyranipocrit*, 48, 54).   [2] *Ibid.*, 23.

[3] *Ibid.*, 43–7, 11.   [4] *Ibid.*, 28–9.   [5] *Ibid.*, 20–1.
[6] *Ibid.*, 31.   [7] *Ibid.*, 16, 19.   [8] *Ibid.*, 23, 50.

are sent to kill one another.[1] Even now, the author says, referring to the peace congress assembled to conclude the Thirty Years War, the agents of Christian princes who are convened at Munster are striving only to advance despotism. Instead of aiming at a universal freedom, they desire to secure the profit of a few, and subject reason to tyranny.[2]

God, however, he affirms, created men free and rational beings, all with an equal right to preservation. It is only by securing to everyone an equal share of earthly goods, therefore, that the law of God and nature can be complied with. This is what the early Christians did, and this alone is true religion.[3] '. . . if you should make and maintaine an equallity of goods and lands, as God and nature would have, as justice and reason doth crave . . . then mankinde might live in love and concord . . . then tyranny and oppression would cease, and the Kingdome of Christ would flourish. . . .'[4]

But his ideas as to the arrangements for effecting communism are nebulous. He seems to have had in mind something like an agrarian law, and says that the magistrate must follow the example of Moses and Paul, Agis and Cleomenes, and the brothers Gracchi, and if he cannot make the poor richer, let him make the rich poorer. '. . . first limit the goods of the rich at ten, twenty, thirty, fourty or a hundred pounds a year,' the author proposed, 'and then share their overplus amongst them that have lesser meanes . . . make an new division againe and againe . . . once in a yeere, or oftener . . . examine every mans estate, to see if they have not made their goods uneven, and if they have . . . make it even againe.'[5] A competent means for every man, he insisted, and an equality of expenditure are the foundations of all justice.[6] 'Take away the name and power of thine and mine,' he pleaded, and establish an 'equallity of all such of Gods creatures, as God hath given for the use and benefit of mankinde . . .'.[7] Yet his suggestion of an agrarian law would scarcely have removed the name of thine and mine. Unlike Winstanley, he gave no thought to the co-operative organization of the sources of production from which the rich men's wealth derived, and though he well understood that a man was not free if he lacked a means of livelihood, his position amounted to no more than a demand that private property be equally distributed.

Tyranipocrit's indignation at the treatment of the poor has undoubted power to move the reader. There can be little question that large numbers of people experienced great economic distress during the revolution, with little effective action taken to relieve them.[8] A writer who supported the Cromwellian government, but who was deeply concerned

---

[1] *Ibid.*, 23–4.   [2] *Ibid.*, 19–20.   [3] *Ibid.*, 19.   [4] *Ibid.*, 32–3.
[5] *Ibid.*, 52, 38.   [6] *Ibid.*, 50.   [7] *Ibid.*, 52–3.
[8] Cf. E. M. Leonard, *The early history of English poor relief*, Cambridge, 1900, Ch. XIII, *passim*.

over the grievances of the time, gives us a revealing glimpse of what the lot of some of the agrarian labourers was. In the North, he says, 'I have seen multitudes of poor people go bare-footed and bare-legged, and scarce a ragge of clothes to cover their nakednesse, or having any bread, or any kind of food to put into their bellies, to keep them from starving. And ask the poor people, whose land they lived in? or who was their Landlord? they would tell us, that it was either the Earl of Northumberland or the Lord Grey. . . '.[1]

The existence of such conditions gave justification to *Tyranipocrit's* denunciations. But the author's plea for communism was no more than a powerful expression of his compassion. It contained no real analysis nor any thoroughgoing suggestions. And, of course, even if it had, it would have been as much at odds with its time as were the ideas of Winstanley.

[1] Francis Freeman, *Light vanquishing darknesse*, 1650, 55–6. It is worth noting that both Northumberland and Grey supported Parliament and, a little reluctantly, the Cromwellian government.

V

THEORISTS OF THE COMMONWEALTH: I

DESPITE the tide of hatred against the royal side which the civil war set flowing, the institution of monarchy itself was too protected by hallowed sentiment and established opinion to be easily swept away. The supporters of Parliament had been bred in a tradition so entirely and unquestioningly monarchical that most of them were simply incapable of imagining England without a king. Parliament, the city of London, for a long time Cromwell himself, almost all but the Levellers, in fact, were royalists, not as a matter of doctrine, but in feeling, and this defended Charles I when his followers no longer possessed the strength to aid him. Thus it was that Cromwell's eventual determination to break with monarchy, resolved on after many back-steppings, was a decision of great daring. It went against the doctrines of generations of English lawyers, political theorists, and theologians. It defied the loyalties that ages had built up, that Tudor greatness and the glory of the defeat of the Armada had sanctified, that Stuart rule had not dissolved.

The acts by which the revolutionary government established itself were, indeed, unparalleled. There was no counterpart for them in the dynastic civil wars of earlier English history. When, previously, had Englishmen seen a military force purge the House of Commons of two-thirds of its members? When had they seen the House of Lords abolished and the country left with a handful of members of the Commons as its Parliament? Above all, when had they seen their legitimate prince brought to a public trial by his own subjects and executed in full view of the populace? It is this last deed which was most astonishing. An age such as ours, which has forgotten the divinity of kingship, may fail to realize the drama of King Charles's trial and execution. The seventeenth century did not. An anointed sovereign, ruler by the grace of God, blood-heir of many princes before him, had been made to stand as defendant on the charge of betraying his trust; found guilty, his crown had been blasted by the executioner's axe. The French monarchy shuddered at the shock. The Dutch government protested, and refused its recognition to the new English republic.[1] And circulating in edition after edition, the *Eikon Basilike* evoked tears and pity for the dead king and created the legend of the royal martyr whose piety and virtue were greatest when his condition was at its most tragic ebb.

It was this audacity in the face of the monarchical past, these revolutionary actions by which the new government sealed its power, that the political theorists of the commonwealth had above all else to reckon with. They were required to vindicate obedience to a political order that was without any precedent in the historic constitution. They had to counter a widespread conviction that the deeds of Cromwell and his followers bore the stain not only of illegality, but of sin.

The doctrines of the theorists who undertook this task fall generally into two categories. The first, which forms the subject of this chapter, was devoid of all revolutionary enthusiasm. Deducing nothing from a right of revolution, it asserted simply that any *de facto* power is entitled to obedience. This was not the view, obviously, which Cromwell and those thinkers close to him entertained, and I call it, therefore, the unofficial theory of the commonwealth. The second category, to be considered in the following chapter, alone employed the repertoire of conceptions clustering round the belief in the people's right to call rulers to account, which the Cromwellians themselves invoked to validate their course. This may therefore be described as the official theory.

The existence of an influential body of ideas advocating obedience to the commonwealth merely because it was the power *de facto* has been all but overlooked. The position has been attributed exclusively to Hobbes.[2] Yet none of the theorists who expressed it in 1649 and 1650 were Hobbesians, though one or two had read, admired, and adopted some of the philosopher's ideas. The most important, Anthony Ascham, was clearly under Hobbes's influence and seems, like him, to have been a personality incapable of a religious *O altitudo*. But there is no evidence that two of the other writers, Francis Rous and John Dury, who expressed views resembling Ascham's, were at all familiar with Hobbes, and both men were of religion and piety. All three, and several others to be noticed, throw into relief an aspect of the thought of the time as different as can be from the ardent proclamations of John Goodwin or John Milton.

---

[1] The reaction of European opinion to Charles's trial and execution has never been adequately studied. Some indications may be found in G. Davies, *The early Stuarts 1603–1660*, corrected ed., Oxford, 1945, 217–18, and G. Ascoli, *La Grande-Bretagne devant l'opinion Française au XVIIe siecle*, 2 vols., Paris, 1930, I, 7–87.

[2] See *Leviathan*, 'A review and conclusion'.

THEORISTS OF THE COMMONWEALTH

1. ANTHONY ASCHAM

Anthony Ascham's is a forgotten name in the history of English political theory,[1] and is obscurely commemorated only as the commonwealth's resident in Madrid who, in 1650, fell beneath the daggers of royalist assassins.[2] Yet he was a writer of decided talent whose ideas are well worth examination. In his own time he was accounted a theorist of importance, and by Sir Robert Filmer he is mentioned in company with Grotius, Selden, and Hobbes.[3] There can be no doubt that he was the most influential of the group of publicists whom we are about to consider. Little is known of his life. He was of an established family and went from Eton to Cambridge in 1634 at the age of sixteen. He proceeded M.A. in 1642, and from 1637 until his death was a fellow of King's College. How he came to support Parliament in the civil war or to be appointed to office by the revolutionary government is not recorded.[4]

Ascham wrote little and published but one work of importance, *Of The Confusions and Revolutions of Governments* (1649).[5] Here the question on which the Cromwellian government had impaled many men's consciences was fearlessly faced: may allegiance be willingly rendered after a civil war to the victors despite the doubts which may be entertained as to the lawfulness of their cause?[6] The answer is given in the affirmative, but the reasoning was such as could scarcely have pleased England's rulers on any grounds but those of expediency.

In the state of nature in which men first lived, Ascham says, discussing the origin of government, all goods were held in common. This condition was not very pleasant, as some have fondly supposed,[7] for those who lived in the woods were more beasts than men. Brutishness prevailed, and natural liberty produced a state of war in which law was unknown. But the weakness of some bred subjection, and the power of others dominion. Thus civil magistracy appeared, and out of fear, men

---

[1] The *D.N.B.* gives his first name as 'Antony', *Alumni Cantabrigienses*, ed. J. and J. A. Venn, Cambridge, 1922–37, as 'Anthony'.

[2] S. R. Gardiner, *History of the commonwealth and protectorate*, 3 vols., London, 1894–1901, I, 342.

[3] *Directions for obedience to government in dangerous or doubtful times*, in *Patriarcha and other political writings*, 231; *Observations upon Aristotles politiques* in *ibid.*, 188.

[4] Biographical details from the *D.N.B.* and *Alumni Cantabrigienses*, *s.v.*

[5] This is the 2nd enlarged edition of a book of 1648, *A discourse wherein is examined what is particularly lawfull during the confusions and revolutions of government*, which was, for obvious reasons, reprinted in 1689.

[6] *Of the confusions . . . of government*, 1–2.

[7] He appears to have had Winstanley and the Diggers in mind, *ibid.*, 18–19.

obeyed. And as individuals began to appropriate the land their own industry had cultivated, possession became the title to property.[1]

In government, also, possession is the strongest title princes can have, for the other reasons usually advanced to validate the right of rulers, Ascham insists, are all dubious. Prescription of long time, for example, is not convincing because if an act was immoral in the beginning, lapse of time does not change its character. Points of fact, too, are scarcely determinable. How can it be known who plotted and who advised, or who gave just grounds for another party's acts? Both questions of fact and of right can be disputed forever without being resolved. Since this is the case, he concludes, 'his [right] is the best who hath possession . . .'. Men may ease themselves of their perplexity about whether or not an invading party has just cause or title by recognizing that 'for a justifiable obedience it is best, and enough for us to consider, Whether the invading party have us and the meanes of our subsistence in his possession . . .'.[2]

But why should such a consideration override all notions of lawful powers men may entertain? Because, Ascham answers, the most 'transcendent right' is that 'which wee naturally have in the preservation of our selves, and of the things without which we cannot be preserved . . .'. Extreme necessity supersedes all else, 'nature itself being more intent to the preservation of particular, then of publike bodyes, which are made out of particulars, and as much as may be for the particular ends and preservation of each singular . . .'.[3]

Forms of government are, in any case, of little significance, he remarks, and are certainly not worth quarrelling over. When a prince is just, monarchy is best. But as no prince has prudence equal to his power, monarchy frequently does great evils. Aristocracy, the mean between the excesses of royal and popular power, often brings with it bloody commotions. Democracy lodges supremacy in the heady and inconstant multitude. And this, Ascham says,

'is the circle which we so painfully move in without satisfying our desires: And no wonder, seeing Nature is in every part sick and distemper'd, and therefore can finde rest in no posture. Humane laws grow out of vices, which makes all governments carry with them the causes of their Corruption. . . .'[4]

Rather than dispute forms of government, men should consider that 'we are now *in faece mundi*, that wee can turne to no sort of government which hath not the power to wrong us in all the parts of Distributive

---

[1] *Ibid.*, 8–10, 18–19, 25, 107. This is a somewhat Hobbesian account of the state of nature. But Ascham criticized Hobbes for asserting that men give up all their rights irrevocably to the sovereign. Certain original rights, he said, are not swallowed up by government, *ibid.*, 120–3. But Hobbes did not deny this; see below, Ch. XIII.
[2] *Ibid.*, 32–4. [3] *Ibid.*, 44. [4] *Ibid.*, 73–4.

Justice, Reward, and Punishment'.[1] Moreover, such justice as is dispensed is not affected by forms of government, since no state can do more than enact or repeal laws, make war and peace, and judge of life and death. Men will not be wrong, therefore, if they accept justice from any state, despite the doubts they may feel as to its legal title.[2]

The only condition of allegiance, then, Ascham affirms, is that those demanding obedience should have plenary possession of power. Before this supreme fact, all antecedent oaths and obligations to previous rulers cease to be binding.[3] Amidst the vicissitudes of life, '. . . we of the People must be contented with those governours into whose full possessions it is our destiny to fall . . .'.[4] When new powers come into being, it should be realized that the event occurs not by chance, but by the providence of God, and the fact accepted that 'the King of Kings hath chang'd our Vice-Roys . . .'.[5] As arguments from title are weak and may err, 'surely we may be excus'd if . . . we determine by the rule of Equity, that his is the best of all who is in possession'.[6]

Was Ascham denying that there existed any difference between lawful and unlawful powers? It does not seem so, since he says, for example, that obedience to those in plenary possession is an acknowledgement of the irresistibility of their power, not of its lawfulness.[7] He never tells us in what the distinction consists, but the unmistakable impression is that he regarded a lawful power as one which acts in keeping with the historic constitution and whose title is valid within that constitution's definition. His main point seems to be, however, that a lawful power and a right to power are not the same thing. Those who have plenary possession may be no lawful power, he was asserting, but may be conceded the right to rule because they control the means of human preservation. And, he added, the right of self-preservation which inheres in all men justifies them in obeying such a power.

This argument, of course, inextricably confuses right and power, and by doing so, renders the notion of a right to rule useless altogether. What point is there in speaking of a right to rule, if any government, by the mere fact of its holding power, has such a right? Moreover, it is obvious that there is a profound difference between an obedience which we give because those above us can compel us, and one which arises from our conviction that those above us have a right to command us. And clearly, that conviction can never be created in us by the bare fact of plenary possession.

In Ascham's book we do not encounter the hopeful sentiments of the revolutionary, but the malaise of the sceptic. One has a glimpse of a feeling that was probably fairly widespread after 1649: weariness of civil strife,

[1] *Ibid.*, 75–6.   [2] *Ibid.*, 131–2, 134, 144–6.   [3] *Ibid.*, 93.
[4] *Ibid.*, 115.   [5] *Ibid.*, 98–9.   [6] *Ibid.*, 116–17.
[7] *Ibid.*, 137–8.

and a sense of mutability and the world's woe which led to a tired ac-quiescence in changes of government as unavoidable. We are struck by the atmosphere of disenchantment, and before Ascham's pyrrhonistic doubting, we see truth become dim and rights indeterminable. The pre-occupation of the theorist with politics has issued only in an advocacy of indifference to politics, since obedience may be given to any power and justice does not essentially depend on forms of government. Such were the thoughts expressed on the commonwealth's behalf when the revolutionary day had scarcely passed high noon!

2. FRANCIS ROUS AND JOHN DURY

A position somewhat similar to Ascham's was taken up by Francis Rous and John Dury. Rous was a true Puritan and the author of many moral and devotional works. An old man in 1640, for he was born when Queen Elizabeth had almost twenty-five years still to reign, he sat in the Long Parliament for a Cornish borough, and held high offices in the interregnum governments until his death in 1659. Dury was a minister, and with unyielding optimism dedicated sixty years of his life to the fruitless task of bringing about a union between the Protestant churches of Europe. The political pamphlets which these two men wrote on the commonwealth's behalf are but minor episodes in their literary activity and have no great merit, but they deserve notice, nevertheless, for the line of argument employed.[1]

Though Rous and Dury both show a clear sense of the doubtfulness of the revolutionary government's title, they were not unwilling to justify its superiority to the previous government and the acts by which it came to power. Thus Rous remarks that the old mixed constitution of king, lords, and commons was more unstable than the rule of commons alone,[2] and Dury that a case can be made for the opinion that the purged members were malignants and the rump parliament of the common-wealth the people's true representatives.[3] But their position does not

---

[1] On Rous's life, see the *D.N.B.*, *s.v.* On Dury, see the pedestrian biography by J. M. Batten, *John Dury*, Chicago, 1944. Rous's tracts vindicating the common-wealth appear to have escaped attention, while Batten scarcely notices Dury's on the subject. A work in which we might expect Dury's political pamphlets to be men-tioned (J. Lindeboom, 'Johannes Duraeus en zijne werkzaamheid in dienst van Cromwell's politiek', *Nederlandsch archief voor kerkgeschiedenis*, New series, XVI, 1921) overlooks them altogether.

[2] *The bounds & bonds of publique obedience*, 1649, 16. This work was published anonymously, but I take it to be Rous's because of its style and ideas, and because it was a defence of his earlier pamphlet, *The lawfulnes of obeying the present govern-ment*, 1649.

[3] *Objections against the taking of the engagement answered*, 1650, 15–16; cf. *Con-siderations concerning the present engagement*, 3rd enlarged ed., 1650, 2–3, where Dury affirms that the king by his actions put himself out of his capacity to rule.

depend on such considerations, and they do not urge them very much. Their chief point is that obedience may justifiably be given to a power in plenary possession, whatever the doubtfulness of its title, provided it issues lawful commands.

Referring to Romans 13, the *locus classicus* of New Testament utterances on subjection, Rous points out that Paul wrote this epistle in the reign either of Claudius or of Nero, both of whom obtained supremacy by military force against the will of the consuls and Senate. Thus, he concludes, 'we see Rulers put by Souldiers into that power which is said by the Scripture to be ordained of God; and even to these Rulers men must be subject for conscience'.[1] Scripture, he insists with Dury, requires that men be subject to whatever powers are in fact placed over them.[2] English history provides many instances, he declares, in which power was forcibly taken without the justification of title through inheritance or proximity of blood. William the Conqueror and Henry VII were such rulers, yet to the very present the nation abides by their laws.[3] A new government has conquered, Dury says, nor is it a disparagement to call the new rulers conquerors, since it was manifestly God's will that they should conquer. Men's duty is to give them obedience whatever may be the titles or claims to right of their competitors for supremacy. These are of no account, because God alone determines changes in states, and all men need do is observe who by God's hand has been given supreme power, and to them render subjection.[4] Neither subjects nor Christian ministers, Dury affirms, may scrutinize the rights and pretensions to rule of the great ones of the world;[5] and all titles are, in any case, so doubtful, Rous remarks, that it is folly to incur death and destruction in vain struggles over them. The only title of which man can be certain is God's.[6]

The fundamental fact, both men contend, is that a government is in plenary possession with no visible force to oppose it. It matters not what form this government takes, for the necessity of states cannot be tied to formalities.[7] Moreover, the supreme power is dispensing justice in the courts, protecting all who will give it allegiance, and commanding

---

[1] *The lawfulnes of obeying the present government*, 2nd ed., 1650, 2–4. This anonymous work reads like Rous's. It is listed among his writings by Anthony Wood (*Athenae Oxonienses*, ed. P. Bliss, 4 vols., London, 1813–20, III, 468). On his copy of *A second part of the religious demurrer*, 1649, which was a reply to *The lawfulnes of obeying the present government*, Thomason wrote that the answer was directed against Rous.

[2] *Ibid.*, 10; J. Dury, *Objections against the taking of the engagement answered*, 22.

[3] *The lawfulnes of obeying the present government*, 4–6.

[4] *A case of conscience concerning ministers meddling with state matters*, 1649, 162–5.

[5] *Considerations concerning the present engagement*, 10–12.

[6] *The bounds & bonds of publique obedience*, 34.

[7] *Ibid.*, 5.

nothing unlawful.[1] Sense, reason, and conscience, therefore, will show a subject what he must do.

'Sense will shew him who is actually in possession of all power . . . over him. . . . Reason will shew him what he who is over him pretends unto; whether yea or no, his pretences are backed with power to maintain his right against all adversaries therein . . . and Conscience will shew, that he to whom God hath committed the plenary administration of publique affairs with unconfrontable power, is Gods Vicegerent over the society of those to whom his administration doth extend it selfe.'[2]

It will be seen that there is much resemblance in these remarks to the arguments employed by Ascham.[3] But Rous and Dury stressed one further condition for subjection that had scarcely figured in Ascham's discussion. Only in lawful commands, they said, is a *de facto* power to be obeyed. 'New or old powers,' Rous declared, 'can never signifie good or bad powers,' and 'we may & ought to submit . . . to those who plenarily possesse, protect and command us lawfull things.'[4] Unless ordered to act unlawfully, Dury similarly affirmed, subjects must obey those in plenary possession.[5] They made no attempt, however, to state the criteria of lawful commands or to suggest who is to judge of the matter. But it is clear that they did not for a moment question the legality of the commonwealth's commands, whatever possible doubt they might feel concerning its right. They seem to have believed that in granting justice according to the known law, in preserving property, and in protecting those who submitted to it, the government was acting in a traditional, a normal, and, therefore, in a legal manner; and they warned that to deny its right to be obeyed was simply to opt for anarchy and confusion.[6]

Rous and Dury, conscientious and religious men both, were certainly sincere in laying down the condition that to merit obedience, the commands of those in plenary possession must be lawful. But from the standpoint of the government's opposition, the qualification had no importance at all, and the position of the two, practically speaking, was indistinguishable from Ascham's. Their critics believed the doctrines of Rous and Dury to amount to nothing more than an advocacy of blind obedience and non-resistance. If those doctrines had been accepted at the outset of the civil war, some Presbyterians pointed out, Charles I

[1] F. Rous, *The lawfulnes of obeying the present government*, 15.
[2] J. Dury, *Considerations concerning the present engagement*, 13.
[3] I do not know whether Dury had read Ascham, but Rous praises him for his judgement and learning (*The lawfulnes of obeying the present government*, 15), and sometimes repeats his arguments almost *verbatim*.
[4] *The bounds & bonds of publique obedience*, 28, 30–1.
[5] *Objections against the taking of the engagement answered*, 20–1.
[6] *Ibid.*, 20–1; J. Dury, *Considerations concerning the present engagement*, 8–9; F. Rous, *The lawfulnes of obeying the present government*, 15, *The bounds & bonds of publique obedience*, 26–7, 33.

would still occupy his throne.[1] One opponent of Rous admitted that between obedience to an unlawful power and anarchy, the choice is hard. But will not compliance with a usurper, he asked, only serve to fasten bonds upon the people? If usurpers may and must be obeyed in acts which are good, then one whose proper right has been injured can never have justice done him.[2]

What Rous and Dury took for granted was precisely what the enemies of the government did not admit: that a distinction existed between a power without authority and the legality of the commands it might issue. A power without authority, the commonwealth's opponents maintained, could not issue a legal command. There was obviously a difference here as to the meaning of legality. On the view of Rous and Dury, it was only the content of a command that determined its legality; on the view of their critics, a command, even if its content were good, would not be legal unless issued by persons who had a right to do so. If the officials of the commonwealth, a group of Presbyterians declared, would proclaim their rule as arising from conquest 'which is a kinde of title, *jure gentium*, we would observe their commands in *licitibus & honestis*, for fear sake. . . . But to a bicipitous and amphidoxous Government . . . we cannot see how it may be done: especially in such acts of obedience as do necessarily ratifie and establish an unlawfull or dubitable Authority.'[3]

The problem really at stake here was whether obligation could be created in the subject by the mere fact of power, and wholly apart from right or authority to rule. The government's opponents thought it could not. Opinions might, of course, vary as to the ultimate norm, adherence to which conveys authority to those in plenary possession. The Levellers would insist that only election by the whole people gives authority. Presbyterians and royalists, despite all their differences, would be unwilling to concede authority to a power which had unceremoniously overthrown the forms and usages of the historic constitution. All the government's enemies, however, were unanimous in the conviction that without authority, a power in plenary possession could not evoke obligation on the part of its subjects, could not issue a legal command, and could rely only on the threat of force to secure obedience.

3. OTHER WRITERS

It is impossible to determine how widely the unofficial theory of the commonwealth was maintained or believed to be an adequate justifica-

---

[1] *A pack of old puritans*, 1650, 34. This work is anonymous.
[2] *A second part of the religious demurrer*, 1649, 6. This work is anonymous.
[3] *A religious demurrer*, 1649, 6. This pamphlet is signed only A. B. C. D. One of its authors was the Presbyterian, Nathaniel Ward; see his *Discollominium*, 1650, 1, 6.

tion for the existing government. The compositions of Ascham, Rous, and Dury, many of which had more than one edition, show that it was not rare, and there were expressions of it in other writings also, and in the sermons of preachers.

One able author who based his argument on it was Lewis du Moulin, Camden Professor of Ancient History in the University of Oxford. Though du Moulin's *The Power Of The Christian Magistrate in Sacred Things* (1650) touched but incidentally on the problem of subjection to the existing government, it was distinguished by its unequivocal employment of the Hobbesian doctrine of sovereignty to justify its position.[1] In du Moulin's mind, there was no confusion as to the nature of law. Law, he was clear, is defined not by its content, but by the fact that it is a command of the sovereign power. '. . . any precept, though morall,' he wrote, '. . . although it bindes the conscience, yet 'tis no Law binding to obedience in *foro humano*, till it be reduced into a Law by the Legislative Power of the Soveraigne Magistrate. . . .'[2] When he takes up the question of subjection to the commonwealth, he insists that St. Paul in Romans 13 required obedience to any power, usurped or not.[3] To interpret the Apostle's admonition as pertaining only to lawful powers would produce absurdities, he points out, 'for first, who shall judge what power is lawfull? shall all joyntly, or every particular man . . . which is to seat The Superior Power no where, and to erect a Tribunall within every particular Dominion, distinct from that of the Supreme Magistrate. . .'.[4] '. . . possession is the great condition required for the duty of Allegiance,' du Moulin affirms, and suggests that this has always been recognized in England, most of whose kings after the Conquest lacked a proper title, but whose laws were and still are taken as valid. The crown in England means whoever is in possession. Even if the Turks were to conquer the country, both Scripture and reason would require obedience to them, because God ordains all powers to their supremacy, and men must be faithful to the power thus ordained. 'I should much doubt,' he says, 'whether Subjects may call any Supremacy of Power unlawfull, or whether a Supreame Governour is not a lawfull Governour. . . .'[5]

Another publicist, while urging that the commonwealth was, in fact, based on popular consent, went on to contend that any power in plenary possession is the ordinance of God and is, therefore, entitled to obedience. 'God himselfe expressly both ownes the giving of power to those who have no Title in point of Right,' he said, 'and . . . commands obedi-

---

[1] du Moulin's discussion of the power of the magistrate in ecclesiastical affairs leaves no doubt that Hobbes was one of his masters.
[2] *The power of the Christian magistrate*, 124.
[3] *Ibid.*, 21.
[4] *Ibid.*, 25–6.
[5] *Ibid.*, 27–32.

ence and forbids disobedience to those who (though God hath alwaies a designe above them) possesse themselves of power by force and Usurpation.'[1] Refusal to grant this position, he warned, entailed 'irrevocably falling into Anarchy and confusion upon every concussion of State . . .'.[2] The same standpoint was taken by still another writer, who pointed out that all governments rise and fall by the will of God, and that 'the prevailing, not the worsted . . . party may lay claim to the signature of Divine approbation, or at least to the concurrence of Gods absolute Will . . .'.[3]

In a sermon delivered before the justices at Exeter, the preacher, one Richard Saunders, expressed the familiar opinion that Romans 13 referred to any power. The only power to be obeyed, he said, is that actually in being and in a position to govern, protect, and back its undertakings with force. The consent of the people is not the sole means of determining that a power is from God, Saunders declared, because any power in plenary possession bears the divine stamp. Christians, he conceded in what amounts to a sop to those who believed in a right of resistance, may and must resist a usurper while in the act of usurpation; but once plenary possession has been obtained, all opposition should cease.[4] A similar doctrine was proclaimed by a Sussex minister, Thomas Carre, who affirmed that whether powers be good or bad, or use or abuse their place, the fact that they have supremacy is enough to entitle them to obedience.[5]

Confronted by such ideas, we inevitably ask whether the defenders of obedience to any power in plenary possession were not, by a supreme irony, pressing into the commonwealth's service the very arguments against a right of resistance which the theorists of the English revolution had all along opposed. They seem, indeed, to have done so, for the analogies between their conceptions and those of the antagonists of resistance from the Reformation right up through the civil war are striking.[6]

The reformer, Calvin, for example, declared that private men have no business inquiring into the rights of rulers. All power is of God, and

[1] *The exercitation answered*, 1650, 29–31. This work is anonymous.

[2] *Ibid.*, 17–18.

[3] N. W., *A discourse concerning the engagement*, 1650, 5, 7.

[4] Richard Saunders, *Plenary possession makes a lawfull power*, 1651, 5–6, 10, 14. But Saunders says also, with a citation from Calvin, that resistance, though sinful in private persons, is not so in the case of inferior magistrates who have been created to curb the exorbitancy of supreme power, *ibid.*, 20.

[5] *A treatise of subiection*, 1651, 6, 14.

[6] It seems scarcely necessary to point out that none of the writers about to be cited denied that commands against the law of God might be disobeyed. But they held that all other commands had to be obeyed and that under *no* circumstances was forcible resistance permissible, at least by private persons.

the fact that God has given power to anyone is sufficient to warrant subjection.[1] There is no tyranny, he remarked, which does not in some respects help to consolidate human society.[2] The Jacobean clergy took a similar view when they laid it down in the convocation of 1606 that after ambitious kings or disloyal subjects succeed in their ungodly design of bringing a country into subjection,

'the authority either so unjustly gotten or wrung by force, from the true and lawful possessor, being always God's authority (and therefore receiving no impeachment by the wickedness of those that have it), is ever, when any such alterations are thoroughly settled, to be reverenced and obeyed . . . not only for fear, but likewise for conscience sake.'[3]

The great ecclesiastic, Lancelot Andrewes, preaching on Matthew 22: 21, declared that the Caesar whom Christ ordered to be given his due was Tiberius, a heathen, an idolater, and an enemy to truth. 'Yet even this Caesar and . . . any Caesar,' Andrewes said, 'will stand with God, and God with them, for all that.'[4] After the outbreak of the civil war, one of the chief royalist writers, Henry Ferne, archdeacon of Leicester and chaplain to Charles I, affirmed that conquest is a justifiable means of translating kingdoms and disposing of peoples. It is 'an uncontrouleable truth', he asserted, that when 'the invading Prince has perfectly subdued a People . . . providence doth sufficiently discover it selfe, and such a people ought to submit, and consent, and take their Prince as set over them by Providence . . .'.[5]

These resemblances are important, and they cast a lurid light on the sort of ideas made use of by some of the defenders of obedience to the revolutionary government. But there is, I think, something in the unofficial theory of the commonwealth which sets it clearly off from the

---

[1] *Commentarius in epistolam Pauli ad Romanos*, XIII, 1; *Institutio Christianae religionis*, IV, xx, 28.

[2] *Commentarius in epistolam Pauli ad Romanos*, XIII, 3. On Calvin's justification of all who hold power, and on Luther's ,which was similar, see the emphatic remarks of G. de Lagarde, *L'Esprit politique de la reforme*, Paris, 1926, 224–48. These statements of Calvin's are quite consistent with his assertion (*Institutio Christianae religionis*, IV, xx, 31) that if a state's constitution provides for the curbing of kings by estates or magistrates, they may do so. What he opposed was all forcible resistance by private persons.

[3] *Bishop Overall's convocation book*, I, Ch. XXVIII. This was not published until 1690, though the canons were drawn up in 1606. I cite it from the edition in *The library of Anglo-Catholic theology*, Oxford, 1844. The convocation's canons never became official, one of the reasons for this being that James I took offence at the doctrine quoted; see his letter printed in *ibid.*, Preface, 7–8.

[4] *XCVI sermons*, 4th ed., 1641, 91.

[5] *A reply unto severall treatises*, 1643, 20.

earlier contentions that all the higher powers are ordained by God and are to be obeyed for this reason.

The difference lies in the unofficial theory's blurring or elimination of the fundamental distinction between the fact of plenary possession and the right to it, that is to say, between power and authority. This is something that none of the earlier writers who opposed resistance would have acquiesced in for a moment. Throughout his discussion of civil government in the *Institutes*, it is evident that Calvin never equated power with authority. Nor did the convocation of 1606, as we may see from its seventeenth canon, where it is unequivocally affirmed that at the death of a king, his heir is successor by right, notwithstanding such efforts as may be made to prevent that right from being realized. Henry Ferne added to his statement quoted above the crucial qualification that it is only when there is no heir apparent to whom the people are bound that they are free to obey a prince whom Providence has permitted to conquer.[1] The remarks both of Ferne and of another important royalist writer, Dudley Digges, on Romans 13, make clear their assumption that the higher powers to whom the Apostle commanded obedience were such only as were invested with authority.[2] The royalist, Robert Sanderson, one of the greatest casuists of the Church of England, was of the same opinion. In lectures delivered at Oxford in 1646, he affirmed that obedience might be given to those in plenary possession for the sake of the public welfare;[3] but he hedged this concession about with numerous qualifications in favour of the rightful ruler who had been dispossessed.[4] Later, after the appearance of Anthony Ascham's book, Sanderson denounced it as tending to atheism, and said that the subjection tendered to those in plenary possession must be limited by a recognition of their lack of authority and by a willingness to assist the dispossessed party to recover its right, should the occasion offer.[5]

Neither Calvin, nor the Jacobean bishops, nor the royalist writers, it is clear, ever identified power with authority. Moreover, we shall not understand their condemnation of resistance unless we realize how entirely and literally they discerned the hand of God upholding all earthly rulers. It was not the bare fact of plenary possession that caused them to oppose a right of resistance; rather, it was their unquestioning convic-

---

[1] *A reply unto severall treatises*, 20.

[2] H. Ferne, *The resolving of conscience*, 1642, 10; D. Digges, *The unlawfulnesse of subjects taking up armes*, 1644, 133.

[3] *Lectures on conscience and human law*, trans. C. Wordsworth, London, 1877, 141–2. Sanderson became Bishop of Lincoln at the Restoration. His life was written by Isaac Walton.

[4] *Ibid.*, The fifth prelection, *passim*.

[5] *A resolution of conscience*, 1649, 2–6. This work is anonymous, but Ascham's answer, *A reply to a paper of Dr Sandersons*, 1650, shows its authorship.

tion that in every earthly power there is really something divine.[1] These religious thinkers regarded power as the creation of God; it was simply inexplicable to them that some men should have sway over others unless God permitted it. Such being the case, there was, indeed, a kind of authority in every power, even a usurped one, an authority deriving from God, by whose will all powers exist. Now this is a genuinely religious attitude towards power, and it is just this that we sense dimmed or non-existent in the unofficial theory of the commonwealth. Despite all their assertions of the presence of Providence in the rise and fall of governments, neither Ascham, nor even the pious Rous and Dury, seem to have felt that in the powers of this world there was present some aura of deity. On the contrary, one has a strong impression that they viewed earthly power disenchantedly, indifferently, and that this is why they evinced such scepticism as to rights and titles and such lack of concern about forms of government. The *mystique* of supremacy had ceased to fascinate them. To Calvin, a supreme power was entitled to obedience because the hand of God was evident in it. To Ascham, a supreme power was just a fact that wisdom suggested could best be reckoned with by yielding subjection.

It was inevitable that the unofficial theory of the commonwealth should evoke criticisms from those who opposed the Cromwellian government but yet claimed to be loyal still to the popular principles put forth by Parliament in the early 1640s. This was precisely the situation of the Presbyterians, and it was, therefore, one of their number, Edward Gee, who dealt most effectively with the issues raised by Ascham and the others who held his position. Gee, a Lancashire minister,[2] is now all but forgotten,[3] but undeservedly, for he was one of the ablest political writers of the interregnum, and his criticism of Sir Robert Filmer is as acute as Locke's.[4] Far more clearly than anyone else, he went to the centre of the arguments employed in the unofficial theory of the commonwealth by contending that power is one thing, and right or authority another, and that only the two conjoined can make a lawful government.

In his most important work, *The Divine Right and Original Of The*

---

[1] This may not be strictly true of Digges, whose writings show traces of Hobbes's influence; cf. J. W. Allen, *op. cit.*, 500, and J. N. Figgis, *The divine right of kings*, 2nd ed., Cambridge, 1914, 239.

[2] See his life in the *D.N.B.*, *s.v.*

[3] There is, however, an appreciative mention of him by Mr. Laslett in his introduction to the writings of Sir Robert Filmer, *op. cit.*, 38; and cf. also J. W. Allen, 'Sir Robert Filmer', *Social and political ideas of some English thinkers of the Augustan age*, ed. F. J. C. Hearnshaw, London, 1928, 45.

[4] In his *The divine right and original of the civill magistrate*, 1658, 144–59 *et passim*.

Civill Magistrate (1658),[1] Gee began by pointing out that force can never be the sole basis of the relationship between ruler and ruled, and that without the willing obedience of its subjects, no government can long endure.[2] He went on then to argue that in the epistle to the Romans, St. Paul was enjoining obedience to just and lawful powers, not to those installed simply by forcible possession.[3] It can scarcely be doubted, he said, that there is a distinction between power and right;[4] and for a government to have right, he insisted, it must be properly invested with its power.[5]

It is, moreover, quite mistaken, he declared, to hold that because all ruling powers come to their ascendancy by Providence, they are, therefore, to be obeyed as originating in the will of God. God's providence manifests itself in various ways, and does not always indicate what men should do.

'We cannot say Providence cals this, or that man to that . . . estate, which the word of God forbids or warrants not unto him. Providence must not be used . . . to lead us there where the will of God in Scripture revealed opens us not a way. This were by consequent to destroy the authority of the word, and to make the most pure and perfect wayes of God the occasions and patronizers of every obliquity.'[6]

The fact that a man takes possession of supreme power without right, Gee says, is not 'ordinative' but mere 'eventual Providence', and no Scriptural injunction to obey the higher powers can apply to such a ruler on the grounds that Providence established him.[7] The Apostle's statement that the higher powers are ordained of God must only be interpreted to signify 'an institutive or legislative, not . . . a meer providential way of ordination'.[8]

Though he meant no more by the 'people' than the prosperous and aristocratic classes in the community, Gee held that '. . . the ordinary means [God] useth for the deputation of persons under himself, and over the people in the office of the Supreme Civil Power, is the vote, elective act, or consent of the body polytique, or people to be ruled'.[9] Conquest in itself can give no right to rule. If the conquest was in a just war, then the right to rule was antecedent to the conquest and in the justice of the cause. If the conquest was unjust, only a subsequent con-

---

[1] Gee had previously written two anonymously published works, *An exercitation concerning usurped powers*, 1650, and *A vindication of the oath of allegiance*, 1650, attacking the views of Rous and Ascham. They can be identified as his by comparing them with his signed work of 1658.

[2] *The divine right . . . of the civill magistrate*, Preface, sec. 6.   [3] *Ibid.*, 7–8.

[4] *Ibid.*, 15–23.   [5] *Ibid.*, 37–9.   [6] *Ibid.*, 37–9.

[7] *Ibid.*, 84.   [8] *Ibid.*, 115.   [9] *Ibid.*, 138.

sent of the conquered can convey to the supreme power a right to rule.[1] It is certainly an error, he says, to distinguish between the power itself and the means used to achieve it. A power wrongfully obtained is not a power at all in St. Paul's sense, and 'a man cannot be a possessor of authority . . . but by lawfull means. . . . Authority consisteth in a right . . . to rule'; without this right, there can be no authority.[2]

To maintain that any possessor is the power spoken of by St. Paul is absurd, Gee declares. It would necessitate that the pope's power is of God. It would frustrate all titles and means of granting authority which the people have constituted. It would make the state a prey to ambitious spirits and call God the author of their unlawful acts. It repudiates the arguments Parliament used against the king, and contradicts the principle of popular sovereignty which 'hath gone of late for a chief Maxime in Politicks'.[3]

Nothing could be clearer than Gee's attack. His arguments were not really answerable by any who supported the commonwealth on grounds of principle. As a Presbyterian, he was attached to the party that opposed religious toleration and whose temporizings and concessions to the king might have thrown away much that the English revolution gained. But this does not detract from the fact that as a theorist, his ideas were far more democratic than the class of doctrines on the revolution's behalf which he assailed.

[1] *Ibid.*, 160–2.   [2] *Ibid.*, 202.   [3] *Ibid.*, 221, 291–5.

VI

THEORISTS OF THE COMMONWEALTH: II

THE republic which was erected on the monarchy's ruins was a military dictatorship. Though sovereignty was now exercised by the House of Commons, the latter, in its truncated condition, was scarcely representative, and was strongly dependent upon the army to maintain it in power. The enmity of royalists to it was inveterate. Left-wing democracy had been estranged by its social policy, Presbyterianism by its religious policy, and both alike, though for different reasons, by its political policy. The reservoir of loyalty on which it could draw was, therefore, small, and many who were not hostile were sullenly indifferent to its fate.

Yet it was with a doctrine of popular sovereignty that the country's oligarchical rulers justified their position. Cromwell himself found sanction for the purging of Parliament and the trial of Charles I in the conviction that in certain cases, any authority might be resisted, and that the army was a lawful power called by God to oppose the king so as to secure the ends for which the war had been fought.[1] The remonstrance in which the army officers announced the fate they intended to visit upon the king took up a similar position.[2] Its writer, Henry Ireton,[3] who was the keenest theorist among the Cromwellians in the army, pointed out that the king's power was a trust which, having been perverted, might be withdrawn and the people absolved from all obedience.[4] Charles must be tried and punished for his tyranny in order to show that no man, not even a prince, is above human justice or unaccountable to earthly powers.[5] 'If . . . our Kings claim by right of Conquest,' Ireton said, 'God

[1] See the important letter of 25th November 1648 to Col. Hammond, *The writings and speeches of Oliver Cromwell*, ed. W. C. Abbott, 4 vols., Cambridge, 1937–47, I, 696–9.

[2] *A remonstrance of his excellency . . . Lord Fairfax . . . and of the generall councell of officers*, 1648. This was presented to the Commons on 20th November 1648. Excerpts are reprinted in A. S. P. Woodhouse, *op. cit.*

[3] Cf. R. W. Ramsey, *Henry Ireton*, London, 1949, 115. Ireton had previously shown his great capacities at the Putney debates.

[4] *A remonstrance*, 22.   [5] *Ibid.*, 47–8.

hath given you the same against him, and more righteous, by how much that on their parts was extended to a forcible Dominion over the people (which originally or naturally they had not) and ours but to a deliverance from that Bondage, into that state of Right and Freedom which was naturally and morally due to us before. . . .'[1] No monarch must henceforth be admitted except by election of the people, the manifesto declared, and only on condition of disclaiming any negative voice in the determinations of the House of Commons, which is to be the supreme power.[2]

These ideas also dominated the arguments which were resorted to during the king's trial. John Cook, the government's solicitor, published a pamphlet a few days after Charles's execution in which he reproduced the speech he had intended to deliver if the king had pleaded to the charge. In England, Cook said, with a buttressing reference to Fortescue, the king has always been subject to law. Furthermore, the people have given him power only so that he will act for their good. As for the law under which Charles stands condemned, it is

'By the Fundamental Law of this Kingdom, by the general Law of all Nations, and the Unanimous consent of all Rational men . . . written in every mans heart . . . in Capital Letters, and a Character so legible, that he that runs may read, viz That when any man is intrusted with the Sword for the protection and preservation of the people, if this man shall imploy it to their destruction . . . by the Law of that Land he becomes an enemy to that people and deserves the most exemplary and severe punishment that can be invented. . . .'

Such a law is unnecessary in writing, Cook declared, because it is self-evident and 'hath a prerogative right . . . before any positive law whatsoever'.[3]

The legislation by which the commonwealth was brought into being also enshrined these conceptions. Early in January 1649, the House of Commons passed resolutions declaring that 'the People are, under God, the Original of all just Power', that the Commons, 'being chosen by, and representing the People, have the supreme Power in this Nation', and that whatever the Commons determines has the force of law without

---

[1] *Ibid.*, 48.
[2] *Ibid.*, 62–9.
[3] *King Charls his case*, 1649, 6–8, 22–3. Cf. the remarks of Bradshaw, the president of the High Court of Justice, in *King Charls his tryal*, 2nd ed., 1649. It might be noted that these same arguments provided the basis of the formal charge under which the king was brought to trial. There it is declared that the people had conferred a limited trust upon Charles to govern by the laws of the land, and that he had violated this trust by attempting to set up an unlimited power; the charge is printed in J. Rushworth, *op. cit.*, VII, 1396–8.

the consent or concurrence of king or peers.[1] Later, the act abolishing monarchy asserted that

'the office of a King . . . is unnecessary, burdensome, and dangerous to the liberty, safety, and public interest of the people, and that for the most part, use hath been made of the regal power and prerogative to oppress and impoverish and enslave the subject; and that usually and naturally any person in such power makes it his interest to incroach upon the just freedom and liberty of the people. . . .'[2]

Numerous pamphlets written in justification of the commonwealth express these same ideas. Among their writers, there is none who can be regarded in any sense as a great political thinker, not even John Milton, whose thought will be treated in another place.[3] Moreover, the arguments which were resorted to were substantially alike. There was little attempt to defend the government on the doctrinaire ground that a republic is superior to a monarchy. The idea does, of course, occur;[4] but it is inconspicuous, and the theory of the commonwealth is distinct from that of the republican movement, which developed separately.[5] The chief theme was that the purge of Parliament and the removal of kingship and the House of Lords arose from an unavoidable necessity which forced the army, acting as the sovereign people's representative, to exercise its right of calling a bad ruler and his accomplices to account. This assertion of the people's supremacy conflicted, however, with the fact that the government was a narrow oligarchy, and with a general awareness that the majority of the people had consented neither to the army's acts nor to the government's rule and perhaps opposed both. In the tension which this conflict created lay the principal problem of the official theory of the commonwealth.

The development of the position might be illustrated from various writers. The theorist who will best serve the purpose, however, is the Independent minister, John Goodwin, who was, with Milton, the ablest and most zealous defender the government possessed.

---

[1] *Commons journals*, VI, 111.

[2] This was passed in March 1649. The text is printed in *The constitutional documents of the Puritan revolution 1625–1660*, ed. S. R. Gardiner, 3rd rev. ed., Oxford, 1906, 384–7.

[3] See below, Ch. IX.

[4] See, e.g., Henry Robinson, *A short discourse between monarchical and aristocratical government*, 1649. This appeared anonymously, but is accepted as Robinsons' by W. K. Jordan, *Men of substance*, 180. See also John Canne, *The improvement of mercy*, 1649, 16–18.

[5] See below, Ch. XII.

THEORISTS OF THE COMMONWEALTH

1. JOHN GOODWIN

John Goodwin was recognized as wielding one of the most effective pens on the commonwealth's behalf, and at the Restoration, the Act of Indemnity expressly named him among eighteen persons who were to be forever disqualified from holding any public trust, civil or religious.[1] He was born in 1594, educated at Cambridge, and became a popular preacher in London. He held Independent principles, and, expelled from his living on this account in 1645, he succeeded thereafter in establishing one of the best attended congregations in the city.[2] A tireless controversialist, he gave his allegiance above all to the principle of liberty of conscience. In its defence, he made, perhaps, the greatest contribution of any writer of his day.[3] It was, primarily, his attachment to this principle which caused him to be concerned with political theory by confronting him with the necessity of defining the relationship between the state and religious groups. His examination of this question issued in a denial of all jurisdiction to the civil power over religious life, and in the absolute segregation of the civil and religious spheres, so that the integrity of the latter might be secured.[4]

Goodwin was well fitted to champion the commonwealth, for his political position was as free from the extremism of the Levellers as it was fearless in defending the course pursued by Cromwell and his supporters. He was, in fact, Cromwellian in his political outlook, and faithfully vindicated every alteration of state, from the commonwealth through the protectorate, which the aristocratic Independents held themselves bound to make. He never fully carried into the secular domain his deep conviction that, in religion, all believers are equal and all privileged to be heard, since truth might emerge from any quarter, even the humblest. He was oblivious in his writings to the political and social grievances which were being so heatedly attacked in his day. Though he wholeheartedly maintained the doctrine of popular sovereignty, he formulated it in a manner compatible with the position of men whose power had been won as much by crushing the Levellers as the Presbyterians and royalists. At the beginning of the civil war, in his passionate pamphlets justifying resistance to the king, he identified the whole nation with Parliament.[5] Later, he strove to identify the whole nation with Cromwell's party, but unsuccessfully, and was compelled

---

[1] 12 Car. II c, 11.
[2] Biographical details chiefly from the *D.N.B.*, *s.v.* A full, up-to-date study of Goodwin's life is badly needed. The old work by Thomas Jackson, *The life of John Goodwin*, 2nd improved ed., London, 1872, is inadequate.
[3] W. K. Jordan, *Development of religious toleration*, III, 376.
[4] *Ibid.*, III, 381.
[5] *Anti-cavalierisme*, 1642, 28; *Os ossorianum*, 1643, 61-2.

to take refuge in ideas at bottom inconsistent with what he most believed.

Shortly after the army's purge of Parliament, Goodwin defended that action in his *Right And Might well met* (1649). His argument was an attempt to overcome the difficulty of reconciling his conviction that the Cromwellian government represented the people with the fact that it enjoyed but little popular support. Those members of the Commons who were forcibly excluded were malignants, he insists, and the case against them as warrantable as was Parliament's against the king.[1] True, the army was raised by Parliament and had no commission to proceed against it. But when the highest magistrates menace the peace and welfare of the people, they forfeit their place and may be removed by inferior magistrates.[2]

Goodwin admits that the army had no formal call from the people. Nevertheless, the army represented the people, whose necessity spoke for them, though they themselves were still.[3] Besides, he declares—and here was the fatal flaw in the position—even if the people judged the army's course to be wrong, it is no matter, because physicians need not have their patients' consent to rid them of distempers. Moreover, '. . . if a people be depraved and corrupt, so as to conferre places of power and trust upon wicked and undeserving men, they forfeit their power . . . unto those that are good, though but a few. So that nothing pretended from a non-concurrence of the people with the Army, will hold water.'[4]

The army's purge of Parliament, he says, was warranted by the law of nature and necessity, and this law is superior to the established laws of the land.[5] Nor is it difficult to judge of necessity. Just as peril of life is an extreme necessity, so was the condition of the people, imperilled by the Parliamentary malignants. This necessity afforded an unquestionable basis for the army's course despite any temporary disobedience to laws.[6]

It will be seen that Goodwin's position was fundamentally untenable. A sincere believer in the people's right to remove unfaithful magistrates, he was certain that the army had acted as the people's representative and in their interest. Yet what if the people did not consent? No matter, he replied, extreme necessity justifies what has been done. His final appeal, therefore, was to necessity, which he accorded precedence even over the sovereign people. It is just at this point that the limitation of the official theory of the commonwealth is disclosed. Whether it was necessity that was invoked, or the people identified, as Milton did,[7] with their virtuous part, however few in number, the consequence was to evade a thorough

---

[1] *Right and might*, 4–5.   [2] *Ibid.*, 6–7.   [3] *Ibid.*, 8–9, 14.
[4] *Ibid.*, 14–15.   [5] *Ibid.*, 15–16.   [6] *Ibid.*, 20–1.
[7] See below, Ch. IX.

application of the very principle which Goodwin upheld—that all power must exist by the people's consent.

This evasion was but the reflection in thought of the commonwealth's position in life. The Cromwellian government could claim with some justification that its elimination of the Presbyterians' influence had removed the danger that the latter might effect a restoration of royal authority without guarantees for the people's religious and political freedoms. But in suppressing the Levellers, it had signalized its refusal to recognize the full implications of those freedoms and had deprived itself of the one means by which it might have won a popular base and thereby, perhaps, stability. Its circumstances made it, consequently, a government of the centre, and to the realities of its situation the doctrine of popular sovereignty had to be adapted. This explains Goodwin's tortuous reasoning. And because of this, too, the official theory of the commonwealth inevitably tended to formulate the doctrine of popular sovereignty in aristocratic terms, emphasizing less the initiative of the people than of their representatives, and praising the government as a balance between regal tyranny and levelling confusion.[1]

In pleading necessity, Goodwin not only avoided drawing the full inferences from his radical theory, but resorted to an expedient which could be used to justify anything. This was recognized by one of the government's supporters, who pointed out that 'if Necessity be not Rightly stated & well limited, I know not how it may prevayl against our greatest Rights and justest Laws . . .'.[2] The government's opponents, of course, would have no truck with the idea. John Geree, a critic of Goodwin, put a question which it is difficult to see how the latter could have satisfactorily answered. '. . . what if the Levelling Part of the Army', Geree asked, 'should have further designs then the Moderater Part, and the heads of the Moderate Party stand in their way, may not they take up this plea, and without Law, or legal processe . . . take them out of their way?'[3] And the Presbyterian ministers who opposed the army declared that any necessity must be 'Absolute, Present, and Clear; not Doubtful, Uncertain, and Conjectural, as that which is alledged in your

---

[1] See, e.g., Henry Robinson, *A short discourse between monarchical and aristocratical government*, 14, 18, 20; John Canne, *The improvement of mercy*, 16–18, *The golden rule*, 1649, 11-12, 32; Eutactius Philodemius, Γένεσις καὶ τέλος ἐξουσίας, *The original & end of civil power*, 1649, 7–8, 28, 34. On the strength of the entry in the Cambridge University Library catalogue, Halkett and Laing (*Dictionary of anonymous and pseudonymous English literature*, new enlarged ed., ed. J. Kennedy, W. A. Smith, and A. F. Johnson, London and Edinburgh, 1926) ascribe this last work to Anthony Ascham. No contemporary evidence in the Cambridge University copy warrants the ascription, however, and it is obviously not Ascham's.

[2] John Sadler, *Rights of the kingdom*, 1649, [4]. This work is anonymous, but Thomson's manuscript inscription gives the authorship.

[3] Καταδυνάστης. *Might overcoming right*, 1649, 33.

case must needs be, it being discerned onely by your selves and your own party.'[1]

Despite Goodwin's inconsistent application of the doctrine of popular sovereignty, we must be careful not to underestimate the democratic character of his position. Just as his advocacy of liberty of conscience was one of the great contributions to the democratic movement of his time, so was his vindication of regicide. This task he undertook in his ὑβριστοδίκαι. *The Obstructours Of Justice* (1649), which was ordered seized and burned at the Restoration.[2] The importance of this work arises not from the originality of its ideas, for they were mostly familiar ones, but from the great cause in which they were uttered and from the uncompromising vigour with which they were laid down. Goodwin knew how audacious and unparalleled it was to bring a king to trial before a court of his own subjects. No wonder the people are troubled by the deed, he told the Commons in his dedication,

'considering . . . 1. how long the judgements . . . of the generalitie of men in the world have been overshadowed with Prerogative Divinitie; 2. how unaccustomed the present Age is to bear the weight of such Heroique transactions; 3. that neither were their Fathers able to report unto them any such thing done in their days. . . .'[3]

Both Scripture and the law of the land, Goodwin says, require that murderers should be put to death. Kings are no more excepted from this law than shoemakers or tailors, and by it, Charles I was justly punished for the blood he was instrumental in shedding.[4] Moreover, kings are not the equals of the people or the people's representatives. They are but servants, and may be removed. 'The people (I mean collectively taken),' he remarks, 'have no Law of nature, or of God . . . which prohibiteth them from laying aside . . . Kingly Government . . . when they have reasonable cause for it.' And reasonable cause exists if the people find kings to be dangerous to their freedom, or if the cost of maintaining royal government is too great, or if another form of government will serve better.

'. . . in all these cases . . . and many like unto these, a people . . . formerly Governed by Kings, may very lawfully turn these servants of theirs out of their doors; as the Romans of old, and the Hollanders of late . . . have done. . . .'[5]

---

[1] *A serious and faithfull representation of the judgements of ministers of the gospell within the province of London*, 1649, 15. This was signed by forty-seven Presbyterian clergymen.

[2] D. Masson, *op. cit.*, VI, 181–2, 193.

[3] *The obstructours of justice*, Dedicatory Epistle.

[4] *Ibid.*, 3–4, 7.

[5] *Ibid.*, 12.

Even if it were granted that the king is the equal of the people's representatives, nevertheless, if he uses his power to oppress the people, he may be resisted. And on the remote supposition that the king is superior, he is, nevertheless, party to a sacred covenant for the breach of which he may be punished.[1] Furthermore, kings are to be distinguished from tyrants. Whatever the people owe a king, they owe him nothing if he becomes a tyrant. No law of God ordains that a 'Tyrant should be the politick head of a body of people (collectively taken) or that such a body . . . shall acknowledge him for their Superiour'.[2] It is not difficult, he points out, to know when a king becomes a tyrant. The laws of the land will generally show it, and if they do not expressly do so, then the people's representatives, who make the law, may decide.[3]

The Parliament which established the High Court of Justice was a true Parliament, Goodwin insists. The members who remained after the military purge were loyal and true, and the absence of the purged members could not invalidate the Parliamentary capacity of those who continued to sit.[4] The Commons violated no fundamental law when they alone, without the peers, erected the tribunal which tried the king. Only that is fundamental law which the people's representatives regard as absolutely necessary to the nation's well-being. Neither the House of Lords nor even trial by jury, in the case of extraordinary delinquents, is fundamental in this sense.[5]

'. . . though the Erection of a Court of Justice by . . . Commons without the Lords be contrarie to the letter and outside the Law; yet a requisiteness of it supposed in order to the people's good, it is of perfect compliance with the spirit and soul of the Law.'[6]

If the Commons, as inferior magistrates, had neglected to execute justice on the king, the duty would have devolved upon any who had the opportunity and means to perform it. But it chiefly concerns inferior magistrates to act when superiors are remiss, and this they must do even if they need to resort to extraordinary courses.[7]

As has been remarked, there is little in Goodwin's stirring pamphlet that is new. Its chief ideas could be found in earlier Parliamentarian writings such as Rutherford's *Lex, Rex*, and further back than this, in sixteenth-century justifications of resistance by the Monarchomachs and others.[8] Its main point of departure was the principle that rulers are the people's servants and may be deposed and punished for misconduct,

---

[1] *Ibid.*, 30–1. [2] *Ibid.*, 31–2. [3] *Ibid.*, 33–4. [4] *Ibid.*, 35–8.
[5] *Ibid.*, 38–9. [6] *Ibid.*, 39–40. [7] *Ibid.*, 40, 43.
[8] See, e.g., the remarks and references in G. de Lagarde, *op. cit.*, 249–68, and in R. W. and A. J. Carlyle, *A history of mediaeval political theory in the West*, 6 vols., Edinburgh and London, 1903–37, VI, Part IV, Ch. II.

the emphasis being placed on the people as a collective body acting through its constituted representatives. This doctrine dominates the work. At the same time, a mixture of *ad hoc* elements was introduced to make the argument fit the circumstances of monarchy's abolition in England. These elements, however, constituted a danger to the central principle and reveal once more the limitations within which Goodwin's democratic outlook was confined. Was he not conceding too much in allowing a Parliament from which a majority of members had been excluded and whose representative character could be doubted, to take any extraordinary measures it deemed fit, even to the extent of dispensing with jury trials? Might not such a concession imperil the very freedom Parliament was ordained to uphold?

There was, it is clear, an insoluble conflict at the core of Goodwin's political thought. The reason for it, as we have seen, lay in the unpopular position of the Cromwellian government. This conflict manifested itself for the last time in his pamphlets supporting the protectorate, which we must briefly note in concluding this account of his ideas. Though Goodwin was somewhat critical of the protectorate's ecclesiastical policy,[1] he maintained, nevertheless, that its constitution, *The Instrument of Government*, well secured the people's rights. He admitted that the protectorate had been set up by acts which transgressed the letter of the law, but held that these had been performed for the people's good.[2] Having said all this, he yet did not scruple to oppose a right of resistance to the government with the very conceptions made use of by Rous and Dury in 1649. It is a pity to see him reduced to the need to maintain such doctrines. Chapter thirteen of the epistle to the Romans, we now find him saying, means that obedience must be shown to all higher powers, irrespective of the way in which they attained supremacy. Was not the higher power in St. Paul's time that monster among men, Nero? Yet to him the Apostle required submission, and as long as the higher powers command lawful things, they must be obeyed.[3]

Here we may leave John Goodwin and the official theory of the commonwealth. Assertor of the right of revolution and of the accountability of kings to human justice, Goodwin was yet incapable of accepting the implications of his democratic position. Prisoner to the contradiction that also held fast the government he defended, in his thought we cannot but see the revolution's illusion of a general freedom fade away, to reveal the narrower freedom which was the Cromwellian power's ultimate achievement for the English people.

[1] βασανισταί. *Or the triers . . . tried and cast*, 1657.

[2] *Peace protected*, 1654, 28; Συγκρητισμός. *Or dis-satisfaction satisfied*, 1653, 5–6.

[3] *Dis-satisfaction satisfied*, 3; *Peace protected*, 44–5. In *Right and might well met*, Goodwin rejected this very interpretation of Romans 13.

VII

THEORISTS OF THE PROTECTORATE

B Y the time of the protectorate's establishment in 1654, political thought was ceasing to be preoccupied with the problem of vindicating the existing government. Almost everything that could be said on this problem had been spoken in the discussion over the status of the commonwealth. Moreover, the revolutionary government of 1649, by its drastic illustration of the principle of the accountability of rulers, evoked from political theorists a passion and concern which the protectorate in its turn was quite unable to command. Henceforth, interest was to shift increasingly to the theory of republicanism, and it was this which dominated most of the important writings of the late 1650s.

Yet the constitution laid down in *The Instrument of Government* required defending, and there were writers to discharge the task. Their works may be dealt with briefly, however, for they were scarcely more than a reproduction of the various ideas that had been expressed earlier on the commonwealth's behalf. There were the same contentions that plenary possession of power in itself warrants obedience, and the same affirmations that the government exists by the people's consent. But while the former were asserted even more unashamedly than before, the latter now lacked the ardency with which the great deeds of 1649 had been defended, and were pervaded, instead, by a pedestrian flatness. The heart seems to have gone out of the writings which sought to justify the Cromwellian rule with democratic arguments, and for reasons that are clear enough. The government's unpopularity was greater than ever, the military basis of its power more conspicuous, and the fiction of legality and consent, in consequence, more threadbare. Cromwell's road to the protectorate was littered with lost supporters. By forcibly dissolving the Long Parliament in 1653, he had alienated Sir Henry Vane; when he shortly thereafter dismissed the Nominated Parliament, which he had himself convened, and gave the quietus to the great reforms that body was preparing, he estranged many religious men in the sects who had been among his most devoted followers; his assumption, finally, of the semi-regal office of

Lord Protector—an office Parliament was denied the right to abolish[1]—gave stimulus to the growth of a republican opposition. How could a sincere doctrine of popular sovereignty accommodate itself to all this? It is no wonder that John Goodwin's writings on the protectorate's behalf were the least effective of his political pamphlets. Even Milton, Cromwell's devout admirer, was unable to conceal his doubts about the government's position.[2]

The official theory, of course, insisted on the protectorate's democratic character and its compatibility with the aims for which the civil war had been fought and won. Cromwell declared that the people had called him to be Lord Protector,[3] and that all just rights and liberties were provided for in *The Instrument of Government*.[4] Such also was the contention of the official pamphlet, *A True State of the Case Of The Common-Wealth* (1654), a workmanlike effort, unrelieved by any flights of enthusiasm, to justify the new constitution.[5] Considering Cromwell's now almost royal pomp and position, it is understandable enough that the anonymous author should emphasize that the war was not fought against any particular form of government, but solely to secure the people's safety and freedom.[6] These are well preserved under *The Instrument of Government*, he said;[7] and if Parliament is forbidden to alter the system by which it must share its power with a single person, this is because there exists no other way 'to keep us from wandring any more in the Maze of our own Contentions . . .'.[8]

Other writers, none of any consequence, sounded a similar note. It was declared by one author that no government had ever been so fully and clearly acknowledged by the people. '. . . this forme of Government we now are under,' he said, '. . . by a single person and a Parliament was sent down into every Shire . . . that none (except enemies and people not worth 200 l.) might . . . be denied his opinion and vote. . . .'[9] He evidently did not pause to reflect how weak was the case for popular consent when not only royalists, for whose exclusion there was some justification, but also those without estates of £200 were denied a franchise

---

[1] *The instrument of government*, Art. XII.

[2] See below, Ch. IX.

[3] *The writings and speeches of Oliver Cromwell*, III, 452.

[4] *Ibid.*, III, 587.

[5] The official character of this work is shown by Cromwell's reference to it in his speech of 22nd January 1655 (*ibid.*, III, 587) dissolving the first Parliament of the protectorate. It was published anonymously, but is attributed to Marchamont Nedham by C. H. Firth, *The last years of the protectorate*, 2 vols., London, 1909, I, 156. The ascription is not improbable, but must remain uncertain. Nedham's work is discussed below, Ch. X.

[6] *A true state of the case of the commonwealth*, 5.

[7] *Ibid.*, 28.

[8] *Ibid.*, 34.

[9] *A letter from a person in the country*, 1656, 17. This work is anonymous.

in county elections.[1] Another anonymous pamphleteer expatiated on the validity of Cromwell's title as Lord Protector.

'... if the People of England, Scotland and Ireland have given his Highness their actual consent and submission; if the Parliament of the three Nations have disannulled the old Title and Line; if they have owned his Highness by the name of Lord Protector ... I may safely conclude ... That whoever hath so much to shew for the Supremacie, hath a good Title to it. ....'[2]

Apart from Goodwin and Milton, the only person of any importance who defended the protectorate with arguments that would have been acceptable to Cromwell was the Baptist, Samuel Richardson. Richardson was a man of somewhat advanced religious views. In the next century, his attack on the doctrine of eternal punishment in hell was translated and reprinted by the materialist, Baron d'Holbach.[3] But he is without significance as a political theorist. Chiefly interested in religious toleration, it was as an advocate of this principle that he made his slight contribution to the thought of the revolution.[4] In 1654, he supported Cromwell primarily because of the latter's tolerant religious policy, and by giving his backing to the government, it is likely that he influenced other Baptists to do the same.[5]

The war, Richardson says, was waged principally for liberty in religion, and this men can enjoy under the protectorate in unprecedented abundance.[6] He himself 'was never against Kingly government, but against their coersive power in matters meerly religious'.[7] There are, he admits, three oppressions which still continue: tithes, corruption in the law, and slowness in the payment of the public debt. But these are legacies transmitted from the past, and will be remedied in time.[8] Moreover, he asserts, the majority of the people support the government, as their payment of taxes and willingness to elect members of Parliament proves.[9] But he was aware how weak this contention was, and contradicted himself when remarking on the opposition to the protectorate's

[1] See *The instrument of government*, Art. XVIII.
[2] *Killing is murder*, 1657, 12.
[3] *A discourse of the torments of hell*, 1660, published in 1769 at Paris as *L'Enfer détruit*. There were other English editions in the eighteenth and nineteenth centuries.
[4] W. K. Jordan, *Development of religious toleration*, III, 515–23, summarizes Richardson's ideas.
[5] *Ibid.*, III, 516. In 1649, in his *An answer to the London ministers letter*, Richardson defended the commonwealth against Presbyterian criticisms.
[6] *An apology for the present government*, 1654, 4–5.
[7] *Plain dealing*, 1656, 14.
[8] *Ibid.*, 20.
[9] *An apology for the present government*, 10–11.

policy of religious toleration. 'There is no ground,' he pointed out, 'to beleeve That the people of this Nation would ever have given us this freedome, or that any Parliament chosen by them would ever give us this freedome. . . .'[1]

Writings such as Richardson's, with their saddening awareness of the government's lack of popularity, were the last faint flickerings of the revolutionary fire in the camp of Cromwell's supporters. Their attempt to justify the protectorate in terms of the great ideas which had inspired the struggle against the king was really an impossible task. Devoid of theoretical substance, dispirited and mediocre, they were proof that the idealism which had earlier sustained the Cromwellian cause no longer possessed much vitality. More interesting, therefore, were the works which continued the argument used in 1649 by Anthony Ascham and urged obedience to the government as the power *de facto*. These were significant as showing how well established the doctrine of sovereignty had by now become. Pervading them all was the conviction that law is only what the sovereign power commands, and that against this command no right can stand.

The most moderate of these writings was *The Grounds Of Obedience And Government* (1655) by Thomas White, a Catholic priest of ancient English family. A good friend of Hobbes, and a philosopher of some contemporary importance,[2] White was one of those scholars, common in the seventeenth century, whose thought, encompassing wide areas of learning, was replete with unorthodoxies. Because of this, his books could please neither his co-religionists, nor Protestants, and were denounced by the latter and censured by the Inquisition.[3]

This is understandable when it is pointed out that his political ideas somewhat resembled those of Hobbes. Imbued with a pessimistic view of human nature, he emphasized man's desire to have his own way, and believed fear and pleasure to be the forces which impelled human beings to create government.[4] The origin of sovereignty he traced to the surrender by men of their wills to one or more persons who were thenceforth to decide all controversies.[5] Like Hobbes, he had only disdain for divines speaking from Scriptural authority alone, and thought lawyers quite incompetent to adjudicate in questions pertaining to the science of politics.[6] He affirmed unambiguously that the magistrate is not under

---

[1] *Plain dealing*, 5.

[2] White is discussed by C. de Remusat, *Histoire de la philosophie en Angleterre depuis Bacon jusqu'à Locke*, 2 vols., Paris, 1875, I, 308–13, and is briefly mentioned by W. R. Sorley, *A history of English philosophy*, Cambridge, 1920, 101. A study of him would be well worth doing.

[3] Biographical details from the *D.N.B., s.v.*

[4] *The grounds of obedience*, 2nd. corrected ed., 1655, 2, 40–4.

[5] *Ibid.*, 45, 47.

[6] *Ibid.*, 158–79.

law,[1] but admitted, nevertheless, that it might be a rational act to overthrow an existing government if the evils resulting from its rule are greater than those likely to arise from a civil war. He was careful to point out, however, that no right of resistance can be traced to any contract. Rebellion, he said in effect, derives not from any right, but is a fact, and originates in the force of nature, that same force which led men to create government in the first place.[2]

White did not descend to particulars in discussing the question of obedience, but it was perfectly evident that the drift of his position favoured the Cromwellian government. Whether a magistrate has been dispossessed for good reasons or not, he said, subjects ought not to hazard everything to restore him, for this would endanger the common good. Indeed, a dispossessed magistrate, however badly treated, should renounce all his claims, and is worse than an infidel if he does not.[3] To act on the principle, *fiat justitia et ruat coelum*, is certainly incorrect, because wise men all agree that the rigour of justice must ever be moderated by charity and prudence.[4] Moreover, a promise to obey a magistrate is binding only while he is an instrument of the common good. Deposed from his magistracy, a man ceases to be such an instrument, and promises made to him, therefore, lose their force.[5] Thus, White concludes, 'a Magistrate actually dispossessed hath no right to be restored, nor the Subject any obligation to seek to restore, but oppose him'. 'Wee know it is naturall', he said, 'that the part should venture for the whole; but that the whole should venture the losse of it selfe to save the part, I cannot understand.'[6]

In advocating submission to the protectorate, White asssumed the role of a disinterested philosopher. Not so John Hall, who in *The True Cavalier Examined by his Principles* (1656), urged that by the very tenets of royalism, the supporters of Charles II were obliged to give obedience to Cromwell. Nothing seems to be known of Hall,[7] and his name does not occur in modern accounts of seventeenth-century political thought. He was, however, an able writer, holding a position somewhat resembling Filmer's, which he expounded in one of the largest books on political theory published during the interregnum. In that book, *Of Govern-*

---

[1] *Ibid.*, 146–7.
[2] *Ibid.*, 114, 121–2.
[3] *Ibid.*, 133–6.
[4] *Ibid.*, 138–9.
[5] *Ibid.*, 140.
[6] *Ibid.*, 142, 143.
[7] His name is given on the title-page of his *Of government and obedience* as John Hall of Richmond. He is not to be confused with John Hall, the poet and Cromwellian pamphleteer (for whom see the *D.N.B.*, *s.v.*), who was admired by Hobbes and died in 1656 at the age of twenty-eight, leaving a great reputation as a prodigy.

ment And Obedience (1654), though he showed many traces of Hobbes's influence, he levelled a very able criticism at the contract theory,[1] and defended monarchy not only as the best, but as the only form of government, other forms being characterized merely as anarchy. That a thinker with such views should come expressly to the protectorate's defence at a time when democratic expressions on its behalf were so ineffectual was symptomatic of the direction events had taken.

Hall dedicated his *True Cavalier* to Cromwell, whom he unblushingly speaks of as king. No party as much as the royalists, he said, 'by their Principles stand more inclined . . . to the present Government, that is, to Monarchy. . . For they fought for their then Monarch, even for Monarchy sake; not for him as he was Charls Stuart . . .'.[2] '. . . as I had from Scripture and Reason,' he added, 'found Monarchy to be the best and only right form of government, so . . . it was not for any one Monarchs sake I did it; but out of a desire to maintain perpetual peace and unity amongst us, I asserted . . . obedience to be continually due to that Person which God . . . should set over us.'[3]

It was with these arguments that Hall went on first to urge his fellow royalists that they were obligated to acquiesce in the protectorate's religious policy, despite its opposition to episcopacy. Quoting from Hooker at length, he pointed out that in Anglican and royalist doctrine, non-conformity in the church has always been considered rebellion in the state.[4] He does not understand, he says, how the lawfulness of the act enforcing the use of the Anglican Prayer Book could be maintained in former days 'if we stick not to our main principle in acknowledging the present supream Christian Magistrate to be head of the Church'.[5] For royalists to depart from this principle, he warns, would justify the earlier recusants and non-conformists. It is true that previously, ecclesiastical supremacy was admitted to be in a chief magistrate styled king or queen. Yet an impartial consideration of the Act of Supremacy will show that the government of the church is united forever 'to the Imperial Crown of this Realm, that is, to the Monarch thereof, although no king . . .'.[6] There is no justification, he says, for denouncing religious opponents as schismatics. Those only are schismatics in religion who do not conform to the rule laid down by the sovereign power, just as 'in State differences, all parties that hold not with the Sovereign Power, are to be called . . . Faction'.[7]

[1] *Of government and obedience*, Ch. 10.
[2] *The true cavalier examined by his principles*, Dedication.
[3] *Ibid.*, Preface [1].
[4] *Ibid.*, 18, and Ch. II, *passim*.
[5] *Ibid.*, 57.
[6] *Ibid.*, 59.
[7] *Ibid.*, 59.

Hall then proceeded to defend the government's position by contending that Cromwell was no usurper. The possession of power by a new ruler is not a usurpation, he declares, otherwise no Christian prince could lawfully begin a royal line, which must necessarily originate in the deposition of the old family. The names, usurper and tyrant, he remarks in words reminiscent of Hobbes, are 'but the remonstrance of discontent . . . as the dispossessed Prince is called Tyrant by one party, so the new one is by the other called Usurper . . .'.[1] Obedience is to be given to rulers irrespective of their titles, else peace would be impossible.[2] While anyone is attempting to seize power, he should certainly be opposed; once successful in his design, however, obedience should be tendered him.[3] Though possession may be unlawful with respect to the deposed ruler, it cannot be so with respect to subjects, who are to regard it 'as an evidence of Right in it selfe . . .'.[4] Refusal of subjection shows a contempt for God's ordinance by which men are raised to power. 'So then,' Hall concluded, '. . . the way to be a constant Royalist, is to be a constant Loyalist; not to respect the power or the place for the persons sake, but the person for the place and power sake. . . .'[5]

This was iron reasoning, indeed. But it is doubtful whether royalists would have been much influenced by it. Perhaps if Cromwell had accepted the kingship which his supporters proffered to him early in 1657, he might have been in a better position to benefit from such opinions as Hall's than while he remained uncrowned and unsceptred. There were, according to Clarendon, some whose allegiance to Charles II 'was more directed to the monarchy then to the person', and who might have acquiesced in Cromwell's rule if he were king.[6] Yet the creed of royalism contained sentiments and ideas against which no utilitarian argument could have prevailed. In the royalists, loyalty to the church and the dynastic monarchy was deeply rooted, and Charles II, as the son of the king who was the hero of the Cavalier poets and the martyr of the *Eikon Basilike*, had a claim on their feelings that a position as cool as Hall's was not likely to dissolve.

A last writer whose views may be noticed was Michael Hawke. Nothing appears to be known of him,[7] and his importance as a theorist is slight. But his works drew on Machiavelli in a manner which, uttered

[1] *Ibid.*, 90; cf. Hobbes, *De cive*, VII, 3.

[2] *Ibid.*, 101.

[3] *Ibid.*, 102–3, 115–16.

[4] *Ibid.*, 116.

[5] *Ibid.*, 108–9.

[6] *The history of the rebellion and civil wars in England*, 6 vols., ed. W. D. Macray, Oxford, 1888, VI, 22.

[7] Hawke describes himself on the title-page of his *The right of dominion* as a Master of Arts and a member of the Middle Temple. I am unable, however, to find his name in the alumni registers of Oxford or Cambridge or in the Middle Temple records.

in defence of the government of Oliver Cromwell, ought not to be passed over without comment.

Hawke's *The Right of Dominion* (1655), in which Cromwell was fawningly addressed as *Pater Patriae* and *Semper Augustus*,[1] and his *Killing Is Murder* (1657), were both devoted to a justification of the protectorate. The latter was written in reply to *Killing No Murder*, the famous republican indictment of Cromwell's rule.[2] In it, Hawke denied that Cromwell was a tyrant, for the Lord Protector, he said, has supreme power by the gift of God, the right of arms, and the consent of the people.[3] He laid most stress, however, on the right of arms, and cited approvingly Ascham's remark that 'possession is the great condition of our obedience and allegiance'.[4] Government originated in force, not consent, he asserted, and from this he concluded that 'Election . . . hath no priviledge in a Commonwealth which was first constituted by force . . .'.[5]

Throughout, Hawke treated Cromwell as king in all but name. He addressed him as prince,[6] and praised monarchy as the best form of government, evidently believing this to be an appropriate line to use on the protectorate's behalf.[7] But it was in his response to the charge of Machiavellianism against Cromwell that his views were most striking. If Machiavelli be read with a 'Chymical Judgement' and refined by religious policy, he said, much that is useful can be learned from him.[8] He went on to urge that a prince should possess cunning and the ability to dissimulate, and may justifiably make use of spies and forged letters to determine the identity of disaffected subjects.[9] Such methods, he declared, do not make a prince a tyrant. Nor is it tyranny to divert the people from domestic discontent by making a foreign war. The avoidance of civil strife by entering a quarrel with an ambitious rival abroad is but good foresight and preventive policy, he urged, which any wise ruler will make use of as circumstances require.[10]

Were these arguments uttered in defence of a Richelieu or a Mazarin, there would be nothing in them to evoke surprise. But expressed on behalf of the protectorate, they were a sure sign something had gone wrong. The Puritan, Oliver Cromwell, had become the beneficiary of doctrines drawn from Machiavelli's *Prince*. He had gone the way of other rulers, and had learned as well as they to mingle the lion and the fox.[11]

---

[1] *The right of dominion*, Preface.
[2] See below, Ch. XII.
[3] *Killing is murder*, 10–15.
[4] *Ibid.*, 4.
[5] *Ibid.*, 8–9.
[6] *Ibid.*, Dedication.
[7] *Ibid.*, 19.
[8] *Ibid.*, 19–20.
[9] *Ibid.*, 21–2.
[10] *Ibid.*, 23.
[11] Cf. Professor Abbott's remarks, *The writings and speeches of Oliver Cromwell*, II, 656. Professor Abbott also notes the interesting fact (*ibid.*, I, 759) that many of Cromwell's portraits are adorned with masks of the lion and the fox.

Carnal, now, was the power of the godly, as the revolutionary government entered the final period of its insecure existence.

Cromwell's primacy had commenced with a great action—the trial and execution of the king—which symbolized the insurgent forces that were to effect the transformation of western Europe and America in the seventeenth and eighteenth centuries. But how sad was the fate of the revolutionary government which, invoking the name of the sovereign people, had done the epic deed. It had become more and more despotic, less and less capable of inspiring the libertarian ideas that gave it birth, more and more the enemy of men still prompted by democratic principles. While democratic theory could produce nothing vital to say on its behalf, it was receiving the support of men whose doctrines Cromwell himself would have rejected with horror.[1] By the time of the protectorate's establishment, the contradictions in which the government was ensnared were sharper than ever, and the revolutionary sky had turned black as night. The power which had begun its eminency with a bang, was nearing its end with a whimper.

[1] This may not be strictly true, however. The republican, Edmund Ludlow, quotes Cromwell as saying to him that even 'if Nero were in power, it would be my duty to submit' (*The memoirs of Edmund Ludlow*, 2 vols., ed. C. H. Firth, Oxford, 1894, I, 434.)

VIII

THE FIFTH-MONARCHY MEN

IN the marvellous victories of Cromwell's army of saints, and in the
miraculous crumbling of a once-mighty monarchy, many radical sec-
tarians joyfully discerned the signs of Christ's imminent return to
rule the earth as king. Taught by their fervid brooding over the books of
Daniel and Revelation to expect Jesus' thousand-year reign, the cata-
clysmic events through which they were living made their hopes white-
hot. The time of the end was near, they rejoiced, and the fulfilment of
the prophecies was about to occur. Crumbled were Babylon's walls!
The lake of fire lay seething to receive the old serpent, and near at hand
towered the beautiful city with its gates of pearl and its walls of jasper.
Was not Charles I the little horn of the beast spoken of in Daniel? Did
not his execution proclaim the fifth monarchy's near commencement,
when Christ would rule in glory with his saints? The year 1648, wrote a
millenarian preacher,

'do I affirm with much assurance was the time when the Thrones were
set, and the ancient of days did sit. . . . Here began the Lord God Almighty to call Kings and Kingdomes to account, to cast down the
mighty from their seats . . . and this work goes forward still, and shall
prevail and prosper, to the utter breaking and destroying of the fourth
monarchy. . . .'[1]

Thus millenarian Utopianism, often an element in sectarian religion,
developed after 1649 into the movement of Fifth-monarchy men. This
movement stood for more than just the hope, held by all Christians, of
Christ's return, for more, too, than the anticipation of his glorious
earthly rule, announced during the 1640s by learned exegetical writings
on the prophetic books of Scripture.[2] It signified, rather, a passionate
determination to pull down all carnal powers in order to prepare the way

---

[1] John Canne, *A voice from the temple*, 1653, 13.
[2] Cf., e.g., John Archer, *The personall reign of Christ upon earth*, 1641, Johann
Alsted, *The beloved city*, 1642, which was a translation of this author's *De mille annis*,
1627, and Robert Maton, *Israels redemption*, 1642.

for the New Jerusalem. As such, it was a fresh outburst of the chiliasm, recurrent in Christian history, which expressed awareness of earthly injustice in apocalyptic visions of Christ's reign of righteousness. Fruitful of heresy, these visions had inspired bitter denunciations of the secularized Church during the Middle Ages.[1] In the sixteenth century, they agitated the Anabaptists of Munster to dream of establishing a communist order.[2] Always when men attempted to act under their impulse, existing institutions were momentarily endangered.

In the Fifth-monarchy men, we see the last wave of burning social protest which the revolution set in motion. The evils they would sweep away—tithes, the oppressions of the rich, corrupt lawyers—were those denounced by the left wing as a whole. But unlike the thinking of the latter, that of the Fifth-monarchy men remained, at bottom, unsecularized. They carried the Puritan emphasis on the believer's inward grace to its furthest point, and required that none but the saints should rule. For them, the endowments of nature were as nothing in comparison with the possession of the spirit of holiness. The latter alone, they held, could qualify men for government in the shadow of the approaching millenium and issue in the social justice for which the world thirsted. Hence, they abstained, essentially, from any secular solutions to the problems of their age. The Levellers had looked to the political remedy of free Parliaments and general manhood suffrage. Winstanley, who had also awaited Christ's return in power, came finally to interpret that event in terms akin to the rationalistic communism of the eighteenth century. The Fifth-monarchy movement, in contrast, desired a theocracy of saints, not a general suffrage, Christ's literal coming in a pomp of glory, not communism. These might have the consequence of rectifying some of the grievances which the Levellers condemned. But the fundamental hope, with all the significance it may have possessed for earthly life, was an other-worldly one.

Owing to this fact, it was impossible for the millenarians to have developed anything distinctive or rich in the way of political theory. This was precluded by the nature of the expectations which they entertained. No basis for systematic political analysis could exist when the real solution to human problems was thought to lie in the momentarily awaited inauguration of Christ's kingdom. Hence, their writings, though very numerous, were generally confused, repetitive, and unoriginal. For most of their political ideas they were indebted to left-wing democracy, drawing freely on its programme and assimilating the borrowings to the tenets of their apocalyptic faith.

[1] Cf. Ernesto Buonaiuti, *Gioacchino da fiore*, Rome, 1931, Part III, and Karl Löwith, *Meaning in history*, Chicago, 1949, Ch. VIII.
[2] Cf. Walter Nigg, *Das ewige Reich*, Zürich, 1944, 231–67, and references there cited.

As the millenarians' hope necessarily nourished itself on extraordinary portents and providences, it could not be of long duration. Its first collective expression seems to have occurred shortly after the king's execution in a petition of Fifth-monarchy men from Norfolk, in which the signers declared that 'we expect new Heavens and a new Earth', and warned against patching up the old government or having any other law but the Bible.[1] Until Cromwell's dissolution of the Nominated Parliament at the end of 1653, and his establishment of the protectorate, the Fifth-monarchy men built their hopes on him. They regarded him as the first of the saints and compared him to Moses, holding his office as the gift of God.[2] His work, they told him, was to execute God's final wrath and vengeance upon 'the two persecuting powers of the world . . . Kingly and Antichristian . . .'.[3]

But their dreams inevitably came into conflict with Cromwell's conservatism. Cromwell might for a time tolerate the millenarians; he could never be an agent in fulfilling the measure of their expectations. In dissolving the Nominated Parliament, he dealt them a sore blow. That body, partially recruited from among the sects and congregations, and some of its members animated by millenarian enthusiasm, meditated great reforms such as the Fifth-monarchy men believed fitting to the time when Christ's return was breathlessly awaited.[4] When Cromwell sent home the Nominated Parliament and went on to become Protector, he incurred the millenarians' bitter enmity. The blessed cause of Christ had been betrayed for the glory of one man, they said,[5] and charged that the government was but a concealed monarchy in which Cromwell made his will and pleasure the only law.[6] 'O our bowels, our bowels,' they lamented,

'our hearts even ake, and are pained within us, to hear the doleful and daily groans of Gods people, crying out, O where are our Deliverers and Saviours! The Reeds that we leaned upon, have pierced our hands, and we bleed! And after our eyes fail with looking for Freedom, Peace, and Light, behold Darkness, Oppression and Distraction!'[7]

[1] *Certain quaeres presented by way of petition*, 1649, 8; cf. L. F. Brown, *The political activities of the Baptists and Fifth-monarchy men*, Washington, 1912, 17–18.

[2] John Spittlehouse, *A warning-piece discharged*, 1653, 10–11.

[3] John Canne, *A voice from the temple*, Epistle dedicatory [3–4].

[4] The millenarian hopes in the Nominated Parliament may be seen, e.g., in *The banner of truth displayed*, 1656, 2, which was published by 'a Certain Number of Christians, who are waiting for the Visible appearance of Christs Kingdome'.

[5] *A declaration of several of the churches of Christ . . . concerning the kingly interest of Christ*, 1654, 13. This was signed by one hundred and fifty members of congregations ministered to by millenarian preachers.

[6] *The protector (so called) in part unvailed*, 1655, 7, 42. This work is anonymous.

[7] *A declaration of several of the churches of Christ . . . concerning the kingly interest of Christ*, 3.

Thenceforth the government was menaced by the threat of a Fifth-monarchist insurrection. The work of the present generation, the millenarians proclaimed, 'is a smiting work . . . wherein the Saints imployed shall visibly appear in a millitary posture for Christ . . .'. 'To your tents, O Israel,' was their exhortation, 'with us arise, for the lot of our inheritance, prepare therefore your victuals, your purse . . . but especially your sword. . . .'[1] But there was no great difficulty in keeping the danger at bay. The chief Fifth-monarchy preachers were imprisoned and their followers held under close surveillance. Thus suppressed, millenarianism lingered on to hope again for something from the government after Cromwell's death,[2] and to make a last appearance in 1661 in a pitiful rising which was, with a little difficulty, bloodily crushed.[3]

The Fifth-monarchy men held that in Christ's kingdom, Scripture would be the only law,[4] and that the godly magistrate could therefore do nothing more holy or more beneficial to the people than to acknowledge Christ's legislative power by making Scripture the law of the land. Would it not be better, a millenarian writer asked,

'for Parliaments to accept of the Legislative Power of Jesus Christ, and of the Law, Statutes, and Judgements ready offered them from God . . . and practicable within one Moneth, and easy to be established: then still to be overturn'd, overturn'd, overturn'd, and trouble and hazard themselves and the Nation, to find out another Legislative Power and other Laws, which last no longer then the Men that make them: nor that but during the Power of the Sword?'[5]

Such a demand carried Puritan bibliolatry to a fanatical extreme, and explains Cromwell's accusation that the millenarians were attempting to foist the Judaic law upon their country.[6] The position certainly had dangerous implications. Thus, William Aspinwall, in calling for the acceptance of the Old Testament legal code, seems humane enough when he denounced the English law's imposition of the death penalty for theft, and pointed out that for theft, the Bible demands only double restitution. But he went on to justify from the Bible the proposal that the death sentence be meted out for denying the being or attributes of God or profaning the Sabbath.[7] This would have involved a far more

---

[1] *The banner of truth displayed*, 28, 14–15.

[2] Cf., e.g., John Canne, *A seasonable word to the Parliament-men*, 1659.

[3] The millenarian plots are recounted by C. H. Firth, *The last years of the protectorate*, I, 207–19.

[4] Cf., e.g., William Aspinwall, *A brief description of the fifth-monarchy*, 1653, 9.

[5] Peter Chamberlen, *Legislative power in problemes*, 1659, 2. Chamberlen was an interesting figure who drew up a remarkable scheme of poor relief and economic reform, *The poore mans advocate*, 1649.

[6] *The writings and speeches of Oliver Cromwell*, III, 438.

[7] William Aspinwall, *The legislative power is Christs peculiar prerogative*, 1656, 30–33.

intolerable infringement upon the consciences of men than was ever committed by Cromwell, whom the millenarians yet denounced during the protectorate as oppressing the people with a national ministry.[1]

Nevertheless, it is important to realize that the invocation of Biblical law was primarily intended by the Fifth-monarchy men as a standard by which to condemn the oppressions of their time. They might be fanatical in desiring to make Scripture the legal code, but their motive was the hope of securing a greater social justice. While '... the Laws of God sayes, Open thy mouth wide for the dumb ... and plead the cause of the poor and needy,' two millenarians wrote, 'the beastly Laws of the World, opens the mouth wide, for those that have a large purse to plead their Cause, whilst the poor are sent empty away'.[2] Another writer emphasized the rationality and love to be found in God's law. No law, he said, is more ancient or more in accord with reason.

'Since then the Law of God is the Law of Nature, the Law of Nations, the Law of Reason, the Law of Precedent, the Law of Antiquity ... Why will some go on to ... Contrive Lawes and Judgements contrary to the Law of God ... ? is not the summ of Gods Lawes, Love & the Execution Do as you would be done by? doth it not end all sutes in a day, & payes all Debts without arrests or Imprisonments ... ?'[3]

But accept God's law, and oppression will cease, he promised, taxes be no more, trade abound, prisons be opened, and 'Peace and safety, plenty and prosperity ... overflow the Land'.[4]

To their proposal to put Biblical law into effect, the millenarians joined the demand that government be exercised by the saints. Not only would the saints rule as Christ's assistants when the thousand-year reign began, but even before this, a godly magistracy was held to be one in which power is wielded by none but those who are sanctified. 'What right or claim', asked the millenarians, '[can] meer natural and worldly men have to Rule and Government?'[5] The saints, they said, are people 'of another Kingdome and world; and are by themselves a Commonwealth and Free-State: And therefore 'tis to be desired ... that they would exercise that Royal Authority which God has given unto them, and invested them with. . . '.[6] In such a government, one writer admitted, there might be a danger of arbitrariness. But this, he was assured, would be avoided by the fact that Scriptural law would make no excep-

---

[1] *The banner of truth displayed*, 8–11.
[2] William Pryor and Thomas Turner, *The out-cries of the poor, oppressed, & imprisoned*, 1659, 10–11.
[3] Peter Chamberlen, *Legislative power in problemes*, 5.
[4] *Ibid.*, 8.
[5] *Certain quaeres by way of petition*, 8.
[6] *The banner of truth displayed*, Epistle dedicatory [6].

tions in its exercise, and by the holiness of the men in whom administration was to be vested.[1]

To opponents, such a position seemed intolerably presumptuous. For men upon the pretence of the fifth monarchy, Cromwell said, '. . . to entitle themselves . . . the only men to rule kingdoms . . . and give laws to the people . . . they had need give clear manifestations of God's presence with them, before wise men will submit to their conclusions.'[2] It is an absurd argument, wrote a government pamphleteer, 'That godly persons, though of small understanding, and little ability of mind in publick affairs, are more fit for Government then men of great knowledg and wisdom, if endued only with natural Parts, and moral vertues . . .'.[3] And a Leveller, who sympathized with the millenarians' detestation of the protectorate, reminded them, nevertheless, that

'the Saints preparation for Christs Kingdome, which God requires, is clothing themselves with righteousness . . . and that no righteous civile powers of governing in this nation can yet be derived from any other fountaine then the peoples consent . . . you cannot be righteous or holy in setting up . . . or adhering to any other civile governing powers'.[4]

Yet if the millenarians wished the saints to govern, it was with no selfish motive, but because only thus did they imagine abundant justice would be given to human kind. Carnal men could be tyrants, but godly men never. And the latter alone, it seemed to them, could do the real work of rulers, which was to care for the oppressed,

'to redeeme again the Vineyard of the poor, which the Ahabs of the earth have taken away; to take away an house from them that have many, and a field from them who have plenty of more, to appoint them for a Portion to supply them that have none, until . . . he that hath most, hath nothing too much, and he that hath least, have nothing lacking, that so . . . the Land may grow up towards her true Sabbath, where she shall no more bring forth her children to Oppression and Bondage . . .'.[5]

A position such as the millenarians held necessarily issued in fanaticism. Its Biblical literalism and its insistence on the rule of those who were considered sanctified made it impossible that it should be otherwise. All the same, we should completely misunderstand the Fifth-monarchy movement if we failed to realize how much it shared the longings of left-wing democracy. This is apparent from some of the writings

[1] William Aspinwall, *An explication . . . of the seventh chapter of Daniel*, 1654, 19.
[2] *The writings and speeches of Oliver Cromwell*, III, 437.
[3] *A true state of the case of the commonwealth*, 25.
[4] *Englands remembrancers*, 1656, 3.
[5] *Sighs for righteousness*, 1654, 14. This work is anonymous.

thus far noticed. The best proof, however, may be found in the most important statement of political principles which the millenarians put forward, *A Standard Set Up* (1657). This statement, a collective declaration signed by one, William Medley, as scribe, shows, if resemblances mean anything, considerable borrowing from the Levellers, and is a certain sign of affiliation with the protest movement of the time.

The declaration begins by tracing the course of events up through the apostacy of Cromwell, who 'Hath left the Cause and Work the Lord so eminently owned him in' by 'establishing and upholding the corrupt interests of the Clergy and Lawyers in these Nations . . . oppressing the people by Taxing them to maintain a constant standing Army to uphold his . . . Lordship over them . . .'.[1] Then follow the principles of government. The supreme and absolute legislative power and authority to make laws for man is acknowledged to be in Christ

'by Right, Conquest, Gift, Election, and Inheritance, who is the onely absolute single person, whom the father hath loved, decreed, sworn to, anointed, and given all power unto in heaven and in earth'.

The Scriptures, which are the revealed will of Christ, are to be accepted as the rule both for the inward and the outward man. By taking the Scriptures as law, a constant administration of justice will be established from which will flow streams of righteousness to ease the poor, needy, and oppressed people.[2]

Exercising the chief magistracy, as princes under Christ, will be a 'Sanhedrim' or 'Supream Councell' of men of spirit and light, of integrity, justice, knowledge, and understanding. These shall be chosen 'according to the principles of Right and Freedome' as the 'Representative . . . of the whole Body of the Saints (whose Day this is,) and people in these Nations'. They will care for the people's safety and welfare, giving judgement in all civil matters without respect of persons, and tolerate all forms of worship.[3]

In each county, courts will be erected to hear cases. The members of these courts are to be elected, and every man will be permitted to plead his own cause.[4] Furthermore, '(it having been found by experience inconsistent with the good and welbeing of the governed)', the supreme council is not to be perpetuated, but elected annually by the 'Lords-Free men (i.e. those that have a right with Christ in and according to the New Covenant)'.[5] It shall have no power 'to violate, take away, give up, or enervate any of the Foundations of Common-Right, and Freedom, which are, or shall be agreed upon; save in case of a further convincing

---

[1] *A standard set up*, 7. [2] *Ibid.*, 15. [3] *Ibid.*, 16.
[4] *Ibid.*, 17–18. [5] *Ibid.*, 18.

light . . .'. And such alterations must be 'according to Law, and the good of the people'.[1]

No person, of whatever rank or quality, is to be exempt from the law. No one is to be imprisoned without a legal cause. Impressment of men for military service will be illegal, excise and customs abolished, and no assessments levied on the people in peace time, nor in war, except with their consent. Tithes are to be taken away, and ministers are to support themselves by their own labours or from voluntary contributions. '. . . all Oppressions and grievances in the tenures of lands, Copyhold, and Customary, Heriots, Fines, Amerciaments, Perquisites, and profits of Courts, customs, services,' are to be abolished.[2]

In this state, the declaration concludes,

'Man shall be blessed . . . he shall be restored by God unto right reason and wisdoms: and that beastlike and brutish nature and principles (from whence has proceeded all Murders, Thefts, Rebellion, Violence, Oppression, Ravenning and Devouring his fellow creatures . . .) shall be in a great measure done away.'[3]

Confused though these ideas are, they clearly involve a carrying over into the fifth monarchy of the principles enunciated in the Leveller *Agreements* of the people. They show the same humaneness, and the same indignation against social wrong. But the Leveller belief in the sovereignty of the people was in contradiction to the millenarian ideal of the government of the saints. The former gave rights to all, excluding the royalists from the franchise for a time, but ultimately admitting them. The latter gave rights only to the sanctified. Up to a point, this category had a political basis, in so far as by their support of tyranny, the royalists, Presbyterians, and Cromwellians had all shown themselves ineligible to belong to the elect. This left the rest of the nation, but even of this remainder, presumably only a minority possessed the grace to be enrolled with the saints. In the end, therefore, political qualifications gave way to religious ones, and the spiritual few were left dominant over the carnal many.

Of the numerous Fifth-monarchy writers, there is only one, John Rogers, who merits individual notice. Rogers, who was born in 1627, was driven from home at the age of fifteen because of his Puritan principles, and by the time he was in his early twenties, was a well-known minister in London.[4] He was one of the most learned and most moderate of the millenarian preachers, and his work, *Sagrir. Or Doomesday*

---

[1] *Ibid.*, 19.
[2] *Ibid.*, 19–20.
[3] *Ibid.*, 21.
[4] See the notice of his life in the *D.N.B.*, *s.v.* Rogers gives an interesting account of his early history in his *Ohel* or *Beth-shemesh*, 1653, 419–39.

drawing nigh (1653), gave the millenarian position as capable an expression as it ever received, particularly with regard to the problem of law.

Laws, he declared, are necessary, but they must be in accord with reason, the intellectual lamp in every soul. When they are not, men may disobey them. Furthermore, laws should not be maintained longer than there is need for them. 'As Reason is restored to more perfection and clearness,' he said, 'all the Laws and results of such Reason must be amended and corrected. . . .'[1] Yet human reason is imperfect, and requires to be supplemented by the law of God, which is divine reason. By deriving all law as far as possible from the eternal law of God expressed in Scripture, he believed that the inadequacies of human reason could be provided against.[2]

The source of law, he points out, is in the people, and tyranny consists in the imposition upon the people of a power not derived from their will. But commensurate with his theocratic doctrines, he adds that by the people he means 'the rationall honest people', 'rightly principled', and 'in their capacity'.[3] The purpose of law is to curb great men and the rich.[4] Since the Norman conquest, however, this purpose has not been fulfilled, and the law has been made an iron yoke upon free-born Englishmen.[5] But now the time of freedom has arrived, and he calls upon Cromwell, not yet the renegade he was soon to become in the millenarians' eyes, to effect broad reforms. These, as Rogers lists them, are much like those demanded by the Levellers, one of them being the abolition of manorial lords.[6] He pleads that England should export its revolution and that 'our . . . Armies, and Navies, and Churches . . . would . . . in the name of Jesus proclaim liberty to the captives and oppressed ones of other Nations . . .'.[7] The fifth monarchy, he exhorts, is hastening on apace to free men from civil and ecclesiastical bondage, and justice and righteousness shall come down to earth as God alone becomes the law-giver.[8]

After Cromwell's death, Rogers, who had been imprisoned for a time during the protectorate, entered into controversy with the republican, James Harrington. From his remarks on this occasion, it is clear that, unlike most other millenarians, he would have given rights to anyone

---

[1] *Sagrir*, 32–6.

[2] *Ibid.*, 36–7; cf. *ibid.*, 105–7, where he quotes Cicero and Aquinas to the effect that the eternal law is reason, and *ibid.*, 138–40, where he declares that Moses' law will be the rule in the fifth monarchy.

[3] *Ibid.*, 46–7.

[4] *Ibid.*, 46.

[5] *Ibid.*, 47–51.

[6] *Ibid.*, 52–9.

[7] *Ibid.*, 14–17.

[8] *Ibid.*, 125, 128–31, 139. Rogers suggested that Christ would come in 1666; see his *Dod, or Chathan*, 1653, 24.

who opposed religious and political tyranny as well as to the saints. He thought Harrington had gone too far, however, in advocating the extension of political rights to all, for the result, he feared, would be a royal restoration.[1] There are two extremes to be avoided, he said, that which makes natural right everything, and that which makes it nothing; as Harrington goes to the first extreme, so some Fifth-monarchy men go to the second.[2] Only those possess natural rights who have not abetted tyrants in enslaving the commonwealth, Rogers declared,[3] and such are the saints and well-affected who will rule in the future 'Christian' and 'Theocratic Government'.[4]

These ideas are certainly unclear enough, wavering unsteadily between the prospect of a supernatural fifth monarchy and a democratic republic in which all men not royalists, Presbyterians, or Cromwellians, would participate. There is something touching in this application of the language of democracy to an earthly theocratic commonwealth established through heaven's agency, something unspeakably pathetic and poignant in the naive and confused hopes of Rogers and his fellows. But however passionate, their aspirations could not endure much longer, for the restoration was at hand. Charles II's accession set a period to millenarianism, and the brief insurrection of 1661 was the last explosion of the Fifth-monarchy men's zeal. Thus, in the few years between Charles I's execution and his son's return, the Fifth-monarchy movement ran its course. In view of the peculiar character of its ideas, it is significant that it appeared as a force only after 1649. Before this time, the struggle for reform and social justice still centred on political and secular solutions. Only when Cromwell had suppressed the Levellers and frustrated their aims did enthusiasm for the thousand-year reign of Christ and his saints begin to spread. It is probable that this would have remained a negligible phenomenon if the Levellers' objectives had been achieved. As it was, however, some religious radicals who, in 1649, were not yet disillusioned with Cromwell, and who were sensible of the heavy burden of terrestrial wrong, threw their dreams of righteousness into chiliastic visions. That their influence grew was chiefly due, I think, to the absence now of a powerful movement oriented to the same goals but without an other-worldly, theocratic outlook. Hence in the 1650s, those cries of social protest which were not still inspired by the impulse emitted from the Leveller movement were for the most part dominated by millenarian ideas. Fifth-monarchism, therefore, was the moan of the distressed creature lamenting the cruelty and heartlessness of the world. In an age still religious, it was an inevitable product of the failure of the left-democratic revolution to consummate itself.

---

[1] Διαπολιτεία. *A Christian concertation*, 1659, 73–4.
[2] *Ibid.*, 59–60.   [3] *Ibid.*, 60, 76.   [4] *Ibid.*, 119–24.

IX

JOHN MILTON

THE vast amount of writing that has appeared, and continues to appear, about Milton, serves, I think, to obscure the fact that as a political theorist and systematic thinker, he was not of the first order. It is no service to an understanding of the poet, nor to his reputation, to attempt, as so many of his admirers do,[1] to discover in his prose a higher quality of political theory than disinterested consideration warrants. There is little Milton said in his political writing that was not spoken by contemporaries, and, in many instances, more theoretically, with a deeper examination of the issues, and an awareness which he, on the whole, lacked, of what could be said on the other side. Moreover, on many important questions with which political thought in his time was deeply concerned—sovereignty, for example, or social reform—he was, except for his divorce writings, either silent or commonplace in his comments. It is significant that we commonly think of Milton's prose rather in terms of a small number of great passages, than, as in the case of a political theorist of first-rate capacity, as a systematic philosophy.

Milton was a supreme poet. And the truth would seem to be that his prose is of far greater importance as illuminating the poet's mind than it is as an exemplification of deep or original political theory. Even the *Areopagitica* (1644), which has justly become a classic, has achieved this status, I suggest, more for those qualities which we should call poetic and which reside in the occasional blaze and wonder of the language and imagery, than for its depth and thoroughness on the problem of toleration and civil liberties. This conclusion seems unavoidable when it is recalled that, though *Areopagitica* was written at a critical moment in the controversy over liberty of conscience, its preoccupation—freedom of the press—was a segmental one occasioned by Milton's personal encounter with the censorship in his divorce pamphlets. Certainly, as

[1] E.g. Arthur Barker, *Milton and the Puritan dilemma 1641–1660*, Toronto, 1942, an admirable work, but which endeavours to the point of tedium to extract more from Milton's philosophy than comprehension of it or justice to it require.

theory, it is clearly inferior to the writings of John Goodwin and William Walwyn, and to Roger Williams's *Bloody Tenent*.[1]

Nevertheless, no account of political thought in the English revolution may overlook Milton. He was the greatest man who wrote on the Parliamentary and Cromwellian side. His defence of the commonwealth was, with John Goodwin's, the most effective it received. Moreover, the judgement of a great artist on the supreme issues of his time must always be full of interest and significance. But all the same, unless we are prepared to treat Milton's prose chiefly as an aid to the understanding of a mighty poet, a loss of perspective will inevitably ensue.[2]

From the very outset of the controversy between crown and Parliament, Milton enthusiastically enlisted himself on Parliament's side. Was he wrong in throwing himself so whole-heartedly into the revolutionary struggle? It has been said that his participation was the prostitution of genius to a party, and that the ideal interpreter of life ought not to be part of it.[3] It has been said also that though he was right in concerning himself with the religious and political conflict, it was a defect in his character that he took an active part in it.[4] My business here is with Milton's political thought, not his poetry, yet I venture to say that these judgments are erroneous. It is difficult to think of Milton writing a poem of the magnitude to which he aspired without the experience he gained by his embroilment in the struggle of his time. The young poet who had left the university for additional study and meditation at Horton was badly in need of further experience of life. The Puritan's profound rejection of experience as an end in itself could have had the unhappy consequence for Milton of truncating his knowledge of life and its depths without which an epic of the sort he wished to write is inconceivable. Let us imagine the effect on him, and on the prophetic role he felt called to perform,[5] had he abstained from mingling in the greatest movement of his time. Let us imagine what the fate of his vast ambition as a poet would have been had he, a Puritan humanist alienated from the cultural atmosphere of the Stuart court, lived through his maturity after Elizabethan greatness had ended and before the revolution had

[1] On this whole subject, see the remarks of W. K. Jordan, *Development of religious toleration*, IV, 203, 210. According to W. Haller (*Tracts on liberty*, I, Appendix B), the contemporary influence of *Areopagitica* was slight. On *Areopagitica's* contemporary influence, see also G. F. Sensabaugh, 'Adaptations of *Areopagitica*', *The Huntington library quarterly*, XIII, 2, which does not, I think, affect Haller's conclusions.

[2] Cf. Douglas Bush, *English literature in the earlier seventeenth century 1600–1660*, Oxford, 1945, 369.

[3] Mark Pattison, *Milton*, London, 1880, 66–7.

[4] E. M. W. Tillyard, *Milton*, London, 1930, 111.

[5] Milton's great idea of the poet's task is discussed by H. J. C. Grierson, *Milton and Wordsworth: poets and prophets*, Cambridge, 1937.

begun. His participation in the struggle was essential for the expression of his profound belief in the poet's sacred mission. It was the very thing that gave him the experience of life necessary for *Paradise Lost* and *Samson Agonistes*.

Milton made his first appearance as a pamphleteer in the discussion over episcopacy which opened when the Long Parliament met. His argument against the bishops, though powerfully presented, was much the same as that of other writers,[1] while his political views were quite conventional. Monarchy, he said, is composed of two essential parts, the king's supremacy and the subject's liberty. The best governments are mixed, and such a government is England's, harmoniously tuned and balanced, 'where under a free and untutor'd Monarch, the noblest, worthiest, and most prudent men, with full approbation, and suffrage of the People have in their power the supreme and finall determination of the highest Affaires'.[2]

With all their strength and ardour, there was something academic in Milton's writings against the bishops. They suggest a mind to which political life is a subject known from afar, and chiefly through the medium of orators and historians. They show us a young genius, full of idealism and passionately absorbed in his country's fate, but clearly not a 'political man', using the term in no pejorative sense to characterize one who possesses an instinctive grasp of politics. This was not merely a matter of inexperience. Milton lacked the political flair, and he never acquired it. Years after his episcopal tracts, when he was fully practsied in controversy and quite accustomed to exchanging insults with opponents, his mind still dwelt on a plane at once exalted and isolated, peopled by thoughts of antique heroes and the virtuous great, and out of touch, somehow, with the essence of political happening.

At the time of the argument over episcopacy, Milton was a moderate Presbyterian,[3] urging how godly and tender Presbyterian discipline would be to those unstained by lust or licence.[4] Yet in temper and many ideas, he was really far from Presbyterianism, as any member of that communion might have seen, had he read Milton's utterances with a

---

[1] W. K. Jordan, *Development of religious toleration*, IV, 203.

[2] *Of reformation, Works*, ed. F. A. Patterson *et al.*, New York, 1931–8, III, 56–7, 63. It is much more likely that Milton took the idea of England as a mixed state from English sources than, as Mr. Zera Fink asserts (*The classical republicans*, Evanston, 1945, 95), from classical ones. Milton's statement cited in the text appears to depend on Sir Thomas Smith's *De republica Anglorum*, I, 9, which the poet noted in his *Commonplace book* (*Works*, XVIII, 176) along with another chapter of Smith's (*op. cit.*, I, 6) to the effect that commonwealths are usually mixed. In general, Mr. Fink greatly exaggerates the importance of the notion of the mixed state in Milton's political thought.

[3] W. K. Jordan, *Development of religious toleration*, IV, 208.

[4] *Of reformation, Works*, III, 36.

view to something more than their immediate effect in the discussion. Milton reveals a lay-pride and an anti-clericalism that indubitably intimate his early break with his Presbyterian friends. He assails the presumption of a usurping clergy who make the term 'laic' a thing of scorn,[1] and the priests who vilify the people as being too low in capacity to search for divine knowledge.[2] He criticizes the 'ignoble Hucsterage of pidling Tithes',[3] remarking that a true pastor requires a very ordinary supply of worldly goods.[4] Such contentions were as fatal to the claims of the Presbyterian ministers as to those of the Laudian clergy. By insisting that 'reason is the gift of God in one man, as well as in a thousand',[5] he was, in effect, defying the conclusions of any corporate reason, Presbyterian or otherwise, which could not persuade his own. Most important of all, his intense optimism and sweeping hopes were far greater than any true Presbyterian could have felt. His belief that he was living in an age of ages,[6] and his passionate exhortation to Christ to perfect the work of reformation[7]—these signify a man to whom truth was progressively comprehended, and who would acquiesce neither in the dogmatic affirmations of Presbyterianism nor in the limited enlightenment of a sect.

Milton's pamphlets on divorce, which followed his writings against the bishops, were his only contribution to the discussion of social problems so widely carried on between 1640 and 1660. His conviction was that incompatibility of mind and temper is at least as justifiable a cause for divorce as adultery, and despite the fact that his position had been adumbrated to some extent by Protestant and Puritan predecessors,[8] no one before had put it forward so fully and uncompromisingly. As his arguments represent, in part, a transfer to the marriage relationship of some of his political ideas, they give us an incidental glimpse into the latter.

His chief contention was that the right of divorce for incompatibility is an essential part of Christian liberty,[9] and behind his ingenious twisting of Scripture lay the conviction that 'no ordinance human or from heav'n can binde against the good of man . . .'.[10] '. . . the great and almost only commandment of the Gospel,' he said, 'is to command nothing against the good of man, and much more no civil command against his

---

[1] *The reason of church-government*, 1641, *Works*, III, 261.
[2] *Of reformation*, *Works*, III, 19.
[3] *Ibid.*, *Works*, III, 75.
[4] *Animadversions upon the remonstrants defence*, 1641, *Works*, III, 163.
[5] *Ibid.*, *Works*, III, 126.
[6] *Ibid.*, *Works*, III, 144–5.
[7] *Ibid.*, *Works*, III, 146–8.
[8] Chilton Powell, *English domestic relations, 1487–1653*, New York, 1917, 93–4.
[9] Cf. A. Barker, *op. cit.*, 110–11.
[10] *Tetrachordon*, 1645, *Works*, IV, 75.

civil good.'[1] Marriage he treated as a contract analogous to the political contract, and subject, therefore, to the same conditions.

'He who marries, intends as little to conspire his own ruine, as he that swears Allegiance: and as the whole people is in proportion to an ill Government, so is one man to an ill marriage. If they against any authority, Covnant, or Statute, may . . . save not only their lives, but honest liberties from unworthy bondage, as well may he against any private Covnant, which hee never enter'd to his mischief, redeem himself from unsupportable disturbances to honest peace, and just contentment. . . .'[2]

He spoke also of the law of nature in the familiar terms of contemporary discourse as something above positive law,[3] and made plain that law for him signified not a command, but a norm whose essence lies exclusively in the justness of its content.[4] These ideas, when pressed into the service of a plea for divorce, were being used for a new end. In themselves, however, they were no more than many another supporter of Parliament was saying. Milton had, in fact, as yet written no political works, and, in the sphere of political theory, was doing scarcely more than assimilate the conceptions of Independency and give them highly personal expression.

Areopagitica (1644) was composed in the same period as the divorce pamphlets. Dealing primarily with the censorship question, it touched the margin of the general problem of toleration then being hotly debated. The majesty and power of this work make it the most superb utterance for freedom of thought in the English language. It radiated a confidence in the people and a hope for their continued growth in knowledge which Milton within a few short years would be very far from feeling. So far as liberty of conscience is concerned, however, his views were not as broad as those of Walwyn or Williams; he denied toleration, for example, to Roman Catholics.[5] Yet he did give a strong justification for religious differences, and defended the sects at a time when they were under fierce attack, declaring that 'out of many . . . brotherly dissimilitudes . . . arises the goodly and gracefull symmetry' of God's house.[6]

Between the appearance in 1645 of *Colasterion*, the last of his divorce tracts, and 1649, Milton engaged in no pamphlet controversies. In the latter year, he dealt for the first time expressly and entirely with political

---

[1] *Ibid., Works,* IV, 137.

[2] *The doctrine and discipline of divorce, Works,* III, 374.

[3] *Ibid., Works,* III, 419.

[4] *Ibid., Works,* III, 434; *Tetrachordon, Works,* IV, 157. Milton's treatment of positive law in these passages is enough to show that he held no theory of sovereignty. I can find no justification for Mr. Fink's assertion (*op. cit.,* 100) that he believed in an indivisible sovereignty.

[5] *Areopagitica, Works,* IV, 349.

[6] *Ibid., Works,* IV, 342.

questions. But already from the commencement of the 1640s, it is clear, the principal element in his political thought had disclosed itself, and this must now be considered, if we are to follow his mind from 1649 to his final political utterance issued on the eve of the restoration.

Milton was a progressive artist who had elected to support revolutionaries engaged in effecting far-reaching changes in church and state. On law, on the law of nature, and on the conditional character of political power, his ideas were familiar ones, held with varying degrees of intensity by all of Parliament's supporters. There was nothing in his views on these subjects either original or from which he drew any too-radical inferences for society at large. Deeply as he subscribed to these doctrines, they do not constitute the essence of his thought. If any conception was paramount for him, and particularly his own, it was the conception of aristocracy. It was this which bulked largest in his mind, assimilating to itself all other elements. Even the idea of liberty, important as it was for Milton,[1] had its content and its claims determined at all times by his aristocratic principle. It has been well said that he 'tried to understand the bourgeois revolution in aristocratic terms',[2] and to this it may be added without exaggeration that the history of his political thought is fundamentally the evolution which his conception of aristocracy underwent.[3]

In religion, where he operated with the Puritan distinction between the regenerate and the unregenerate,[4] and in politics, where he emphasized that the best government is ruled by the noblest men,[5] Milton's outlook was aristocratic through and through. His view of the function of education embodied entirely the ideal of aristocratic public service.[6] Deeply tinged with Platonic and humanist notions,[7] his belief, of course, was in an aristocracy of virtue, not of birth. The liberty he demands in the divorce tracts is for those who are virtuous and guided by reason.[8] They are the true aristocrats, and it is they, we are told in the astonishing prayer which concludes *Of Reformation*, who in Christ's kingdom 'shall receive above the inferiour Orders of the Blessed, the Regall addition of Principalities, Legions, and Thrones . . .'.[9]

[1] A. Barker, *op. cit.*, Ch. VII.

[2] Malcolm Ross, *Milton's royalism*, Ithaca, 1943, 61 n.

[3] The importance of the aristocratic idea in Milton's work has been discussed, though superficially, and with some unfortunate racist assertions, by H. Brunner, *Miltons persönliche und ideele Welt in ihrer Beziehung zum Aristokratismus, Bonner Studien zur englischen Philologie*, XIX, Bonn, 1933.

[4] Cf. A. S. P. Woodhouse, 'Milton, Puritanism, and liberty', *The university of Toronto quarterly*, IV, 4, 496–7.

[5] *Of reformation, Works*, III, 63.

[6] *Of education, Works*, IV, 280.

[7] Cf. A. Barker, *op. cit.*, 183–4.

[8] Cf., e.g., *Tetrachordon, Works*, IV, 74.

[9] *Of reformation, Works*, III, 79.

But there is always a close relationship between the conception of an aristocracy of virtue and the historically existing aristocracy of a time. This must be so, if only because those in the latter class alone command the means by which to perfect themselves to the point where they become aristocrats in the Miltonic sense. Milton clearly recognized this,[1] and it is evident that between his ideal aristocracy and the dominant social class on the revolutionary side an intimate connection existed; indeed, in his last political writing, the two are all but identified.[2] This connection is manifest in the low opinion which he entertained both of the luxurious rich and of the shopkeepers and workmen of London,[3] and in his bestowal of praise exclusively upon 'the middle sort, amongst whom', he declared, 'the wisest men and most skillful in affairs are generally found; the rest are commonly diverted, on the one hand by luxury and wealth, on the other by want and poverty, from achieving excellence, and from the study of civill prudence'.[4] Though written in 1651, these words are characteristic of his position at all times. They signified that Milton's orientation was entirely towards the men of independent means, neither plebeians nor corrupt and effeminate courtiers[5] —men, in fact, such as headed the struggle against the king. These were the likeliest to qualify for membership in the Miltonic aristocracy.

It was of the essence of Milton's aristocratic principle that it should issue in a demand primarily for the liberty of this class, idealized as the wise and good, and that it should concede liberty to the generality of people only so long as they gave their approbation to the former's rule. '. . . just and naturall privileges,' he declared, 'men can neither rightly seek, nor . . . fully claim, unless they be . . . ally'd to inward goodnesse, and stedfast knowledge. . . .'[6] It was, therefore, only within the limits of its concern for the liberty of the virtuous that this principle could serve as a solvent of the existing order. This was the function it performed when its edge was turned against the church and state organization which the first measures of the Long Parliament struck down. In this period, Milton identified the aristocratic element with the entire Parliament.[7] The people have not yet become the obnoxious rabble of his later writings, but are praised as keen-spirited,[8] and shown giving a willing

[1] He declared that high nobility and well-reputed ancestry are 'a great advantage towards vertue . . .', *An apology against a pamphlet*, 1642, *Works*, III, 335.

[2] See below.

[3] *First defence of the English people*, 1651, *Works*, VII, 357.

[4] *Ibid.*, *Works*, VII, 393.

[5] In *Eikonoklastes*, 1649, *Works*, V, 172, Milton referred to the 'dissolute rabble of . . . Courtiers . . . both hees and shees, if there were any Males among them'.

[6] *Tetrachordon*, *Works*, IV, 74.

[7] *An apology against a pamphlet*, *Works*, III, 334–41.

[8] *Areopagitica*, *Works*, IV, 339–40.

subjection to the rule of the noblest and best.[1] The liberties he then claimed, however, even though their operation might be general, were particularly for men like himself, who, as true aristocrats, ought not to be subjected to tyrannous restraints. His attack on the bishops in *Lycidas* (1637), for example, was on behalf of those of 'clear spirit', raised 'to scorn delights and live laborious days'. The censorship he denounced in *Areopagitica* was oppressive above all to those to whom truth has first spoken and 'whom God hath fitted for the speciall use of these times with eminent and ample gifts . . .'.[2]

It is evident that this aristocratic idealism was not anything democratic. If it served as a basis for rejecting the despotism of the Stuart state, it could also deny liberty to the majority of men the moment they should cease to acquiesce willingly in the government of the aristocrats. For this reason, it was less and less capable of furthering democratic ends after 1649. Once the revolutionary coalition of the earlier 1640s was disrupted, it could work only for Cromwell and the grandee Independents. These were, socially and economically, from the class with which Milton's fancied aristocracy had the greatest affinity. By 1649, they were the only ones who could qualify, the Presbyterians having excluded themselves, first by opposing liberty of conscience, later by condemning the sentence visited upon the king. In thus linking his aristocratic doctrine with Cromwell and the Independents, Milton was obliged to adapt it to their circumstances after 1649, and from that time forward, therefore, it manifested increasingly conservative overtones. This was the inevitable consequence of supporting Cromwell. For the latter, in whom Milton discerned the most complete embodiment of aristocratic virtue, was the head of an increasingly unpopular government, and in identifying his aristocratic idealism with the Cromwellian state, Milton made it serve undemocratic ends. This is not how he himself saw his role, of course. Up on his exalted height, he considered himself the enunciator of 'real and substantial liberty'.[3] But, objectively, this meant that the few should rule the many, even against the latter's will.

With these considerations in mind, we are in a position to understand Milton's ideas between 1649 and 1660. This was a period of growing disillusionment for him. That the commonwealth should be so widely opposed led him to conclude that the majority of men had servilely rejected the liberty offered them by the Independents. The Presbyterians he now conclusively removed from the elect of which they had seemed to be part in the earlier years of the Long Parliament. They had but posed as good patriots, he says, in order to rectify their own grievances, 'of purse especially', and now they have deserted those, who 'endu'd

[1] *Of reformation, Works*, III, 63.
[2] *Areopagitica, Works*, IV, 350, 351.
[3] *The second defence of the English people*, 1654, *Works*, VIII, 131.

with fortitude and Heroick vertue', strive on to effect England's deliverance.[1] The people, because of their tepid reception of the revolutionary government, are described as 'besotted', degenerate and base in spirit, 'exorbitant and excessive in all their motions . . .'.[2] As for the age, once thought so golden in its prospects, it is now 'graceless', one in which wisdom, valour, and justice are counted as schism and faction.[3]

Early in 1649, Milton published *The Tenure Of Kings And Magistrates* in vindication of the monarchy's removal. This work, the first of his purely political writings, was not a systematic treatment of the origin of political power or the basis of political obligation. It was, rather, a bold and uncompromising assertion of the right of revolution. Men are by nature free, he said, and rulers are subject to law.[4] Kings may be deposed even if they are not tyrants, but merely by the right which free men have to be governed as seems best to them.[5]

'. . . they that shall boast, as we doe, to be a free Nation and not have in themselves the power to remove, or to abolish any governour supreme, or subordinat, with the government itself upon urgent causes, may please thir fancy with a ridiculous and painted freedom, fit to coz'n babies; but are indeed under tyranny . . . as wanting that power, which is the root and source of all liberty, to dispose and oeconomize in the Land which God hath giv'n them, as Maisters of Family in thir own house and free inheritance.'[6]

These were high and stirring words, and bold enough in the seventeenth century. But Milton made no effort to argue that the commonwealth was, in fact, the people's government, acting in the people's name and responsible to it. This, he well knew, was impossible to prove, and with his aristocratic principle, he did not consider it necessary. His assertion of the right of revolution was kept entirely within the confines of his aristocratic standpoint.[7] The leader of the commonwealth was, after all, Cromwell, of whom Milton wrote in 1649 that he 'hath done in few yeares . . . eminent and remarkable Deeds whereon to found Nobility in his house . . . and perpetuall Renown to posterity . . .'.[8] It was therefore enough for Milton to say that the determination of who are tyrants he will leave 'to the Magistrates, at least to the uprighter sort of them, and of the people, though in number less by many, in whom faction least hath prevaild above the Law of nature and right reason . . .'.[9]

---

[1] *The tenure of kings and magistrates*, 1649, *Works*, V, 1–2.
[2] *Eikonoklastes*, *Works*, V, 68, 69.   [3] *Ibid.*, *Works*, V, 73.
[4] *The tenure of kings and magistrates*, *Works*, V, 8–9.
[5] *Ibid.*, *Works*, V, 11–14.   [6] *Ibid.*, *Works*, V, 40.
[7] Cf. H. J. C. Grierson, *op. cit.*, 62–3.
[8] *Observations on the articles of peace*, *Works*, VI, 252.
[9] *The tenure of kings and magistrates*, *Works*, V, 7.

To such only would he concede the right of changing their government.

All this is made even clearer in his *First Defence Of The People Of England* (1651). This work is Milton's most important defence of the commonwealth, and is also the first time in which he writes as a republican. A commonwealth is superior to monarchy, he now declared, for royal government, though not evil in itself, most commonly degenerates into tyranny.[1] It is doubtful if much importance should be attached to this new-appearing republicanism, since Milton seemed much less concerned with the superiority of republics than with his aristocratic ideal of government by the virtuous. It was this, and not a doctrinaire preference for republics, which he invoked to defend the Cromwellian government.

The establishment of the commonwealth was the people's doing, he said, 'For whatever the better, that is, the sounder part of the Parliament did . . . why may not the people be said to have done it?'[2] Yet he contradicted himself, since he admitted that the king's removal was the act of only a small number; but that minority, he asserted, 'were worthy to have dominion over the rest . . .'.[3] Those who voted for the king's death were the only ones who remained faithful, he declared. They played their parts like men, outdoing all their ancestors and previous Parliaments in wisdom, magnanimity, and constancy. Deserted by a great part of the people, they defended that part which remained sound.[4] Blindly identifying the nation with its leaders who embody aristocratic virtue, Milton praised the glory of the English, who '. . . struggled with, and overcame, not only their enemies in the field, but the hostile, that is, superstitious, opinions of the common people'.[5]

Milton's aristocratic doctrine was thus the means by which he strove to resolve the contradictions in the commonwealth's position and to evade, as John Goodwin had evaded, the full implications of the principle of popular sovereignty. That principle Milton adapted to his deeply rooted belief that the virtuous minority should rule the unenlightened majority. As a defender of the Cromwellian government, he could vindicate a right of revolution for none but the virtuous minority alone. He must refuse to defend 'seditions rashly kindled by the heat of a mad multitude', and must justify a summons to arms only by 'magistrates . . . senates . . . Parliaments . . .'.[6]

Milton was straying a long distance from the popular principles of

---

[1] *First defence of the English people, Works,* VII, 77, 123. This work and the *Second defence of the English people* were written in Latin. In citing them, I have occasionally altered the English readings as given in the translation printed in Milton's *Works.*
[2] *Ibid., Works,* VII, 357. [3] *Ibid., Works,* VII, 63. [4] *Ibid., Works,* VII, 511.
[5] *Ibid., Works,* VII, 65. [6] *Ibid., Works,* VII, 247.

the 1640s. This becomes even more apparent in the *Second Defence Of The English People* (1654), written in justification of the protectorate. That he should write on the protectorate's behalf is another indication that his republicanism at this time could not have been very deep. As far as a republican movement existed, it was in opposition to the government,[1] and so ought Milton to have been if his republicanism had been something vital. Another thing which must be observed is that at the time of the *Second Defence*'s appearance,[2] some of the men Milton most respected as aristocrats in his sense had broken with Cromwell. Sir Henry Vane the younger, the subject in 1652 of a famous laudatory sonnet, was among the Protector's enemies. So were Bradshaw, Robert Overton, and Sidney, three of the very group celebrated with Cromwell in the *Second Defence*. Yet Milton himself remained loyal, a fact which seems to have caused disturbance to his friends, if we may judge from a letter written to him by Moses Wall, one of the protectorate's opponents. In this letter, sent in 1659, Wall tells Milton, '. . . I was uncertain whether your relation to the Court . . . had not clouded your former light,'[3] a clear indication that the poet must have been somewhat distrusted for a time because of his acquiescence in Cromwell's semi-regal position after 1654.

In Cromwell, however, Milton discerned the highest fulfilment of aristocratic virtue, worthy to rule others because so much the master of himself. The Lord Protector, he declared, is a supreme statesman and soldier,

'above all others the most exercised in the knowledge of himself; he had either destroyed, or brought under his control, all enemies within his own breast—vain hopes, fears, desires. A commander first over himself, the conqueror of himself, it was over himself he had learnt most to triumph.'[4]

With this went an affirmation stronger than ever of the right of such men as Cromwell to exercise power over the carnal majority.

'There is nothing more agreeable to nature, nothing more just; nothing more useful or more for the interest of man, then that the less should yield to the greater; not number to number, but virtue to virtue, and counsel to counsel. Those who excel in prudence, in the management of affairs, in industry and virtue, will . . . however few their number, prove to be the majority, and will be everywhere weightier in their suffrages. . . .'[5]

---

[1] See below, Ch. XII.
[2] Thomason's copy is dated 30th May 1654.
[3] Printed in *Works*, XII, 334.
[4] *Second defence of the English people, Works*, VIII, 215.
[5] *Ibid., Works*, VIII, 155.

Notwithstanding his overall support of the protectorate, however, it appears that he was somewhat troubled by the political situation, as he could not help but be, seeing that men like Vane were in opposition. One senses Milton's misgivings in his admonition that Cromwell should join to himself colleagues of reputable and noble birth such as have been his associates from the beginning,[1] and in his advice (which Cromwell signally ignored) that civil and ecclesiastical power should be kept distinct, tithes abolished, and persons engaged in free inquiry left unhindered by censorship.[2] Milton admitted that the government was not all that could be wished, and said that it was only the best which existing conditions permitted.[3] He doubtless hoped that any drawbacks in the situation would be temporary, and that Cromwell, whom he addresses as 'father of his country', and *'auctor libertatis'*,[4] would, like a Solon or Lycurgus, eventually inaugurate a superior order.[5]

But if he felt misgivings in 1654, they must have grown stronger during the ensuing years, as he contemplated the government's ecclesiastical policy, Cromwell's regal pomp, and the offer of the crown to the Lord Protector in 1657. Such things as these must have greatly disturbed the poet. Otherwise we could not explain why, after Cromwell's death, Milton should denounce government by a single person,[6] and condemn Cromwell's dissolution of the Long Parliament six years before.[7] In vindicating the commonwealth and protectorate, these were, after all, the very things he had defended. Milton was not the sort of man ever to admit that he had been mistaken in anything. Yet it is impossible to avoid the conclusion that the events of the protectorate had disillusioned him. No doubt, Cromwell's pre-eminence kept Milton loyal. But it is understandable why, after Cromwell's death, in his final political work, he should attack government by a single person. Scarcely anyone, he must have felt, was great enough to rule alone. It was unfeasible to build political schemes on the hope that men of Cromwell's calibre would appear or that even such as these would remain wholly invulnerable to the temptations offered by great power. Besides, he was too proud and aware of his own worth to think very highly of government by a single person.[8] Men such as he, the gifted minority, could rule themselves, and were thus fitted to rule others without submitting to a single person.

It is the rule of this minority which Milton makes the foundation of

[1] *Ibid., Works,* VIII, 229–31.
[2] *Ibid., Works,* VIII, 235–9.
[3] *Ibid., Works,* VIII, 238.
[4] *Ibid., Works,* VIII, 224.
[5] Cf. Z. Fink, *op. cit.,* 104–5.
[6] *The readie & easie way to establish a free commonwealth,* 1660, *Works,* VI, 104.
[7] *Considerations touching the likeliest means to remove hirelings out of the church,* 1659, *Works,* VI, 43; *The readie & easie way, Works,* VI, 125.
[8] Cf. *The readie & easie way, Works,* VI, 121–2, 123–4.

his republican proposal in *The Readie & Easie Way To Establish A Free Commonwealth* (1660), his last political utterance. As this was the first time that he elaborated his republican ideas, it seems likely that only now did they come to have real importance for him. In part, this was due, as he himself said, to the fact that a republic was the only means by which a return to kingship could be avoided.[1] In part, it must also have been due to the fact that, after Cromwell's death, the minds of all who opposed a restoration were so dominated by republican schemes,[2] above all, by James Harrington's, that none but these would have been likely to obtain a hearing. So now, on the very eve of the restoration, Milton carried his aristocratic principle to the limit by proposing the lifetime rule of a council of oligarchs. This was the platform which he offered as a substitute for a servile return to monarchy. If his position was impossible, it was not because he was advocating a republic in the shadow of the returning Charles II. A good cause is not disgraced by defeat, and may have its day again, as the great ideas of the revolution certainly had theirs. It was because Milton conceived the alternatives so unacceptably that his position was hopeless. A republican oligarchy was no improvement over a Stuart restoration; his aristocratic ideal, full of illusions, was no basis upon which to found a government. This was the heart of his difficulty.

Milton's proposal, in brief, was for the establishment of an elected council or senate consisting of the ablest men. This council, he says, will possess sovereignty '. . . not transferred, but delegated, and as it were deposited . . .'.[3] By this, he seems to have meant that power would be fundamentally in the people and only exercised by the council. But this intention was vitiated by his suggestion that, once elected, the council should be perpetual. Successive Parliaments breed commotions, he asserts, and a perpetual senate alone can provide the stability and the experienced men which the state requires.[4] In a grudging concession to the ideas of James Harrington (who is not named, however), Milton says that if a lifetime council wounds some men's ambition or seems to set up too absolute a power, then rotation of one-third of the senate's membership annually or longer might be resorted to. But if at all possible, this should be avoided, he declares, for it will remove too many of the best and ablest persons from office.[5]

In justice to Milton, it must be pointed out that he did not think a perpetual senate would be dangerous so long as the well-affected among the people possessed arms.[6] Moreover, the proposal of a senate, or

[1] *Ibid., Works*, VI, 124–35.
[2] See the remarks of Edmund Ludlow, *op. cit.*, II, 98–9.
[3] *The readie & easie way, Works*, VI, 126.
[4] *Ibid., Works*, VI, 127.
[5] *Ibid., Works*, 127–9.
[6] *Ibid., Works*, VI, 128.

some other body vested with extraordinary powers, if not with life tenure, was made by other republican writers at this time.[1] He was perfectly aware that the greater part of the people seemed to desire the return of kingship,[2] and he regarded the senate as the means by which such a dreaded eventuality could be avoided. He saw no reason why the minority which still valued freedom should permit itself to be dragged back to the thralldom of monarchy by the majority.[3]

Yet the fact remains that he allowed almost no scope for democratic rights. Not only did he deny the desirability of successive Parliaments, but he rejected popular assemblies as troublesome and hazardous.[4] And from his remarks on the franchise, and on local government, it is clear that he now virtually identified the rule of the ablest with that of the upper-class persons who still opposed a restoration. The right to vote and to sit on the supreme council is not to be committed to the rude multitude, but primarily to those of 'better breeding'.[5] Moreover, each county is to be a kind of little commonwealth, in which the nobility and principal gentry are to head the administration, preside over assemblies (their nature is unspecified), and act as judges without appeal in civil cases.[6] Thus, at the last, Milton fell back on the aristocracy of blood, and ability and social position, virtue and breeding, go cheek by jowl.

Such was the poet's final political counsel. We may praise the courage with which he opposed the revival of kingship and the devotion to liberty of conscience which he manifested.[7] Yet even if the restoration had not been imminent, his proposals were too impracticable to be accepted by other republicans. From the experience of twenty years of revolution, he had drawn only the conclusion that popular assemblies were hazardous and successive Parliaments not to be trusted. He never understood that the failure of the commonwealth and protectorate to survive was caused by their refusal to grant liberty and reform in measure large enough to win the people's support. At the end, the best form of republic he could suggest was one which granted almost no popular rights and fastened permanently upon the all-but-unrepresented people the rule of the aristocracy and its satellites, the very first to acquiesce in the restoration of Charles II. To think, as Milton, no doubt, sincerely did, that this was the sovereignty of the people, was mere self-delusion.

The poet had thrown himself with heroic energy into the revolutionary struggle. Through twenty years, he sought the realization of an

[1] See below, Ch. XII.
[2] *The readie & easie way*, *Works*, VI, 134.
[3] *Ibid.*, *Works*, VI, 140–1.
[4] *Ibid.*, *Works*, VI, 130–1.
[5] *Ibid.*, *Works*, VI, 131.
[6] *Ibid.*, *Works*, VI, 144.
[7] *Ibid.*, *Works*, VI, 142–3.

ideal, and remained loyal to his principles to the very last. At the expense of great labour and danger to his health, he became, to the audience of Europe's intellectuals, the spokesman of revolutionary England. In an age when the extent of liberty demanded by the Levellers and the Diggers was scarcely thought of, and when the trial and execution of an anointed king by his own subjects were enough to stir any disciple of freedom to the soul, Milton proclaimed the people's right to remove their rulers, and justified the sentence visited upon Charles I.

Yet his case was now a sad one, for, spiritually, he had become a displaced person. In the world of the restoration, he would be an alien, and from the memories of those to whom he had looked in the past, he could take but little comfort. All had disappointed him—the people, the Presbyterians, the Long Parliament, even Cromwell. His disappointment was a foredoomed thing, however, and fated to result from the illusions bred by his aristocratic idealism. The meaning of the revolution did not lie in the effort to reform England by lodging government in the virtuous few. It lay in the seizure of power by the gentry and wealthy merchants, aided by the masses of small men whom the great hopes of the early 1640s set in motion. The leaders of the commonwealth were not Miltonic aristocrats, nor was the liberty they demanded that submission to reason's sway which Milton called 'real and true liberty'. What they strove for was the realization of the political and economic arrangements which would best serve their interests. They sought to establish their own power, and were bound to disappoint the poet's idealistic definition of their role. As for the people, Milton never knew them. How could he, with his breeding and education? Even when, in *Areopagitica*, he celebrated the nation rising like a strong man after slumber, the people remained a mythical entity to him. As long as they obeyed his fancied aristocracy, he praised them; when they did not, he condemned them. But they were not the besotted mob he believed them to be. He thought them servile for not supporting the commonwealth, yet many of them had stood by John Lilburne's side to demand a larger freedom than the commonwealth would grant.

It was inevitable, therefore, that Milton should be disillusioned. His aristocratic principle misled him; it was inadequate to comprehend the nature of the events through which he had lived. Thus, in 1660, he was left isolated, to be sustained in the future by the consciousness of his own fortitude and greatness, and by the recollection of how once, in an heroic time, he had defended the great deed of regicide to all of Europe.

X

MARCHAMONT NEDHAM AND FRANCIS OSBORNE

Republicans of a sort, yet wholly detached from the republican movement of the time, Marchamont Nedham[1] and Francis Osborne have a place of their own in the political thought of the revolution. Excellent stylists and, though not deep, exceedingly clever, their preference for a republican form of government was probably sincere. But it was outweighed by a cynicism which too-close proximity to the centres of political influence had made razor-sharp. They were 'acquiescers', not enthusiasts, and Machiavelli seems to have exercised a strong influence over their minds. While Harrington and his disciples had visions of an immortal commonwealth, Nedham and Osborne were exponents of the tough-minded school of politics. Their sense of mutability was too great, and their view of man too low, to permit them to indulge in golden dreams. Their attitude to power was utilitarian, not reverential. Power was a brute fact in which not even the slenderest ray of divinity could be perceived. But that it had a great capacity to injure, they were well aware, and so they were circumspect, risking nothing for an idea, and accepting the supremacy of any upon whom fortune had bestowed its accolade.

Nedham, who was born in 1620 of a gentle family, studied at Oxford, and in 1643 began a career as journalist by becoming editor of an anti-royalist news-sheet. Four years later, he turned king's propagandist. After 1649, he changed sides again, and was the commonwealth's chief hired writer, editing the official organ, *Mercurius Politicus*, under Milton's supervision. He continued to serve in this capacity during the protectorate, wrote in 1659 against the desirability of a royal restoration,[2] and fled the country when Charles II came back. But he soon returned home, began to curry favour with the royalists, and before his death in 1678 was employed by the government to write against Shaftes-

---

[1] Sometimes rendered as 'Needham'.
[2] *Interest will not lie*, 1659.

bury and the opposition.[1] Anthony Wood's characterization of him as a wholly mercenary penman seems just enough.[2]

Because of the variety of opinions Nedham was obliged to vent on behalf of his several employers, it is difficult to disentangle those to which he himself subscribed. An antagonism to religious fanaticism, however, and an attachment to a prudent toleration seem to have been constant elements in his thought.[3] His praise of a republic as a superior form of government also appears genuine enough, though this did not prevent him from serving either Charles I or Cromwell as Lord Protector.

The earliest of Nedham's writings worthy of any notice is *The Case of the Kingdom Stated* (1647),[4] a most characteristic production. Issued in the midst of hot religious and political wranglings, it was intended as a cool, factual analysis, in terms of reason-of-state, of the interests of the chief parties. Machiavelli seems to have been the principal influence in this approach, and in his preface, Nedham commends to all factions the remark of the important reason-of-state theorist, the Duke of Rohan,[5] concerning the princes of Europe, 'that according as they follow their proper Interests, they thrive or faile in Successes'; and he suggests that 'the Parties now on foot in this Kingdom, must look to stand or fall upon the same Ground'.

Detaching himself thus from any merely moral standpoint, Nedham presents himself as the counsellor who will advise each party how best to achieve its aims. For the royalists, he proposes the adoption of 'what Machiavel sets down as a sure Principle toward the purchase of Empire', namely, divide and rule. Let the king sit by while his enemies disagree, 'and then his only Interest will bee, to close with that Party which gives most hope of Indulgence to his Prerogative, and greatest probability of favour to his Friends'.[6] This party will be the Independents, he suggests, for while the Presbyterians are noted enemies to monarchy, the Independents are not. If but granted freedom of conscience, they will assist in reinstating the king.[7]

The Presbyterians' interest, he says, is to secure an alliance with the Independents before the king does so, by abandoning compulsion in

---

[1] Biographical details from the *D.N.B.*, *s.v.*

[2] *Op. cit.*, III, 1183.

[3] Cf., e.g., *The case of the common-wealth of England stated*, 1650, 88–91, and *The excellencie of a free-state*, 1656, 146–52.

[4] This was published anonymously, but is certainly Nedham's. It was attributed to him by Anthony Wood (*op. cit.*, III, 1184), and is accepted as his in C. H. Firth's life of Nedham in the *D.N.B.*

[5] On Rohan, see Friedrich Meinecke, *Die Idee der Staatsräson in der neueren Geschichte*, 3rd ed., Munich and Berlin, 1929, 203–45.

[6] *The case of the kingdom stated*, 1.

[7] *Ibid.*, 3–6.

religion. But he regards it as unlikely that they will do this, since their zeal for religious uniformity is too great.[1] As for the Independents, they have no special system of politics, and stand as the 'ballancing power' between the king and the Presbyterians, their only interest being to embrace whatever party will grant most liberty of conscience. This party, Nedham thinks, is likely to be the royalists.[2] Finally, there is the City of London. Its sole interest is trade, and so it ought to show neutrality to all parties and make itself odious to none. Above all, it should cool towards Presbyterianism.[3]

Interesting as this effort was to treat the issues at stake in a purely practical manner, the analysis proved, in the main, to be erroneous. Independency, contrary to Nedham's notion, did imply a political philosophy, and this philosophy was essentially inimical to the king's claims. As the issues grew sharper, it was in the Presbyterians that the king began to find support; and instead of the Independents allying themselves with Charles I, they put him to death. The iciness of Nedham's approach deprived him, in fact, of insight into the revolutionary implications of Independent and sectarian religion. It might, nevertheless, be said on his behalf that at the time he wrote his pamphlet, he reflected faithfully the intention of Cromwell and the leaders of the Independents to reconcile the king to themselves if they could. In addition, whatever its mistakes, his method of dealing with political problems was quite distinctive in the literature of the 1640s, and marks the entrance of an unfamiliar note.

After he took employment with the revolutionary government, Nedham published a capable work advocating submission to it, *The Case Of The Common-Wealth Of England Stated* (1650).[4] His chief arguments are already familiar to us from their similarity to those in the writings of Anthony Ascham, and are just the sort we should expect him to use. The sword, he declares, has always been the foundation of all titles to rule. After the flood, when the world became heavily populated, men were so vicious that they could no longer be controlled by heads of families. Then Nimrod established his government by force. Thus, 'the Power of the Sword [was] the Originall of the first Monarchy, and in-

---

[1] *Ibid.*, 6–9, 11.
[2] *Ibid.*, 10–12.
[3] *Ibid.*, 12–16.
[4] Published anonymously, but acknowledged by Nedham in *The great accuser cast down*, 1657, 88. Owing to the fact that extracts from *The case of the commonwealth* subsequently appeared in *Mercurius politicus*, which Nedham edited under Milton's supervision, the latter's hand was mistakenly discerned in some of these articles by Masson (*op. cit.*, IV, 327–35) and Gardiner (*History of the commonwealth and protectorate*, I, 412–14). This was not the case, however; see J. M. French, 'Milton, Needham, and *Mercurius politicus*', *Studies in philology*, XXXIII, 2, and E. A. Beller, 'Milton and *Mercurius politicus*', *Huntington library quarterly*, V, 4.

deed the first politicall Form of Government that ever was'.[1] And since then, force alone has been the dispenser of titles to commonwealths and kingdoms.[2] Eliminating, as Ascham had, the distinction between power and authority, he points out that

'those whose Title is supposed unlawfull, and founded meerly upon Force, yet being possessed . . . may lawfully be obeyed. Nor may They onely, but they must, else . . . such as refuse may be punished as seditious and Trayterous ; the Victors being ever allowed (*Jure gentium*) to use all means for securing what they have gotten, and to exercise a Right of Dominion over the Conquer'd Party.'[3]

It is not surprising that these conceptions should be enveloped in a thick atmosphere of pessimism occasioned by the same awareness of the mutability of human affairs which had oppressed Machiavelli. All things move in cycles, Nedham remarks, and are corruptible. So, too, with the 'huge Bodies of Common-wealths', which share the same fate as plants, brutes, and men, 'and this by a certaine destiny, or decree of Nature, who in all her Productions, makes the second moment of their perfection the first toward their dissolution'.[4] Changes of government, therefore, are a consequence of those hurricanes of fatal necessity which blow on human affairs from all points of the compass.[5] As other powers have had their day, so now, after six hundred years, a period has been set to the English monarchy. A new power has risen to supremacy which it would be madness to resist, for 'when all is done, we shall find it but labor in vain; that we have but fortified Castles in the Aire against fatall Necessity, to maintain a Phant'sie of pretended loyalty . . .'.[6]

Besides all these considerations, Nedham urged briefly that, because it is a republic, the commonwealth is a superior form of government.[7] But this was merely an afterthought, and his arguments for a republic only assumed significance later, in his most important work, *The Excellencie Of A Free-State* (1656).[8] This was an able book, and won a certain later renown, as appears by the fact that it was reprinted in France during the revolution,[9] and was also singled out for extensive discussion

[1] *The case of the common-wealth*, 6.
[2] *Ibid.*, 8.
[3] *Ibid.*, 16.
[4] *Ibid.*, 1.
[5] *Ibid.*, 2.
[6] *Ibid.*, 5.
[7] *Ibid.*, 80–93.
[8] This was unsigned, but it is surely his, judging both by its style and the fact that it is made up of articles which first appeared in *Mercurius politicus*.
[9] *De la souveraineté du peuple et de l'excellence d'un état libre*, trans. Th. Mandar, Paris, 1790. See the laudatory introduction.

by John Adams, second president of the United States.[1] It is impossible, however, to believe Nedham sincere in all the ideas he now set down. His contention, for example, that the origin of all just power is in the people,[2] he had denied earlier, and was to deny again.[3] His condemnation of Machiavellian reason-of-state is also not credible in so mercenary a writer who had himself engaged in reason-of-state theorizing.[4] Yet there is no need to doubt his preference for a republic, for it fits in well with the influence exercised over him by Machiavelli, and with the impression made upon him by the Greek and Roman political writers, to whom he frequently refers.

In vindicating a republic or free-state, Nedham's concern was not with constitutional devices, and he presented no detailed scheme of government. His aim was primarily that of inculcating a few basic principles and defending them against criticism. These principles were, as a whole, democratic in character, and if taken at their face value, they constitute a notable statement for a popular republic based on the tenets which had been emphasized by the Independents during the 1640s.

A rightly constituted commonwealth, Nedham says in what is surely an echo from Machiavelli's *Discourses on the First Decade of Livy*, must be founded on the proposition that 'the People . . . are the best keepers of their own Liberties'.[5] These liberties, he affirms, consist in wholesome laws, an easy and cheap administration of justice, a power to alter governors and government, an uninterrupted course of successive Parliaments or assemblies of the people, and a freedom of electing members to Parliament.[6] The basic consideration in establishing these liberties, he repeatedly insists, is 'a due and orderly succession of the Supreme Authority in the hands of the Peoples Representatives . . .'.[7] In a free-state where this principle is carried out, the people's good is best secured, since it is the people themselves who are most likely to provide remedies for their own relief. Moreover, it is only reason that none should be admitted to power but by the people's consent, and that those so admitted should return again to the condition of private men where they can themselves feel the benefits and burdens of what they have ordained.[8] Where due succession of authority by the people's consent is made the foundation of the commonwealth, the door of advancement is open to all without exception, and thus men become valiant and aim at great

[1] John Adams, *Works*, ed. C. F. Adams, 10 vols., Boston, 1850–6, VI. Adams says Nedham's book was well known in America, *ibid.*, VI, 6.
[2] *The excellencie of a free-state*, 130–6.
[3] *The great accuser cast down*, 88–90.
[4] See below.
[5] *The excellencie of a free-state*, 24; cf. Machiavelli, *Discourses*, I, 5.
[6] *Ibid.*, 4–5.
[7] *Ibid.*, To the reader.
[8] *Ibid.*, 35–7.

actions.[1] And, in addition, such an arrangement alone accords with reason and nature, for to deprive a people of their choice of governors is 'destructive to the Reason . . . and Majesty of that Noble Creature, called Man . . .'.[2]

By the consent of the people, Nedham seems to mean a general suffrage, for he rejects the criticism that confusion would result if all men without exception are given the right to elect and be elected.[3] He is at pains also to deny the other criticisms customarily made of popular rule. Thus, free-states do not level property, he points out, but rather preserve it against its chief enemy, royal tyranny.[4] They do not encourage calumnies against good men, though they must preserve a right of accusation if the intrigues of the ambitious are to be guarded against and all persons kept accountable.[5] Nor are they ungrateful and inconstant; the people know well how to reward eminent persons, even if the latter must sometimes be dealt with harshly lest they become too powerful.[6]

In a final section, Nedham discusses some of the things a free-state must take care to do or avoid if its liberties are to be preserved. It must not, he says, impose any religious orthodoxy or allow the clergy to establish a separate interest of their own, for this has been the main cause of civil wars in Europe.[7] The people should beware lest tyranny be imposed on them in a disguised form,[8] and should never permit authority to continue long in one man or family, or let the control of the militia out of the hands of their supreme assembly.[9] Most important of all, they should be honest in their dealings, rejecting Machiavelli's reason-of-state and his counsel that promises may be broken.[10] The Italian *ragione di stato*, he says, is but the statesman's lust making ambition, power, profit, and revenge a justification for any design, however contrary to common honesty and the law of God.[11]

Such, in brief compass, are Nedham's ideas on behalf of a popular republic. They are strange coming from one who was then serving the protectorate, a government republicans opposed. Some of his propositions, even if they did not descend to particulars, bore implications

[1] *Ibid.*, 39–40, 54–5.
[2] *Ibid.*, 67.
[3] *Ibid.*, 93–8.
[4] *Ibid.*, 83–93.
[5] *Ibid.*, 111–16. These remarks seem to depend on Machiavelli, *Discourses*, I, 8.
[6] *Ibid.*, 119–27; cf. Machiavelli, *Discourses*, I, 29, 58.
[7] *Ibid.*, 146–52.
[8] *Ibid.*, 152–60.
[9] *Ibid.*, 163–5, 173.
[10] *Ibid.*, 205–31. The reference is to *The prince*, Ch. 18, which Nedham reprints in full, *ibid.*, 234–40.
[11] *Ibid.*, 205–6.

against Cromwell himself, whose status under the *Instrument of Government* gave him powers which Nedham warned ought not to be devolved on any man. But Nedham seems to have been a complete cynic who might employ his fancy in advocating republican doctrines, and even, perhaps, believe them true, but whose wit was ever subservient to power. And so within a few months of the appearance of *The Excellencie of a Free-State*, when a move was on foot to make Cromwell king, we may take a final glimpse of him, pliant as ever, hinting broadly at the desirability of a return to monarchy. Men are as free under a monarchy as under a republic, he now wrote, and right reason shows that all forms of government are but as planks which men seize upon after shipwreck. Experiments have been in vain, he said, and the best thing is 'to revert upon the old bottom and Foundation'.[1]

The tendencies visible in Nedham's political ideas were carried to a higher pitch in the thought of Francis Osborne, for in the latter, scepticism and an insight into the adversity of fate and the precariousness of human existence were even more deeply rooted. Perhaps this was because Osborne spent much of his life before 1640 in the service of the great. Born the son of a royal official in 1593, he was employed first by the Earl of Pembroke and then at court, and the intrigue and insecurity of court existence may have contributed to forming his philosophy. During the commonwealth and protectorate, he held minor posts, and expressed a preference for a republican form of government.[2] But everything doctrinaire and positive in his outlook was outweighed by his profoundest conviction : 'that nothing would accept of Life upon such hard conditions as the Creature doth undergo, if it lay in its power to refuse . . .'.[3]

Like Hobbes, whose 'great acquaintance' he was,[4] Osborne was utterly void of religious zeal, and was suspected of atheism.[5] If he chose to believe in God, it was solely because this was safer, he said, than to risk the hope of future beatitude in atheism.[6] Sin he regarded as determined by law, all actions being indifferent in themselves.[7] He was also thoroughly Erastian and declared that '. . . the Keyes of the Church can hang no where so quietly, as at the Girdle of the Prince . . .'.[8] Unity in

---

[1] *Mercurius politicus*, 26th March–2nd April 1657; cf. all Nedham's articles in *ibid.* between 5th–12th March and 2nd–9th April 1657.

[2] Osborne's life is noticed in the *D.N.B.*, *s.v.*

[3] *Advice to a son, The second part*, 1658, 156.

[4] John Aubrey, *Brief lives*, ed. A. Clark, 2 vols., Oxford, 1898, I, 370.

[5] *The life and times of Anthony Wood*, ed. A. Clark, 5 vols., Oxford, 1891–1900, I, 257.

[6] *Advice to a son, The second part*, 188.

[7] *Advice to a son*, 6th ed., 1658, 87–8. All subsequent references to this work will be from this edition, which is somewhat enlarged over earlier ones.

[8] *Politicall reflections*, 1656, 29.

religion was best, he held, but if this is unobtainable, then toleration should be granted.[1] He denounced the clergy as arrogant and hypocritical, making it their task to go about like 'burning glasses', to

'cast the Rayes of a Celestiall Fire, into the Consciences of others, carrying in the meane time, themselves, a cold, Chrystalline, and Fragil Creed . . . taking upon them a publick cure of Soules, out of a no more religious respect, then to provide against their private wants . . .'.[2]

But the clergy perform an important function, he conceded, provided 'they keep close in their Doctrine, to Reason of State . . .'.[3] For sin ce miracles and the audible voice of God are silent, 'nothing is so likely as a Sanctified Policy, to . . . maintain so much Probity, as is requisite . . . to keep us from murdering one another, upon the instigation of Covetousnesse and Revenge'.[4]

As befitted a friend of Hobbes, Osborne was a partisan of the new philosophy, and condemned religious enthusiasts as 'anti-Veritarians', because of whom 'The Students of Reason in our days [lie] under the heavy fate the Mathematicians did of old, in being thought Conjurers and Atheists . . .'.[5] There is no justification for adhering to the judgement of antiquity, he said, for 'There may . . . lye as vast a World of Truth beyond this rotten Barre, as Experience hath shewn us of Land and Nations, which never fell within the Compasse of the Old Maps. . . .'[6] But these elements of enlightenment in Osborne's thought were in conflict with his sense of disenchantment and the vanity of things, and this was far stronger than his belief in new truth. Hence, much more in keeping with his outlook was his remark that '. . . what is, was before us, and will be, when we are no more; Warre followes peace, and peace warre, as summer doth winter, and foule weather faire . . .'.[7]

Osborne's view of political life was a dark one. Not only are men vicious, he felt, but they must always be in conflict with one another owing to the impossibility of the world's resources to maintain them all. A kind of seventeenth-century Malthusianism was his creed, and he regarded tyranny as natural and necessary, since 'if the stronger Creatures did not spoile and devour the weaker, the whole mass of Animalls would perish by famine; or stifle for want of roome'. Hence Providence is wise, he said, in causing man to be actuated

---

[1] *Ibid.*, 71–2; cf. W. K. Jordan, *Development of religious toleration*, IV, 240–9, for a full discussion of Osborne's views on liberty of conscience.
[2] *Ibid.*, 21–2.
[3] *Ibid.*, 19–20.
[4] *Ibid.*, 31.
[5] *Advice to a son, The second part*, 170, 172.
[6] *A miscellany of sundry essayes*, 1659, 102.
[7] *Advice to a son*, 99.

'by such Impetuous Passions and brutish Desires, as, through the Mediation of excesse, Covetousness, and Ambition, he becomes the Moderator, no lesse than the Destroyer of his own kind. . . . And when this is too little to ballance the Incomes of Lust . . . and over-repletion calls in Pestilence and famine to turne the Scales.'[1]

There was never a golden age, he asserted, and men were as malignant at the world's beginning as at any other time. But when the earth was young, it had few inhabitants and there was enough for all. Soon, however, the earth became overcrowded, and then want and struggle appeared, and this it was that made government and law necessary.[2]

Osborne's moral insights being what they were, it is not strange to find him justifying Machiavelli, for whom he had a profound admiration. The Italian, he said, does not deserve the censures cast upon him, for why should one man inherit 'the mass of Reproaches due to all Princes and Statesmen in generall'?[3] Machiavelli but undertook to make a grammar of politics, and must not be condemned 'for setting down the most generall Rules, and such as all Statesmen make use of . . .'.[4] The body politic, declared Osborne, is like a man outwardly beautiful but inwardly filled with filth. History is the story of pride, murder, and ambition, and because Machiavelli realized this, and raked more deeply than his predecessors in the entrails of the state, he smells in the nostrils of the delicate and ignorant.[5]

Living through the years when the revolutionary governments held power, Osborne saw no reason for refusing obedience to them. Changes of government are in the care of Providence, he affirmed, and when a new power has been placed in the saddle of sovereignty, it should be obeyed without concern for title or right.[6] 'He that suffers his conscience to mislead him in civill Obedience,' Osborne declared, '. . . doth not consider that All States and Kingdomes now extant, had their foundations laid in the dirt, though time may have dried it up by oblivion, or flattering historians lick't it off.'[7] Yet with all this, he suggested that a republic is a superior form of government, and that the commonwealth ought to be accepted for this reason. This republicanism was too passionless to cast a glow of hope into the gloom that invested Osborne's ideas, yet it seems to have been a genuine element in his thinking.

---

[1] *Advice to a son, The second part*, 155–6.

[2] *Ibid.*, 124–5.

[3] *Politicall reflections*, 127–8. Osborne's remarks on Machiavelli in this work are virtually identical with an anonymous pamphlet of 1642, *The atheisticall politition*, which I therefore take to be his.

[4] *Ibid.*, 145.

[5] *Ibid.*, 140–1, 146–7.

[6] *Advice to a son*, 90–1, 96.

[7] *Ibid.*, 98–9.

K

Osborne was somewhat under the spell of Venice, as were other seventeenth-century Englishmen,[1] and he declared that Venice's progress and virtues prove a superiority in republics which monarchies lack. Though small in comparison with her neighbours, she has withstood great coalitions, turned back the Turks, and gotten the best of the papacy.[2] In a republic, he said, the senate may possess the same great power as princes have in monarchies, but will use it more judiciously, since its exercise must reach the senators' children, who are mingled among the people. A republic is also immune from the sad effect of hereditary succession in monarchies, and its highest bodies are always occupied by worthy men.[3] Republics are always more favourable to persons of talent than monarchies, where a pleasing face or the recommendation of the king's mistress are the usual road to advancement. The ancient English nobility, he declared, will prosper more under a free-state than it did in the past under kings, when it suffered because of the royal patronage extended to low-born favourites.[4]

At other times, however, Osborne expressed adverse opinions about republics. Thus, they are notorious for their ingratitude, he said, rarely rewarding the merits of their greatest friends, and are also very vulnerable to tumults and civil strife.[5] The truth would seem to be that his preference for a republic, though probably genuine, was tepid and of little importance in comparison with his cynical conception of political life. The essence of political wisdom for him lay in the recognition that ill things are, and ill will they ever be; his sincerest feeling, no doubt, was in his remark that to a wise man, it makes no difference 'what card is Trump . . . neither ought he to be troubled, whether his Fetters consist of many linkes, or but One'.[6]

Such an attitude Nedham in his cynicism shared with Osborne. It is this that sunders them from the republicanism of the time. Both might bring forward arguments to prove the superiority of a free-state, but at bottom, they remained sceptical and indifferent. Their outlook was therefore alien to the true republican. The latter believed in progress, and contrived political schemes with the expectation of ameliorating the lot of man. For him, forms of government were of the greatest moment, things on which human liberty depended. Like Harrington, he either considered politics a science, or, at least within broad limits,

---

[1] Cf. Z. Fink, *op. cit., passim.*

[2] *A perswasive to a mutuall compliance under the present government*, 1652, 26–7; cf. *Politicall reflections*, 94–5. The former work appeared anonymously, but was acknowledged by Osborne in an unnumbered edition of 1656 of his *Advice to a son*, Preface to the reader.

[3] *Ibid.*, 25.

[4] *Ibid.*, 37–9.

[5] *Advice to a son*, 105–6, 109.

[6] *Ibid.* 97.

subject to design and control. Quite otherwise was it for Nedham and Osborne. In their deepest conviction, they held that though forms of government should be changed, it would only be as sick men change their beds, for life's fevers and distempers would remain. To them, politics was the profane realm, dark and unredeemable, presided over by malignant forces, and victim of a destiny beyond human power to foresee or prevent.

XI

JAMES HARRINGTON

THE foremost of the republican theorists was James Harrington. In the pages of his penetrating work, *Oceana* (1656), the political ideal of classical antiquity lived again, and the commonwealth of the republicans' dreams was given palpable shape and provided with a systematic rationale. Probably because its ideas stood in opposition to the protectorate, *Oceana* was cast in the form of an elaborate Utopian romance. In a style as often dull as not, things English were exhibited under outlandish names and political proposals presented with a super-abundance of fantastic detail. Yet the fantasy displayed an insight into the contemporary situation that gave Harrington an unrivalled ascendancy over the republicans. To them, he held forth, as his intention was, the possibility of an English free-state incorporating institutions so perfectly contrived that it could be as long-lived as the world. Between 1656 and 1660, he propagated his views with unwearying zeal and such success that for a moment it really seemed as if England might be reconstituted somewhat along the lines he laid down. Then came the restoration, and in the great gust of enthusiasm for the returning Charles II, the republicans' schemes were swept away like dust. Yet Harrington remained undaunted, for more clearly than any other thinker he understood that the revolution was the product of forces too powerful and deeply rooted for its essential work ever to be reversed. With keen prescience, he realized that the future belonged to the class which, in the extremity born of civil war, had smashed the monarchy.[1] 'Well, the king will come in,' he said in 1660. 'Let him come in, and call a Parliament of the greatest Cavaliers in England, so they be men of estates, and let them sett but 7 yeares, and they will all turn Common-wealthe's men.'[2]

This unshaking confidence in his position was no mere consequence

[1] Cf. R. H. Tawney, 'Harrington's interpretation of his age', *Proceedings of the British Academy*, XXVII, 1941, 223.

[2] J. Aubrey, *op. cit.*, I, 291.

of a heedless and arbitrary optimism, but arose, rather, from the depths of his political theory. For Harrington was a thinker of a new type in England, and the spirit of his thought was that of the new philosophy.[1] Rigour and demonstrability, and the establishment of principles upon necessary premisses were its aims.[2] On the precedents which law or custom might yield, it set no value at all, and it felt only contempt for the feudal polity in which the crabbed learning of the common lawyers discerned the pattern of English liberty.[3] Politics it conceived on mechanical lines as 'art' and as 'architecture',[4] and its desire was to comprehend the political order systematically by means of a unitary theory, and to create a commonwealth founded upon procedures as rational and infallible as those of mathematics.[5]

But if Harrington was animated by the spirit of the new philosophy, there was a respect in which he differed from it, and which constitutes at the same time both the chief peculiarity of his ideas and the source of their strength and persuasiveness. It is well known in what low estimate the philosophy of the seventeenth century held the study of history. To Hobbes, as later to Locke, history was but experience, not ratiocination from necessary principles. Its results, consequently, could admit only of probabilities, not of exact demonstration, and its rank in the scale of knowledge was accordingly an humble one.[6] Harrington's attitude was different. To him, it was history, and history alone, that could provide the principles on which the science of politics was to be established. Hence, the essence of his thought was the notion of a necessity, or a causal nexus, sure and demonstrable, governing political life, embedded in the historical process, and there only to be sought for. This necessity was the root cause of political change, and it was reason's task to apprehend it, and thereby to grasp the conditions of effective political action.

Harrington thus arrived at the conception of historical necessity—a force discernible within the social order and determining political development. This idea was his own; but it seems clear that it was owing to the influence of Hobbes and of Machiavelli upon his mind that he

---

[1] Cf. R. H. Tawney, *op. cit.*, 204–5.

[2] Cf., e.g., *The prerogative of popular government*, 1658, *Works*, London, 1771, 248. Except for *Oceana*, all subsequent references to Harrington's writings will be from this edition of his *Works*.

[3] *Oceana*, ed. S. B. Liljegren, Lund and Heidelberg, 1924, 47–8. All subsequent references to *Oceana* will be from this edition.

[4] *The art of lawgiving*, 1659, *Works*, 367.

[5] *The prerogative of popular government*, *Works*, 248.

[6] Thomas Hobbes, *De corpore*, I, 8; John Locke, *An essay concerning the human understanding*, Book IV, XVI, 9–11. The Cartesian view of history was similarly contemptuous.

was enabled to achieve it.[1] Although he criticized Hobbes, he also admired him profoundly.

'It is true I have oppos'd the politics of Mr. Hobbs. . . . Nevertheless in most other things I firmly believe that Mr. Hobbs is and will in future ages be accounted the best writer, at this day, in the world. And for his treatises of human nature, and of liberty and necessity, they are the greatest of new lights, and those which I have follow'd, and shall follow.'[2]

From Hobbes more than from anyone, it would appear, he learned to treat politics mechanistically and to seek for a deterministic explanation of the political order based on demonstrable principles.[3] Moreover, he accepted, as we shall see, Hobbes's view of sovereignty, and like him, strove to make the sovereign power the rational expression of the common interest.

It was by Machiavelli, on the other hand, that he was led to turn to history for the correct principles of political science. Harrington's respect for the Italian thinker was unbounded. He considered him 'the onely Polititian of later Ages' and 'the greatest Artist in the modern World'.[4] He regarded him, not as a corrupter of states, but as an analyst or physician with the help of whose doctrines a cure for political evils could be effected.[5] Above all, he believed him to be the great restorer of the republican tenets of classical antiquity—that ancient prudence which ended with the establishment of the Caesarian monarchy at Rome, and which established government upon common right and not, as did the modern prudence that succeeded it, upon the interest of a minority.[6] At the very commencement of the *Discourses on the First Decade of Livy*, Machiavelli had insisted on the indispensability of history for the understanding of politics.[7] In this, Harrington entirely concurred.

'No man can be a Polititian except he be first an Historian or a Travel-

---

[1] This has been stressed by Richard Koebner, 'Die Geschichtslehre James Harringtons', *Geist und Gesellschaft, Festschrift für Kurt Breysig*, 3 vols., Breslau, 1927–8, III, 15–19; and cf. the same writer's '*Oceana*', *Englische Philologie*, LXVIII, 1933–4, 364–8. Professor Koebner's articles are far the most penetrating analyses of Harrington's thought that I know of.

[2] *The prerogative of popular government, Works*, 241.

[3] Harrington had read both Hobbes's *De cive* and *Leviathan*. For some obvious connections with Hobbes's mechanistic standpoint, see, e.g., *Oceana*, 207, *The prerogative of popular government, Works*, 248, and *A system of politics*, n.d., *Works*, 468 (Ch. IV, Aphorism 10).

[4] *Oceana*, 13, 135.

[5] *A system of politics, Works*, 482.

[6] *Oceana*, 12–13.

[7] *Discourses*, Preface to Book I.

ler; for except he can see what Must be, or May be, he is no Polititian: Now if he have no knowledge in story, he cannot tell what hath been; and if he hath not been a Traveller, he cannot tell what is: but he that neither knoweth what hath been, nor what is; can never tell what must be, or what may be.'[1]

Like Machiavelli, he sought in the history of republican governments for the constitutional devices by means of which the state could be preserved. But in the end, as we shall see, he diverged fundamentally from his master for reasons that are contained in the very core of his political thought.

We have in Harrington, then, a profound preoccupation with history: raised from its low estate, history becomes a philosophical principle designed to serve the purposes of demonstration. It is this which has led to his being customarily characterized as an exponent of the inductive or historical method in politics.[2] The characterization is ill-formulated, however. It overlooks the extent to which he was dominated by the ideal of basing the state upon eternal principles of reason, and leaves out of account the mechanistic spirit in which his ideas were conceived. To this spirit, his concern with history, unique and fruitful as it may have been, was entirely assimilated. From history, he wished to distill the underlying cause by which political development was determined. This done, he would be able to lay the foundation of a commonwealth that could live forever. Such a commonwealth would be a product of art, a mechanism so balanced that it need never run down.[3] No aspiration could show less regard for the relativity of historical circumstance or place greater trust in reason's power to create an edifice that would permanently withstand the ravages of time. It represented a complete departure from Machiavelli's view of life. The Italian thinker, with all his confidence in the statesman's craft, had never entertained such a hope, for he knew too well the corruptibility of things and the fickleness of fortune.[4] But that Harrington should do so was a perfectly logical outcome of the mechanistic assumptions by which his attitude towards history was conditioned.

The decisive factor in politics Harrington held to be the distribution of property, above all, property in land. Those who possess the balance of property in a state must inevitably possess sovereignty. If one man is sole landlord of a territory, or himself holds the greatest proportion of the land, the government will be an absolute monarchy. If the land is

---

[1] *Oceana*, 175.
[2] Cf. G. P. Gooch, *op. cit.*, 252; H. F. Russell Smith, *op. cit.*, 17–20; G. Sabine, *A history of political theory*, New York, 1937, 497.
[3] *Oceana*, 207.
[4] Cf. e.g., *Discourses*, I, 16, III, 1; *The prince*, Ch. 25.

in the possession of a minority, the government will be a regulated monarchy in which power is shared between the crown and the aristocracy. And if the ownership of land is dispersed throughout the entire people, the government will be a commonwealth.[1] The balance of property, therefore, is the foundation, and upon it is reared the form of government as the superstructure.[2] The root cause of political disturbance lies in a discord between the two. For as landed property gradually passes to new social groups, the existing superstructure ceases to be stable and can be maintained only by force. It is the violent preservation of the superstructure against a new balance which brings on civil war. The essence of political prudence, consequently, consists in the raising of such superstructures as will be compatible with the distribution of property.[3]

This is the famous theory of the balance which Harrington claimed as his great discovery and described as 'that principle which makes the politics . . . the most demonstrable of any [art] whatsoever'.[4] It is easy to see why history should be so important in this theory. Without a knowledge of the antecedent social changes which have effected a redistribution of property, it will be impossible either to understand the reasons for the rise and fall of states or to frame a stable government. The analysis, therefore, takes the balance, or what may be called economic facts, as primary, and political facts as secondary. Ascertain the former, and the latter can be inferred. Should the state decline, it is clear that political arrangements have ceased to reflect economic realities. Devise a constitution in which economic facts are rendered invulnerable to change, and the political sphere will be mastered and placed on a permanent foundation. Thus, it seemed, nothing was left indeterminate,and politics made a science based on demonstrable principles.

His own country, which he describes under the name of Oceana, had reached the crisis of civil war, Harrington held, because the monarchical constitution had ceased to conform to economic facts. Ruled after the Norman conquest by the king and the few lords who controlled all land, England had been founded on a feudal balance. But the crown strove against this balance by aspiring to be absolute, and the government became nothing but a wrestling match between king and nobility.[5] To abate the latter's power, Henry VII took measures which made him supreme, but whose long-run effect was to place the balance in the people, thereby begetting the force which was to blow up the monarchy itself. His Statutes of Population, Retainers, and Alienations created a

---

[1] Oceana, 14–16; cf. The art of lawgiving, Works, 368–9.
[2] Oceana, 15; The art of lawgiving, Works, 368.
[3] Oceana, 15–16, 53; cf. The art of lawgiving, Works, 362.
[4] The prerogative of popular government, Works, 226.
[5] Oceana, 46–8.

new class of 'yeomanry' or 'middle people' and undermined the feudal lords, transforming them into courtiers who sold their lands and bankrupted themselves to maintain their position at court. While the old nobility declined, the new class grew, enhancing its power with the possession of the estates of the Church, which fell to it when Henry VIII dissolved the monasteries. Thus the balance passed by degrees to the people, who, to contend for sovereignty, needed only to become aware of their own strength. When they did, the civil war was the result. It was, therefore, not the war which had caused the disintegration of the monarchy, Harrington concluded, but the disintegration of the foundations on which the monarchy stood that had caused the war.[1]

From this analysis, it followed irresistibly that only a commonwealth or republic could be compatible with the new balance which had emerged in England. Property being diffused among the people, there was no basis left upon which a monarchy could continue as a stable and peaceable government. This was the fact. To urge the divine right of kings against it, or to invoke the oath of allegiance, was merely to pursue chimeras. Failure to recognize it entailed the prolongation of civil discord and the postponement of a settlement. The English monarchy had died a natural death, and in the course of its decline, the prerequisites for fashioning a republic had come into being. There was no other practicable alternative.[2]

The logical starting-point, then, of Harrington's republicanism was not any abstract notion of rights or of natural law; it was the conviction that an ascertainable historical necessity made a republic the only possible form of government which could bring his distracted country to a settlement. But more was required than a demonstration of what was politically possible. Before Harrington could describe the institutions of his desired republic, it was essential also to show that, in this case, to bow to necessity was to be moral, and that a rightly framed republic is the best of state-forms with respect to reason and justice. To fail to do this would have meant acquiescence in any government simply because the balance requires it, and would have entailed turning away from what political philosophy had traditionally cherished as its chief aim, namely, the establishment of the state upon justice.

Harrington undertook, therefore, to demonstrate the superior virtue of a republic. He began by affirming that there exists a common or public interest and that the just state is one in which this is best secured. Such a state, he said, may be described as an empire of laws rather than of men; for though law is admittedly the command of men, its true essence is the rational and impartial care of the general good, and where this is fulfilled, law may be said to hold sway. Then, following the utilitarian ethics of Hobbes, he pointed out that since both men's reason and

---

[1] *Ibid.*, 48–50.　　　　[2] *Ibid.*, 53–5.

their wills are moved by interest, a political order can be just only when law is made by the reason and will of all. If law is made by a minority, it must necessarily reflect a partial interest. When the whole people make law, however, the common interest is given expression, and justice and right reason prevail.[1] This, then, it seemed to Harrington, was the ethical validation of his republic, that it would transmute the pursuit of a private into the securing of a public interest, and enable the sovereign power to act as the rational agent of the general good.

Suffused by his dream of harmony, he could see no reason why his republic, firmly fixed as it would be, should have anything to fear from granting royalists their full rights. Though they had supported the monarchy, their interests would be completely secured in the new state, and they would have no motive to act against it.[2] Nor need the republic anticipate any danger from the gentry. On the contrary! Born into this class himself, Harrington was at pains to make clear how indispensable its services would be. 'There is something,' he said, '. . . in the making of a Common-wealth . . . in the governing of her, and . . . in the leading of her armies; which . . . seems peculiar unto the Genius of a Gentleman.'[3] Wisdom and virtue, he believed, were most likely to be embodied in gentlemen. Possessed of leisure, they could devote themselves to the study of politics, a subject not to be mastered except by diligent labour. Commanding independent means, they did not need to earn a living, and could give themselves fully to the public service. They were, accordingly, the exemplars of political sagacity and patriotic spirit, and, for this reason, the natural leaders of the people. And as long as the republic's institutions prevented them from overbalancing the people, their leadership would produce nothing but good.[4]

A balance invulnerable to change, popular sovereignty with an admixture of aristocratic elements, and class peace—such were the chief requirements of the republican polity Harrington now proceeded to delineate. Of its various institutions, two were fundamental, and in the first of these, his independence and boldness were strikingly displayed. It was to be an agrarian law limiting the value of land any single person might hold to £2,000 per annum in England and Ireland, and £500 per annum in Scotland.[5] By means of this limitation on land ownership, the popular balance would be preserved and kept sufficiently equal so that 'no one man or number of men within the compass of the Few or Aristocracy can come to overpower the whole people by their possessions in Lands'.[6] With its foundation thus fixed, Harrington declared, the government will be secure and incapable of suffering change.[7]

[1] *Oceana*, 20–3; *The prerogative of popular government, Works*, 224–5.
[2] *Oceana*, 55, 217.　　[3] *Ibid.*, 34–5.　　[4] *Ibid.*, 118–19, 18, 34.
[5] *Ibid.*, 85–6.　　[6] *Ibid.*, 32–3.　　[7] *Ibid.*, 91

To understand the daring of this proposal, we need only be reminded that there was almost no measure that had incurred more disapproval and censure from political theorists and historians than a *lex agraria*. Cicero had denounced it.[1] Livy had emphasized the civil strife which it excited in Rome.[2] Machiavelli called it the first cause of the destruction of the Roman republic.[3] It was, however, a necessary inference from the theory of the balance, and Harrington did not hesitate to advocate it. He denied that it was responsible for the evil consequences ascribed to it, and maintained, on the contrary, that republics in the past had survived only while they had had an agrarian law, or something that had produced the same effect of keeping possessions relatively equal.[4] It was, he insisted, the only cure for remedying the instability of government,[5] its virtue being such 'that wherever it hath held, that Government hath not altered . . .'.[6]

The second of the fundamental institutions was to be rotation in office. This Harrington defined as 'equal . . . Succession unto Magistracy, conferred for such convenient terms, enjoying equall vacations, as take in the whole body by parts, succeeding others through the free election . . . of the People'.[7] Without it, he warned, there could be no equal access to office, and the commonwealth would come under the domination of parties.[8] And that rotation might achieve its full effect, he borrowed a device from the Venetian constitution, for which he had great admiration, and decreed that the people should give their suffrages in the form of the ballot. By this means, they could vote their minds freely, unintimidated by the fear of offending anyone.[9]

Within the framework of the agrarian law and rotation, the various organs of the government were to operate. Of these, only the most important need be considered, otherwise we should be overcome by the plethora of details with which Harrington harassed his readers. The leading bodies were to be an elected popular assembly and senate, and an executive magistracy.[10] For election purposes, the people were first to be divided into freemen and servants, the latter being described as those dependent on others for a livelihood. Then the freemen were to be distinguished into horse and foot, according to whether or not they were possessed of annual incomes of more than £100.[11] There were to be fifty counties, or tribes, as Harrington called them,[12] and in each two knights would be elected to the senate and seven deputies to the assembly. All freemen had the right to vote. But only those in the horse were eligible to sit in the senate, and of the seven deputies from each county, three

[1] In his three consular orations, *De lege agraria contra Rullum*.
[2] *Ab urbe condita*, II, 41. [3] *Discourses*, III, 24; I, 37.
[4] *Oceana*, 89–91. [5] *Ibid.*, 91.
[6] *Ibid.*, 16. [7] *Ibid.*, 32. [8] *Ibid.*, 107.
[9] *Ibid.*, 101–2, 33. [10] *Ibid.*, 33. [11] *Ibid.*, 64–5.
[12] *Ibid.*, 73.

were also to be of the horse.[1] Thus the senate would be the aristocratic body in which the gentry would have precedence of place.

Together, the senate and assembly made up Parliament and constituted the sovereign power.[2] Their functions, however, were carefully differentiated. To the former, the wiser of the two, belonged the sole right of debating matters; to the latter, the more representative of the two, the sole right of deciding them. As the senate was strictly denied the power to make law, so the assembly was strictly denied the power to discuss it. The procedure would be that the senate would first consider a measure, and having adopted it, propose it to the assembly. There, without the slightest discussion, it would be voted upon, and if accepted, would become law.[3]

By thus distinguishing between senate and assembly, Harrington seems to have thought that he was accepting Hobbes's theory of sovereignty, while eliminating its dangers. Like Hobbes, he believed that the sovereign power must be absolute and that there could be no right of resistance against it, otherwise government could not exist at all.[4] In his republic, he pointed out, sovereignty would be as absolute and unbounded as in any monarchy; but it would be so 'librated' or 'ballanced' between the leading organs of the state that there would be nothing formidable in it. The people, in whom lay the power to vote law, would never use that power against themselves; while the senate's proposals would have to express the people's interest as well as its own, otherwise they would not be approved.[5] This, however, ignored some obvious problems: what if the senate should falsely persuade the assembly that something was in the general interest which, in reality, was not? Or what if the senate and assembly disagreed so fundamentally that the government broke down? Harrington did not face these questions. But he would doubtless have taken the optimistic view that no motive for deception by the senate or for an irreconcilable difference between the two bodies could ever arise.

Completing the national government would be an executive magistracy which was to be elected by the senate and include military, financial, and other officials, as well as a system of councils vested with jurisdiction over the main departments of administration.[6] In emergencies, it was provided, with Roman precedent in mind, that a dictator in the form of a special commission named by the senate should be instituted for three months.[7] In all official bodies, rotation was, of course, to be the

---

[1] *Ibid.*, 80–1.
[2] *Ibid.*, 103.
[3] *Ibid.*, 116–17, 143.
[4] *The art of lawgiving, Works*, 404.
[5] *Oceana*, 84–5; *The art of lawgiving, Works*, 404.
[6] *Oceana*, 105–6.
[7] *Ibid.*, 111–14; cf. Machiavelli, *Discourses*, I, 34.

rule, so that a part of the senate, assembly, and magistracies would quit office annually to be replaced by an equal number of incoming members. Finally, all public officials were to receive moderate salaries for their services.[1]

There remain only the ecclesiastical arrangements to consider, and these are just what we should expect from a student of Hobbes and Machiavelli. Strongly anti-clerical, Harrington thought nothing more dangerous to civil peace and to free inquiry after truth than that the clergy should have power.[2] '... if you know not how to rule your clergy,' he said, 'you will be like a man that cannot rule his Wife; [and] have neither quiet at home nor honour abroad.'[3] He provided, therefore, that there should be an established church entirely under state control, but with toleration granted to those who would dissent from it. Without toleration, he declared, civil liberty would be precarious and incomplete.[4] Hence, attendance at the national church was to be strictly voluntary, and all but Catholics, Jews, and 'idolaters' left unmolested in the exercise of their religion.[5] The national worship was to be determined by act of Parliament,[6] and was to be supervised by the state down to its smallest details. In the government's council of religion would be vested the duties of protecting liberty of conscience, hearing ecclesiastical causes, settling disagreements in doctrine, and providing ministers.[7] The latter were to be obtained from the universities, but would have to be elected by the parish before being confirmed in their benefices.[8] They were, of course, prohibited from holding any state office, lest secular preoccupations corrupt them.[9]

Such, in broadest outline, was the commonwealth Harrington delineated with so much care. Given the stability and harmony which its institutions enforced, he was sanguine enough to think it could live forever. Founded upon its equal agrarian law, it would be incapable of swerving from the infallible principles it incorporated.[10] If Venice, he said, had survived fresh and unchanged for a thousand years despite the imperfections of her constitution, then his own republic 'may for any internal causes be as immortal, or longlived as the World'.[11] This will

---

[1] *Oceana*, 150–1.

[2] *Pian piano*, 1658, *Works*, 519; *Oceana*, 37–8.

[3] *Oceana*, 173.

[4] *Ibid.*, 37; *Valerius and Publicola*, 1659, *Works*, 459. Harrington's Erastian and tolerationist views are discussed by W. K. Jordan, *Development of religious toleration*, IV, 281–91.

[5] *Oceana*, 69.

[6] *The art of lawgiving*, *Works*, 422.

[7] *Oceana*, 109–10.

[8] *Ibid.*, 69.

[9] *Ibid.*, 110.

[10] *Ibid.*, 185–7.

[11] *Ibid.*, 185–6.

be true, he added, even if the corruptibility of human nature is conceded. For as the world is perfect though man be a sinner, so the state can be perfect though the citizen is a sinner.[1] But men are usually bad, he suggested, because they are under bad government; give them a government founded, like Oceana, upon a popular balance and the public interest, and they will quickly acquire the virtue of commonwealthsmen. It is, in fact, good laws that make good men.[2]

As if this vision of Oceana's immortality were not enough, he held forth the dazzling prospect of her great imperial mission. In Machiavelli's terminology, she was to be a commonwealth for increase, not for preservation,[3] and with her citizen army, would aspire to rule the world so that all might know the beneficence of her power.[4] Her method of governing her empire would be Roman, and based on unequal alliances. Her provinces would be made members of a league of which Oceana would be the head, and given autonomy, though remaining subject to levies of men and money. Freedom of conscience was to be granted the people in the provinces, and wherever possible in the conquered territories, the agrarian law was to be instituted.[5] Thus, to all oppressed peoples, Oceana would export the freedom of a commonwealth, and her armies would wield the sword in the interests of God and mankind.[6]

But how were all these proposals to be translated into life? By what means were the institutions of England's greatness to be introduced? At first, Harrington seems to have thought Cromwell might be the agent. Following Machiavelli's opinion, he believed the establishment of a republic best done all at once and by a single person;[7] and so, under the name of Olphaus Megaletor, Cromwell was depicted in *Oceana* as a connoisseur of the ancient republican prudence, erecting, like Lycurgus, a commonwealth which would make his name famous forever.[8] Needless to say, however, the Lord Protector had other fish to fry, and would not—as he was reported to have remarked upon reading Harrington's book—quit the power won by the sword for a little paper shot.[9]

Thereafter, Harrington carried on continuous propaganda, and his views were brought by him and his disciples before the public and the Parliaments that sat after Cromwell's death.[10] Though he won many

---

[1] *Ibid.*, 185–6.
[2] *Ibid.*, 53–4, 56.
[3] *Ibid.*, 133; Machiavelli, *Discourses*, I, 6.
[4] *Oceana*, 193.
[5] *Ibid.*, 195–6.
[6] *Ibid.*, 194.
[7] *Ibid.*, 58; Machiavelli, *Discourses*, I, 6.
[8] *Oceana*, 58–9.
[9] John Toland, *Life of James Harrington, Works*, xvii.
[10] Instances are given in H. F. Russell Smith, *op. cit.*, Ch. IV.

supporters, a host of critics sprang up to engage him.[1] Even among the republicans, those who agreed with him on most matters questioned the wisdom of granting full rights to royalists.[2] By other writers, the presuppositions of his republican model were rejected altogether. The most capable of his opponents was Matthew Wren, son of the Bishop of Ely, devotee of experimental philosophy, and disciple of Hobbes. Wren directed a searching criticism against the agrarian law,[3] and warned that sovereignty divided between senate and assembly would cause quarrels which might destroy the state.[4] He could see no reason why the members of a popular assembly should discern their true interest,[5] and affirmed that there will always be men irrational enough to think it to their advantage to subvert the supreme power.[6] Because of the nature of man, it seemed to him impossible that any government could be perfect or immortal.[7] '. . . the Fate of Empires,' he gloomily remarked, 'has not born a proportion to the Perfection of their Government,' and instanced China succumbing to the Tartars and Rome to the barbarians.[8] He also made the interesting observation that Harrington overvalued Greece and Rome. There is as much to be learned, he said, from the practices of the Babylonians, Persians, and Egyptians, and from recent discoveries made in Chinese history, as from classical antiquity.[9]

But to all such criticisms Harrington was impervious, and the only concession he would make to opponents was one sparing existing life interests in land by postponing the date at which the agrarian law was to take effect.[10] Convinced that his ideas were deductions from necessary premises and that they had nothing in common with the heated slogans of a party, he was sure the future would vindicate him. 'If this Age fails me,' he declared, 'the next will do me Justice.'[11] When he died in 1677, at the age of sixty-six, his position still had many adherents, and his thought in one or another of its aspects continued to exercise influence and to be accorded respect right through the seventeenth and eighteenth centuries. In England, he remained a prime inspiration of such republicanism as continued to exist after 1660; in America, his impress was

---

[1] Among them, Richard Baxter, John Rogers, and Peter Heylyn, Presbyterian, sectarian Fifth-monarchist, and Anglican, respectively; cf. H. F. Russell Smith, *op. cit.*, Ch. V.

[2] See below, Ch. XII.

[3] *Monarchy asserted*, 1659, Ch. XI.

[4] *Ibid.*, 52.

[5] *Ibid.*, 58.

[6] *Ibid.*, 79.

[7] *Ibid.*, Ch. VIII.

[8] *Ibid.*, 123–4.

[9] *Considerations on Mr. Harrington's commonwealth of Oceana*, 1657, 2–3.

[10] *The art of lawgiving, Works*, 409.

[11] *Ibid., Works*, 361.

felt on some of the colonial constitutions; and in France, political theory took note of him down to the great revolution.[1]

Harrington's achievement was to formulate, though in a highly rigid and doctrinaire fashion, the connection between economic and political life. This enabled him to understand that his age had witnessed the birth and the triumph of a new social order. Mistaken in thinking a monarchy impossible in England, he was certainly correct in his belief that the pre-revolutionary kingship was dead and never to be revived. Even if in a form unforeseen by him, the substance of his outlook was verified by political development. Under a monarchy, and without an agrarian law or the other devices he set such store by, England after 1660 did become a kind of commonwealth ruled by the gentry and the mercantile elements which were continually assimilated into it—by the class, that is, which had risen to economic supremacy out of the ruins of feudalism.

Needless to say, Harrington was no democrat. It was to the gentry that he was primarily oriented, and he shared the belief of his class that there was no substitute for good broad acres. He well understood that in such commercial centres as the Low Countries, other forms of wealth might be more important than land. Yet land seemed to him the most stable and solid kind of property, and that is why he made it the basis of his theory of the balance.[2] Because his outlook was basically that of the gentry, his advocacy of popular sovereignty was framed in a distinctly aristocratic spirit. His would have been a popular, but an aristocratically led republic. Though he would have established a wide suffrage and modified landownership with his agrarian law, he hoped by these means to consolidate the political and social influence of the gentry on a secure basis. He had no radical social policy, and such alterations as he proposed to make in agrarian arrangements did not extend to the abolition of the hardships imposed on the peasantry by the vestiges of the manorial system.

Despite Harrington's firm understanding of the forces at work in his time and the confidence which he felt in the practicability of his proposals, his thought was shot through with utopian elements. The latter were inextricably bound up with his richest insights. It was his mechanical philosophy with its peculiar historical emphasis that led him to formulate the theory of the balance, and to apprehend a causal connection between economic and political development. But it was this philosophy also that led him to put forward eternal principles of reason by means of which history could be arrested and an immortal commonwealth established. This was surely utopian. Utopian, too, was his be-

---

[1] For details, see H. F. Russell Smith, *op. cit.*, Ch. VI–IX; R. Koebner, '*Oceana*', *loc. cit.*, 377–96; S. B. Liljegren, *A French draft constitution of 1792 modelled on James Harrington's Oceana*, Lund, 1932; Z. Fink, *op. cit.*, Ch. V.

[2] *Oceana*, 16.

lief in the social harmony his republic would incorporate. By the simple acceptance of popular sovereignty, and by the contrivance of a senate proposing and an assembly deciding, class peace was to be won and the general good secured. The economic order whose victory Harrington intended to perpetuate was to have its cake and eat it, too. It was to permit accumulations of property which, even within the limit set by the agrarian law, were large and substantial; it was to leave untouched manor-lords, monopolies, and most of the other social grievances which the left-wing had repeatedly condemned; yet it was to maintain tranquillity and the common interest. It is scarcely necessary to remark how unreal such a prospect was.

What is most interesting in Harrington is his attempt to give an historical basis to his formula for comprehending politics. He was, of course, no historian, and it is easy to find frequent appearances in his work of tendentiousness and error.[1] Yet within the mechanistic limitations of his philosophy, he succeeded in putting forward a general theory of historical development. History was conceived as process (cut short, it is true, by the establishment of the immortal commonwealth), the cause of whose evolution is contained within itself; and this cause was rendered as something abstract and comprehensive, operating through specific persons and events. In this way, he rose to a degree of sophistication in his historical thinking that makes even the greatest historical work of his time seem primitive by comparison. For the latter, despite its occasional feats in narrative presentation, and with all its wonderful accomplishments in the handling of texts, was too enveloped in empiricism to entertain any but the most commonplace theoretical notions of its subject matter, if it had any such notions at all. Of first-rate historical scholarship in the seventeenth century, there was plenty; of first-rate historical thinking, almost none. Perhaps Harrington's achievement, then, may best be suggested simply by pointing out that we shall learn the nature and causes of the English revolution far better from his work than from Clarendon's great *History of the Rebellion*. The latter is one of the classics of historical literature. Yet despite Clarendon's political experience, his knowledge of concrete circumstance, and his masterly portrayal of character, he understood his time, its significance, and the forces that had shaped it, far less than did the doctrinaire author of *Oceana*.

---

[1] Thus, he maintained, despite ample evidence to the contrary, that Venice had never experienced civil strife (*Oceana*, 31). Moreover, he wrongly characterized the agrarian changes of the sixteenth century as a general diffusion of property among the people. In reality, they were an enriching of the gentry and part of the yeomanry at the expense not only of the feudal dynasts, but of the smaller peasants and copyholders, pushed out by enclosures and harassed by rack-renting.

XII

THE REPUBLICANS

REPUBLICANISM, on the negative side, signified a doctrinaire antagonism to all forms of kingship, and, on the positive side, the quest for a free commonwealth in which the sovereignty of the people would be untrammeled by any species of royal rule, under whatever guise or conditions. It represented the annexation to Independency's political creed of a further article of faith which pronounced anathema on monarchy as such. It was the hardening of anti-royalist principles into the unqualified conviction that monarchy is an inferior form of government either evil in itself, or, at least, evil for England. This is probably the simplest general criterion by which republicanism is to be distinguished from viewpoints in other respects similar. Republicans did not only believe in the sovereignty of the people and its representatives, or merely oppose a Stuart restoration and the protectorate of Cromwell. They condemned, as well, any rule by a single person as fatal to liberty and fit only for slaves.

Owing to the strength of the monarchical tradition in England, republican principles were slow to develop. The process of their growth was not decisively assisted by analagous doctrines to be found in the political thought of classical antiquity. For classical republicanism to take effect, the ground needed to be prepared, and this could not be until considerable tension and conflict had arisen between the monarchy and the social elements that were to make the revolution. During the Tudor period, the agreement of interest between the crown and the gentry offered no room for republican notions. The dominant political theory reflected this agreement by stressing the unity and harmony of the state under the sovereign, and by treating the great prerogatives of the ruler as quite compatible with liberty.[1]

This theory, however, was gradually undermined, as class antagonisms and their attendant religious differences began to sharpen during the reigns of James I and his son. Its place was taken by ideas which

[1] Cf. J. W. Allen, *A history of political thought in the sixteenth century*, London, 1928, Part III.

either exalted Parliament against the crown, or the crown against Parliament.[1] Nevertheless, it required the shock of revolution to destroy the permutations of the organic theory of the Tudor age once and for all. And yet, even under the impress of the civil war, years elapsed until republicanism became a force. In the early 1640s, most of the chief men on the Parliamentary side, both Presbyterian and Independent, regarded their struggle as being waged against Charles I, not monarchy. With all its misdeeds, the monarchy was something to which the revolutionary leaders were bound by sentiment and interest alike. It was, after all, the paramount symbol of order and social hierarchy, and the capstone of a system of privileges which, however they might be rearranged, the Long Parliament had no intention of abolishing. Moreover, in troubled times, the monarchy's existence would help to keep political and social change within what men of substance considered reasonable limits. It was, no doubt, partly for these reasons that such extended efforts were made to reach an agreement with the king long after his armies had been swept from the field and he himself left militarily powerless.[2]

In the forefront on so many other issues, the Levellers were also among the first to call for the abolition of kingship. Since their programme involved the establishment of a democratic commonwealth without crown or House of Lords, they may be considered republicans. But the heart of their position lay in their left-wing principles, and their inferences from the doctrine of popular sovereignty were more sweeping than those of the republican writers of the later 1650s. By 1649, their theory was complete and their movement disrupted, while the republican theory influential in the last years of the revolution had still to be formulated.

Apart from the Levellers, there was also a small minority in the Long Parliament which, at an early date, seems to have desired that monarchy should be dispensed with. One of its outstanding figures was Henry Marten, member for Berkshire. Marten held republican views from the beginning of the struggle, and in 1643, was temporarily expelled from the Commons for some remarks which he made against the king.[3] He and those who entertained similar opinions were characterized by Edmund Ludlow, one of the group, as 'Commonwealthsmen'.[4] It was they

---

[1] Cf. M. Judson, *op. cit.*, Chs. IV–VI.

[2] There is an interesting remark on this point by Clarendon (at that time, plain Mr. Hyde). Writing in 1647, he says that it is unthinkable 'that those who have good fortunes and excellent understandings [should] have a design to dissolve monarchy and change the government which would carry away with it so much of the common law, as would shake their own property and every part of their condition, which made life pleasant to them . . .' (cited in B. H. G. Wormald, *Clarendon*, Cambridge, 1951, 187).

[3] See Marten's life in the *D.N.B.*, *s.v.*

[4] Edmund Ludlow, *op. cit.*, I, 184.

who failed in 1647 to persuade the Commons to pass the vote of no addresses, by which it was proposed to break off all further negotiations with Charles I.[1] These Commonwealthsmen, however, were not political thinkers, and whatever may have been their importance in practical politics, they never gave their ideas any significant expression in the theoretical realm. According to Ludlow, they maintained that 'monarchy is neither good in itself, nor for us', and proposed that Stuart rule should be succeeded by an 'equal commonwealth founded upon consent of the people, and providing for the rights and liberties of all men . . .'.[2] Though these specifications were certainly not met by the revolutionary government of 1649, they nevertheless took part in it,[3] even if with some reservations.[4] But Cromwell's expulsion of the Long Parliament in 1653 alienated them completely, and they became bitter enemies of the protectorate.

Even when the commonwealth had been established, republican thought remained undeveloped and the republicans themselves a minority. The men who created the revolutionary government were not, for the most part, republicans. They put Charles I to death, not out of an antagonism to kingship, but because they had concluded that no other alternative was left them. This was how Cromwell looked at the matter.[5] In 1648, he declared that any form of government might be good in itself and for England, according as Providence should direct.[6] He justified the king's trial in the name of the principles of *salus populi* and the right of resistance to rulers who become tyrannical.[7] At no time was he addicted to republican doctrines. Moreover, though the state of which he was the leading figure was called a commonwealth, this did not mean that it was erected according to systematic republican principles. On the contrary, it was an *ad hoc* creation, the offspring of expediency. It has already been remarked in an earlier chapter that the chief writings in defence of the commonwealth were not written from a re-

[1] S. R. Gardiner, *The great civil war*, III, 366–7.

[2] *Op. cit.*, I, 185.

[3] Marten, for example, was a member of several of the commonwealth's councils of state (*The writings and speeches of Oliver Cromwell*, II, 14 n., 501 n.), and Ludlow was lieutenant-general in Ireland (Edmund Ludlow, *op. cit.*, I, 248–9).

[4] See Ludlow's remarks, *op. cit.*, I, 245–6. There was a definite distrust of Cromwell.

[5] I do not see how any other conclusion can be drawn from the long reluctance of Cromwell and his party to break with the king.

[6] Edmund Ludlow, *op. cit.*, I, 184.

[7] *The writings and speeches of Oliver Cromwell*, I, 697. According to Bishop Burnet (*History of my own time*, ed. O. Airy, 2 vols., Oxford, 1897, I, 70–1), Cromwell drew his ideas of regal power from Buchanan and Mariana. It is worth pointing out that the *Remonstrance of the army* (1648), which Ireton drew up, though it declared the army's determination to break with the king, did not reject the possibility of a future monarchy, provided it was elective; see above, 79.

publican standpoint. There was, of course, a small number of works which praised the commonwealth as a parliamentary republic and superior, therefore, to monarchy.[1] But as theory, these were quite insignificant and need not be noticed.

It was only during the protectorate that republican thought first obtained any noteworthy expression. The reason for this was that Cromwell's military dictatorship made it impossible for the republicans to continue in support of the government as they had hitherto done. Until the protectorate and the events which led to it, they had, on the whole, merely acquiesced in existing arrangements. They had regarded the commonwealth, creature of expediency though it was, as a type of republic, and had failed to offer any constitutional platform of their own. In 1653, they were ready, despite widespread demands for a new election, simply to perpetuate the Long Parliament, which had already been sitting for thirteen years.[2] But when Cromwell expelled the Long Parliament by force in the spring of 1653, they were thrown into unrelenting opposition. To them, that act, and the protectorate which followed it after a few months, marked the end of Parliamentary government in England, the subordination of the civil power to the army, and the fixing of a Cromwellian tyranny upon the country. Their hatred grew when the office of Lord Protector was made hereditary in the family of Cromwell, and when the latter was offered the crown. Now for the first time, they were compelled by the force of circumstance to devise a distinctive political settlement of their own and to give substance to the ideal of the free commonwealth in which they professed to believe.

The violence of the republican reaction to the protectorate may be judged from the indictment which was drawn up by John Wildman, the former Leveller, who had now become a republican plotter. His manifesto, a broadside which was scattered about the streets to incite opposition to the government, was headed, *A Declaration of the Free-born people of England, now in Armes against the Tyrannie . . . of Oliver Cromwell* (1655).[3] Condemning Cromwell as a usurper whose pride and am-

---

[1] See, e.g., Henry Robinson, *A short discourse between monarchical and aristocratical government*, 1649, and John Cook, *Monarchy no creature of Gods making*, 1651. Some other writings between 1649 and 1654 in support of the commonwealth which contain republican ideas are: Eleutherius Philodemius, *The armies vindication*, 1649; N. T., *The resolver continued*, 1649; Albertus Warren, *The royalist reform'd*, 1649; John Hall, *The grounds & reasons of monarchy considered*, 1650; Peter English, *The survey of policy*, 1654.

[2] *The writings and speeches of Oliver Cromwell*, II, 573.

[3] According to Bulstrode Whitelocke (*Memorials*, 2nd ed., London, 1732, 618), Wildman was dictating this manifesto at the time of his arrest by Cromwell's soldiers. M. Ashley is wrong, however, in saying that it was not published (*op. cit.*, 90) for there is a copy dated 16th March 1655 in the Thomason collection, with Thomason's MS. note declaring that it was scattered about the streets.

bition had reduced Englishmen to slavery, Wildman declares that '. . . we could not think it possible that a man of such mean quality and estate as he, should aspire to make himself an absolute lord and tyrant over three potent nations . . .'. But by his false professions of godliness, his hypocritical prayers and fastings, Cromwell deceived the people. Now he is supreme over Parliaments, so that Englishmen have their lives, liberties, and estates merely by his grace and favour. The only course left open, therefore, Wildman urges, is revolution to secure the abolition of all usurped powers and free and successive Parliaments.

A year after this denunciation, the first attack on the protectorate from a Harringtonian standpoint was published. Signed only R. G., this pamphlet was entitled *A copy of a Letter from an Officer of the Army in Ireland* (1656). Curiously enough, it appeared before Harrington's *Oceana*. But it is obviously plagiarized from the latter, and so must have been written by one of Harrington's associates.[1] The *Instrument of Government*, its author says, plainly provides for a monarchy maintained by the sword.[2] Such a régime will never work, because, insensibly, the conditions for a free-state have been created, and against these it is useless to strive. Henry VII and Henry VIII enriched the Commons in order to debase the nobility, with the result that a force was brought into being which struck at the root of monarchy itself. '. . . the riches of the people,' he points out, '. . . is the natural cause of destruction to all Regal States. . . .' And now that the lands of the king, the Church, and the royalists have been redistributed, '. . . we are farther off from a capacity of being governed by Monarchy . . . then when we first began this quarrell. . . .'. The consequence, therefore, is that England must be a commonwealth, for 'it is wholly impossible to make it any other, without an excessive force and violence . . .'.[3] For this reason, the writer tells Cromwell, '. . . nothing can be more pernitious . . . then for you to govern well . . .'. Just as only the happy reign of Augustus Caesar could have given Roman liberty its final blow and opened the way to the monsters that succeeded him, so for Cromwell to be a successful ruler 'would Palliate the assumed Power, and . . . hide it from

---

[1] Professor Wormuth has failed to note (*op. cit.*, 131–2) that *A copy of a letter* is probably a plagiary. *Oceana* appeared in November 1656 (C. H. Firth, *Last years of the protectorate*, I, 68); Thomason's *A copy of a letter* is dated 8th June 1656. Toland says (Harrington, *Works*, xv–xvi) that *A copy of a letter* was thought by many to be plagiarized from Harrington by Henry Neville or John Wildman. The author of the pamphlet declares that he wrote it long before publication, in 1654 (*A copy of a letter*, Postscript, 21); but Thomason, underneath the latter date, wrote, 'A feigned Date'. W. T. Whitley (*A Baptist bibliography*, 2 vols., London, 1916–22, I, 63) ascribed the pamphlet to one Richard Goodgroom, on what grounds I cannot tell. M. Ashley (*op. cit.*, 133) is, of course, wrong in saying that *A copy of a letter* has not survived.

[2] *A copy of a letter*, 3.

[3] *Ibid.*, 9–11.

the just indignation of this age . . . and be a bribing us out of our Rights and Liberties with a seeming justice . . .'.[1]

The most inflammatory republican attack on the government was, of course, the famous pamphlet, *Killing Noe Murder* (1657), written by Edward Sexby and Silius Titus.[2] The latter was a Presbyterian, and the former had been a Leveller spokesman during the 1640s who was now involved in ceaseless plotting against the Lord Protector.[3] *Killing Noe Murder* was in no way novel in its ideas, but it was startling in its unrestrained call for Cromwell's assassination as a glorious act of tyrannicide. The classical influences on it were pronounced, its authors feeling themselves kin to Brutus and Cato, stern republicans who preferred liberty before life.

The pamphlet began by raising three questions: is Cromwell a tyrant? If he is, is it lawful to kill him? If it is lawful, will his demise be beneficial to the nation? Naturally, all three questions were answered in the affirmative. 'Who made thee a Prince . . . over us?' the authors asked Cromwell. 'If the people, where did we meet to doe it? Who took our Subscriptions? To whom deputed we our authority? And when and where did those Deputies make the choice?'[4] It is clear, they said, that Cromwell reveals all the marks of a tyrant, as Plato, Aristotle, and Machiavelli listed them. Both the law of nature and good precedents in history and Scripture leave no doubt of the lawfulness of slaying him.[5] If he is not removed, his rule will debase Englishmen's spirits, and 'by degrees we shall, after the example of our Master, All turne perfidious, Deceitfull, Irreligious, flatterers, and whatever else is villainous and Infamous in Mankind'.[6] Duty and honour, therefore, and safety and interest require that the viper be put to death. Other nations must not be allowed to think meanly of the English, 'as if we were resolved to sit still and have our Eares bored: or that any discouragement . . . can ever make us desist from attempting our Libertie till we have purchased it, either by this Monsters death or by our own'.[7]

These denunciations show how much hatred the republicans felt towards the Cromwellian regime. It had betrayed their hopes and led them back into Egypt. It had made a mockery of the cause for which men had taken up arms against the king. But denunciations were one thing, and constructive schemes of government another. The great need

---

[1] *Ibid.*, 18–19.

[2] On its authorship, see C. H. Firth, '*Killing no murder*', *English historical review*, XVII, 66, 308–11.

[3] *Ibid.*; Sexby was one of the Leveller agitators, and took an effective part in the Putney debates.

[4] *Killing noe murder*, 3.

[5] *Ibid.*, 6–11.

[6] *Ibid.*, 12.

[7] *Ibid.*, 14, 15.

was for the latter, for some solid alternative around which the opponents of kingship and protectorate might, perhaps, be able to unite. Of suggestions to this end put forward while Cromwell lived, two alone were of importance. One, of course, was *Oceana*. The other was *A Healing Question*, by Sir Henry Vane the younger, which appeared in May 1656, several months before Harrington's book.

Vane was one of the revolution's great political leaders, and had been an intimate collaborator of Cromwell's, with whom he broke, however, when the Long Parliament was expelled. Strictly speaking, he ought not, perhaps, to be called a republican, though this is how he is usually characterized.[1] His great political principle was the supremacy of Parliament, and in the 1640s, at least, he does not seem to have thought this incompatible with the fact of kingship. To the last, he opposed all proposals to break off negotiations with Charles I, and during the king's trial and execution, he absented himself from all public business.[2] But in 1649, he took office in the commonwealth's council of state, believing that the king had lost his right by making war against the people's representatives, and that the people were therefore free to frame a government without monarchy.[3] Until thrown into opposition by Cromwell's *coup*, he was an important member of the government. Thereafter, he opposed both the protectorate and a Stuart restoration, and in 1662, was executed as a regicide.[4]

Vane's doctrines were those of the Independents. He maintained an unwavering allegiance to liberty of conscience, and a contractual theory of government. Men, he said, are rational creatures and can give subjection only by their own consent.[5] Government originates in a conveyance of power from the people to their rulers, and when commands are unjust, the people may disobey them.[6] But he did not interpret the notion of the sovereignty of the people in any radical way. In 1653, he voted that only those with real or personal estates worth £200 should possess the suffrage in elections to Parliament.[7] Popular rule he regarded as equivalent, practically speaking, to the supremacy of Parliament, and declared that the common consent of the people as given through their representatives is the only means warranted by the law of nature for ad-

---

[1] Cf., e.g., F. Guizot, *History of Richard Cromwell and the restoration of Charles II*, trans. A. Scoble, 2 vols., London, 1856, *passim*; H. A. L. Fisher, *The republican tradition in Europe*, London, 1911, 43; J. Willcock, *The life of Sir Henry Vane the younger*, London, 1913, 273 *et passim*; G. P. Gooch, *op. cit.*, 239.

[2] J. Willcock, *op. cit.*, 168–9, 173, 179–80.

[3] *The tryal of Sir Henry Vane*, 1662, 101–2, 106–8.

[4] Details in J. Willcock, *op. cit.*, *passim*.

[5] *The retired mans meditations*, 1655, 384–5.

[6] *The tryal of Sir Henry Vane*, 98, 110–12.

[7] *Commons journals*, VII, 273.

mitting the exercise of a supreme authority.[1] He never seems to have considered it possible that the people might justifiably act apart from Parliament. When a prince is to be resisted, he asserted, it must be done only at the call of the 'publick Trustees', 'the Tutors and Maintainers of the State . . .'.[2] Above all, he held that '. . . none are Judges of the Power . . . of Parliaments but themselves. For admit once that their Judgment may be called in question, and disputed by private persons . . . [and] the Fundamentals of Government are plucked up by the roots.'[3]

It is easy to see why, with these views, Vane should have regarded Cromwell's use of the army to expel the Long Parliament as a crime, and the protectorate as a military despotism. To restore Parliament's supremacy seemed to him the prime task of the hour and the chief point on which any republican scheme must centre. It was to achieve this great objective that he advanced the proposals contained in *A Healing Question*.

Vane commenced by pointing out that liberty of conscience and the right to be governed by Parliament together comprised the 'good cause' for which the 'honest party' had engaged against the king.[4] The army, he declared, had fulfilled a great purpose when winning mighty victories over the people's enemies. But it may under no circumstances subordinate the civil power to itself.[5] Its task is to serve the people's safety and welfare, and this it can never do 'while the soveraignty is admitted and placed any where else, then in the whole body of the people that have adhered to the cause, and by them be derived unto their successive Representatives . . .'.[6] In a concession to Cromwell, he remarked that he did not oppose the vesting of executive power in a single person, nor even the promulgation of laws in this single person's name. But no constitution can be compatible with a free-state, he emphasized, unless all persons are made subordinate to the legislative power.[7]

Vane recognized that the turn of events had made extraordinary measures necessary if Parliamentary government were to be restored. He suggested, therefore, the convening of a special assembly freely chosen by the whole body of adherents to the cause. This assembly, he said, will signify 'the people represented in their highest state of Soveraignty, as they have the sword in their hands, unsubjected unto the rules of Civil Government . . .'. Its function will not be that of exercising legislative power, but of framing a fundamental constitution by means of which the people will once more mould themselves 'into a Civil and Politique Incorporation . . .'. To this constitution, those in the honest party will individually subscribe their consent, and thereafter,

---

[1] *The tryal of Sir Henry Vane*, 106. [2] *Ibid.*, 124.
[3] *Ibid.*, 38. [4] *A healing question*, 2–8.
[5] *Ibid.*, 11. [6] *Ibid.*, 15. [7] *Ibid.*, 18.

the sword will subject itself to the civil power, and love, peace, and righteousness prevail.[1]

Here, once more, as before in the Leveller *Agreement of the People*, we see the social-contract idea at work in all its force. Cromwell's rule of the sword, Vane seems to have thought, was a kind of state of nature from which the people could extricate themselves only by the extraordinary constitutional convention which he advocated, and to whose work men would need to give their personal consent. This convention, however, was to represent only the 'honest party'; the people were limited to those who had remained true to the cause. But what were the criteria for precisely distinguishing those in the 'honest party'? And how was the 'honest party' to choose the delegates who would represent it? Vane did not even raise these questions, much less answer them. No doubt, he meant to include only those who had supported liberty of conscience and opposed the rule of a single person. Royalists, Presbyterians, and Cromwellians had all lost their birthright by aiding tyranny, and could have no representation—at least, temporarily—in any commonwealth which the assembly of the 'honest party' would frame. But when, and under what stipulations would the excluded elements be finally brought in? On all these matters, Vane was silent.

Despite his vagueness, Vane's advocacy of a free-state confined to the 'honest party' took account of a contemporary reality which was inescapable. His scheme was based on the recognition that if rights were granted to all, even to enemies of the republic, the latter would use the opportunity thus provided to reintroduce the Stuarts. For this reason, no commonwealth could be an equal one until adequate security for its survival was assured. It was on just this vital point that Harrington disagreed, and as we have seen, his republic made no distinctions between the parties, all men being at once granted the same rights. This was to become the chief immediate cause of disagreement among republican writers.

While Cromwell lived, however, censorship and repression prevented much discussion of this and other matters. But in September 1658, he died, and was succeeded by his son. Richard Cromwell had neither his father's ability nor any control over the army, and within a few months he was forced to resign his power. Thus the protectorate drifted to an inglorious end. All the hitherto-submerged opposition had now come into the open, and there began a babel of argument and controversy concerning the government which should rule the disordered and uneasy country. While the anti-royalist politicians in Parliament and the army successively quarrelled with one another and blended into shifting and momentary alliances, numbers of republican pamphlets appeared, most of them merely brief effusions, but all expressing the hope that a

[1] *Ibid.*, 20–1.

154

free commonwealth would at last be instituted. So 1659, the year of anarchy, became republicanism's *annus mirabilis*, as England seemed a *tabula rasa* upon which any constitution-maker might try his hand.

Because of the scientific foundation upon which Harrington's thought seemed to rest, he exercised immeasurably greater influence upon the republicans than did any other writer. It is, indeed, no exaggeration to say that he was the creator of republican theory. The small number of important republican writings of the year 1659 all stand within the circle of his ideas. His views were echoed in many a pamphlet, and the doctrine of the balance accepted as an unanswerable argument for a commonwealth. An anonymous writer remarked,

'. . . it is evident that we are now upon a Popular balance . . . and being so, cannot admit of any other form of Government then such as is Popular, without violence and force offered to propriety: which once rightly perceived . . . would . . . soon put a stop to the proceedings of the most violent Assertors of Monarchy. . . .'[1]

His scheme for a commonwealth was brought before the public and urged upon Parliament. A statement published by a prominent group of Harringtonians, after demonstrating from the balance the futility of attempting to re-establish monarchy,[2] advocated the lodging of supreme power in a senate proposing and an assembly resolving.[3] Other writings offered similar proposals for a Harringtonian bicameral legislature.[4] In July 1659, the same demand, together with suggestions for rotation and a state church, was presented to Parliament by a group of Harrington's supporters.[5]

Within the framework of Harrington's fundamental principles, extensive reforms were suggested. Among the most interesting were those embodied by William Sprigge, a fellow of Lincoln College, Oxford, in his *A Modest Plea For An Equal Common-wealth Against Monarchy*

---

[1] *A commonwealth and commonwealthsmen, asserted*, 1659, 5; cf. *XXV queries modestly and humbly propounded*, 1659, 11. It is worth noting that, in the life of her husband which she wrote after the restoration, Mrs. Hutchinson explains the cause of the civil war in terms of Harrington's theory of the balance, with which she was obviously familiar (Lucy Hutchinson, *Memoirs of colonel Hutchinson*, Everyman ed., London, 1936, 59–60).

[2] *The armies dutie*, 1659, 14–23. This bore the initials of Henry Marten, Henry Neville, John Lawson, John Wildman, John Jones, and Samuel Moyer.

[3] *Ibid.*, 24–8.

[4] *A model of a democraticall government*, 1659, 3–4; *The leveller*, 1659, 7. The latter pamphlet may be, as M. Ashley has suggested (*op. cit.*, 136–7), by John Wildman. Harrington said its principles had been gathered from *Oceana* (*The art of lawgiving, Works*, 404).

[5] *The humble petition of divers well-affected persons*, 1659, 8–9.

1659).[1] Sprigge believed that the balance of property made monarchy mpossible in England,[2] but he warned that the traditional institutions which support monarchy must also be uprooted, if a true free-state is to be instituted.[3] He then went on to deal critically with problems that Harrington had almost wholly neglected. Because he thought tithes an exploitation of the free man's labour, he proposed their abolition, though with reasonable compensation for impropriators.[4] He denounced lawyers as 'Professors . . . of iniquity that live upon the sins of the people', and, to reduce the cause of litigiousness, called for the setting up of county registers to record all property transfers.[5] He advocated the establishment of workhouses as the most humane and efficient means of poor-relief, for '. . . the deafness of this uncharitable age to the cryes of the poor', he said, 'is one of the crying sins of this Land'.[6] He also suggested elaborate reforms in the universities. Their administration, he held, should be democratized, and colleges founded in various parts of the country. Moreover, the curriculum should be overhauled to include science, useful arts, and modern languages, so that students might be enabled to make 'new and further discoveries into the America of nature . . .'.[7]

On some subjects, Sprigge was more radical than Harrington, or disagreed with him altogether. Thus, he opposed a professional clergy and a national church as infringements upon liberty of conscience.[8] He intended the agrarian law not merely as a way of preserving the popular balance, but to check the covetousness of the rich. How can there be a righteous government, he asked, 'while those worms of the earth, that Possess the greatest dunghills, must be our Senators, because they have the greatest rout of tenants to voyce them into the saddle of authority'?[9] He desired, too, that primogeniture and entail be abolished, and the old Kentish custom of gavelkind restored, whereby land would descend in equal shares to all the sons.[10] And to strengthen the freedom of the agrarian population, he believed that all tenures of land should be converted into freehold.[11]

[1] This appeared anonymously, but Sprigge's authorship is attested by Anthony Wood, *Athenae Oxonienses*, IV, 560.

[2] *A modest plea for an equal common-wealth*, 12–14.

[3] *Ibid.*, To the reader [1–2].

[4] *Ibid.*, 39–41.

[5] *Ibid.*, 71–5. It is an interesting fact that a great royalist nobleman, the Duke of Newcastle, made the same proposal; cf. The Duchess of Newcastle, *The life of William Cavendish, duke of Newcastle*, ed. C. H. Firth, London, 1886, 240.

[6] *Ibid.*, 43–4.

[7] *Ibid.*, 49–55.

[8] *Ibid.*, 21–3.

[9] *Ibid.*, 86.

[10] *Ibid.*, 58–70.

[11] *Ibid.*, 56.

The same reforming zeal which animated Sprigge was also at work, though with more tenderness to the landowning class, in the author, regrettably anonymous, of *Chaos: Or, A Discourse, Wherein Is presented . . . a Frame of Government by way of a Republique* (1659). The writer did not by any means take over Harrington's views wholesale, though he reproduced such details as rotation, the ballot, and a modified form of agrarian law.[1] His great concern was with removing the irrationalities in the law and economic life, and it was to these subjects that he devoted most attention. He began by outlining a vast scheme for a system of registry offices throughout the land, arranged hierarchically from the parish through the hundred and shire up to a national registry office at Westminster. In these were to be recorded within a fixed date all titles to land, records of debt, contracts of hire, and other agreements. In this way, he thought, fraud would be reduced to a minimum, litigiousness checked, and a considerable revenue derived from the fees which would be paid for entries made in the registers.[2] Parallel with the registries was to run a series of courts culminating in a 'National Registerial Court'. By establishing long court terms and setting a limit to the period in which replies to actions could be made, he expected that justice would be rendered quick and easy.[3]

Besides these innovations, he proposed extensive changes in the methods of holding and transmitting land. Primogeniture was to be abolished, and the freedom of inheritance thereby achieved would operate, he expected, with the effect of an agrarian law.[4] All copyholds were to be converted into freeholds by reasonable composition with lords of manors, and reliefs, heriots, ancient services, and manorial jurisdictions were also to be done away with, though with compensation to lords.[5] As his willingness to grant compensation shows, the author had no desire to harm landowners. In recognition of their importance, he suggested that only those with incomes of £1,000 per year or more should be eligible for election to Parliament as county members.[6] Moreover, he thought it good that there should be a nobility based on wealth, and that Parliament should confer lordships on persons with £10,000 per year and knighthoods on those with £1,000.[7] It is difficult to see, however, of what advantage any agrarian law would be which permitted incomes of £10,000.

Among the republicans generally, the most pressing problem was to

---

[1] *Chaos*, 42, 53–4, Preface [3]. The scheme for the national church (*ibid.*, 53–4) is much less tolerant than Harrington's, and resembles a Presbyterian establishment.
[2] *Ibid.*, 5–19, 24.
[3] *Ibid.*, 32–3.
[4] *Ibid.*, 25, Preface [3].
[5] *Ibid.*, 26.
[6] *Ibid.*, 44.
[7] *Ibid.*, 44.

reconcile their allegiance to a free commonwealth with the generally accepted fact that in any open election, men would be returned who favoured a Stuart restoration. An anonymous writer put the issue clearly when he remarked, 'it is hard if the people cannot be trusted with Election'; yet if trusted now, he said, they would 'elect such as would deprive them of the blessed Government of a Free-State'.[1] To deal with this problem, it was widely recognized that special provision would have to be made, and that it would be utterly impractical to ignore the distinction between the friends of the republic and its enemies. It was, of course, suggested that until royalists should prove their approbation of the government, the franchise should be denied them.[2] Besides this, the commonest recommendation advanced was for the institution of some extraordinary constitutional device charged with the duty of safeguarding the state. Some Gloucestershire republicans proposed that at every election to Parliament, the well-affected should also elect a special body to sit during the session and take all necessary steps in the event that the Parliament men should promote any measures against the commonwealth.[3] To the same end, a petition from officers of the army advocated the establishment of a 'select Senate, Co-ordinate in power' with the representative body, and composed of godly and faithful persons adhering to the cause.[4] By Edmund Ludlow, the suggestion was put forward for a twenty-one man commission to be called the Conservators of Liberty and among whose duties would be to see that 'the government should not be altered from a commonwealth by setting up a King, single person, or House of Peers'.[5] Even some of the Harringtonians, though they would deprive no one of his civil rights, were prepared to graft on to the republic's constitution a temporary committee of twelve vested with the responsibility of seizing anyone suspected of treasonable practices against the state.[6]

There could be no doubt of the existence of a real danger in 1659 of a Stuart restoration effected by force. Presbyterians were plotting with royalists, a widespread insurrection was in preparation, and though it did not materialize as planned, in August, the royalist, Sir George

[1] J. S., *Government described*, 1659, 8.

[2] Cf., e.g., *Englands safety in the laws supremacy*, 1659, 17–18, and *A model of a democraticall government*, 8.

[3] The Gloucestershire address was reprinted in *ΠΑΝΑΡΜΟΝΙΑ, or, the agreement of the people revived*, 1659, 1 ff. Despite its title, this anonymous pamphlet is not a Leveller writing, as Professor Wormuth has erroneously asserted (*op. cit.*, 149). It is chiefly a plea for liberty of conscience by a Socinian, and its author was very likely the well-known Socinian, John Biddle, who himself came from Gloucestershire. I am indebted to Professor A. S. P. Woodhouse for making available to me a photostat of this tract.

[4] *The humble petition and address of the officers of the army*, 1659, 10–11.

[5] Edmund Ludlow, *op. cit.*, II, 172.

[6] *The humble petition of divers well-affected persons*, 10–12.

Booth, rose in Cheshire.[1] This rebellion was put down, but it was a warning of what might happen in the future, and with larger success, unless the greatest vigilance was exercised. All such signs Harrington himself refused to take seriously. Throughout 1659, he reiterated his opposition to any curtailment of privileges in the republican constitution. Even by his own principles, a monarchy could be maintained against the balance through the employment of force. Nevertheless, he had no fears. 'In the present case of England,' he said, 'commonwealthsmen may fail thro want of art, but royalists must fail thro want of matter; the former may miss thro impotence, the latter must thro impossibility.'[2] He attacked the army officers' proposal for a select senate, warning that such a body might become an instrument for minority control; and he pointed out that there could be no danger in free elections, since no one could contract an interest to destroy the republic.[3]

It was Harrington's fatuous refusal to concede any danger of a restoration which precipitated the disagreement between him and Henry Stubbe, his ablest disciple. Stubbe was a character, a remarkable personage in his own right, and need not stand in Harrington's shadow. Described by Anthony Wood as 'the most noted person of his age that these late times have produced',[4] he was only twenty-eight when the restoration occurred. As a boy he was taken up because of his intellectual gifts by Sir Henry Vane the younger, with whose aid he was sent to Christ Church, Oxford. Though a republican, he was, like Harrington, a great admirer of Hobbes and the new philosophy. It was he who undertook the task of translating the *Leviathan* into Latin,[5] and when the great philosopher got involved in controversy with the Oxford mathematicians, Stubbe defended him.[6] He was also uncompromising in his support for liberty of conscience, urging toleration not only for Anglicans, Catholics, and Quakers,[7] but even writing a work in vindica-

---

[1] F. Guizot, *op. cit.*, I, 186–9, 204–9.

[2] *The ways and means whereby an equal and lasting commonwealth may be suddenly introduc'd*, 1659, *Works*, 507.

[3] *A discourse upon this saying: the spirit of the nation is not yet to be trusted with liberty*, 1659, *Works*, 570–1.

[4] *Athenae Oxonienses*, III, 1067. Stubbe's life is recounted in the *D.N.B.*, *s.v.*

[5] He translated at least ten chapters; see F. Thompson, 'Lettres de Stubbe', *Archive de philosophie*, XII, 2.

[6] Θερσίτης ἀκριτόμυθος. *Or an exact account of the grammatical part of the controversy betwixt Mr. Hobbes and J. Wallis D.D.*, 1657.

[7] *An essay in defence of the good old cause*, 1659, 131–2; *Malice rebuked*, 1659, 37; *A light shining out of darkness*, 1659. This last work appeared anonymously in two somewhat different editions. It is accepted as Stubbe's by Wood, *Athenae Oxonienses*, III, 1076–7, and F. Madan, *Oxford books*, III, 2428. *A light* contains a notable defence of the Quakers, and though not mentioned in Professor Jordan's study of religious toleration, is probably one of the finest writings on liberty of conscience that appeared during the revolution.

tion of Mohammedanism.[1] He desired toleration partly because he felt a Hobbesian scepticism as to the possibility of ascertaining religious truth.

'The unsupplyable defect of common evidence in the delivery of Spirituall matters [he declared] is of that nature, as it would suffice to the enforceing of a Toleration. For though it be a confessed principle that whatsoever the prime verity doth say is an uncontroulable truth, yet the course whereby he discovers himself . . . is followed by so much ambiguity . . . as inquisitive men, and sober, if destitute of the highest gifts may upon a rationall ground . . . suspect the sincerity [of] the Revelation in the word, and if he assent thereunto strongly and firmly, he is rather to be accounted resolved then certaine.'[2]

It is a sign of the persuasiveness of Harrington's theory that it obtained Stubbe's support. 'I admire [Harrington's] modell,' he said, 'and am ready to crye out as if it were the pattern in the Mount. . . .'[3] With Harrington, he considered that the fact of sovereignty would be least dangerous in a republic. '. . . in all Governments,' he pointed out, 'some must be Judges in their own Case. . . . The question is . . . seeing Arbitrary power . . . must reside somewhere, where then is it best fixed? I suppose in the people; and that it is . . . impossible for a Democracy to be partial. . . .'[4] 'I never yet read of a Monarchy,' he asserted, 'which did not in its tendency corrupt the best men; nor can I imagine a regulated Democracy, upon a ballance, ballot, and rotation of Governours which will not amend the worst of men.'[5]

But he thought it mere folly on Harrington's part to imagine that the republic could at once be free from the menace of a royal restoration. A people under good orders, Stubbe declared, and

'convinced of their interest in this, or ignorant of any other Government may be serene and prudent, voide of discord. . . . But a people unconvinced of their interest, nor unanimous in any common concern . . . not instructed in, yea averse from a Republick, that such a people put into orders (in which no over-ruling power must retain them, for they must be their own army) should be serene and calme, it is unimaginable. . . .'[6]

[1] *An account of the rise and progress of Mahometanism*, first published from Stubbe's MS., London, 1911.

[2] *An essay in defence of the good old cause*, 40–1; cf. his *Legends no histories*, 1670, Preface [13], where he says that he was addicted to the new philosophy partly because he hoped it would render the clergy contemptible and destroy the authority of antiquity in spiritual affairs.

[3] *An essay in defence of the good old cause*, Preface [14].

[4] *Ibid.*, Preface [40–1].

[5] *Malice rebuked*, 41.

[6] *An essay in defence of the good old cause*, Preface [16].

At present, he warned,

'it is not in the interest of all . . . to promote a Republick: nor are all whose interest it is . . . sufficiently convinced thereof: It is evident then what course must be taken, unlesse we limit our Commonwealth unto the honest and faithfull party, leaving the residue so much liberty as they are now capable of, or may prove hereafter.'[1]

Here Stubbe was proposing exactly what Vane had suggested three years before. But, as we shall see, he was clearer concerning the methods by which the honest party was to be secured in its conquest. The denial of rights to disaffected persons he justified by a contractual theory of government which, in some of its aspects, would appear to owe something to Hobbes. All men are born free and equal, he said, and it is the people who erect and set limits to government. When a government is broken, men are thrown back into their natural freedom, and then the victorious part of them may set up a new government. In such a case, the new power must give as much liberty as is compatible with its survival, and no more. To grant a liberty which may result in the destruction of the supreme authority is not merely folly, it is a breach of trust, because the sovereign power may not throw away the sovereignty with which it has been vested. Moreover, to preserve their government, those who had brought it to power may suppress those who oppose it; and in doing so, their conduct should not be judged too rigorously, for within a wide latitude, all their actions taken in self-defence are just.[2] The people's good, it is true, is the end of all government. But the question is, who are the people? Only those, Stubbe answers, 'who upon the erection of a Government have impoured the Legislatours to act, being avowedly ready to stand by and uphold them in their actings'. In England, the people include only those who supported Parliament in its time of trial against Booth's rebellion.[3] As long as those who are not part of the people acquiesce simply because of force, and withhold their free consent, the republic has no obligation to grant them privileges.[4] If it should do so, its constitution, however good, will be of no avail in saving it from destruction.[5]

What was required, Stubbe thought, was to accept Harrington's model, but with special provision made to guard the state against subversion.[6] For this purpose, he offered his own scheme. All persons who are part of the people, he suggested, should be listed in county registers

---

[1] *Ibid.*, Preface [19].
[2] *A letter to an officer of the army concerning a select senate*, 1659, 49–50.
[3] *Ibid.*, 52–3.
[4] *Ibid.*, 55.
[5] *Ibid.*, 57.
[6] *An essay in defence of the good old cause*, Preface [25].

as Liberators of their country. These, and these only, would be permitted the use of arms. Of the working classes, he seems to have had little fear, for he was willing that they should be given arms and admitted to privileges as a matter of course, after a period of time had elapsed. But gentlemen were not to be admitted until they had proved their affection to the commonwealth, and then they were to be noted in the registers as 'imprivileged'. Finally, the armies in England, Scotland, and Ireland were to be included among the Liberators.[1] This done, the militia of the three nations would elect, at their musters, a number of deputies, who would, in turn, choose from their ranks a senate of Conservators of the liberties of England. The senators so named were to sit for life, but they were to be subject to the biennial investigation of a commission elected by the militia. Both senate and commission of investigation, Stubbe believed, should be composed only of persons from the parties which support the commonwealth: Independents, Baptists, Fifth-monarchy men, and Quakers. The senate was not to have any executive or legislative function, its sole task being that of securing the republic in its constitution. In discharging this duty, it was to have supervision over the militia, the ministry, and the universities.[2]

Once this platform was put into effect, then Stubbe believed that Parliament might be elected by the entire nation. And short of infringing on the fundamental constitution and the senate's authority, it was to have the full law-making power. But for greater security, the members of the senate were also to sit in Parliament.[3]

This scheme was, perhaps, the most practicable of any suggested in the year 1659. It attempted to combine some of the good features Harrington's republic was acknowledged to possess with measures designed to reduce the danger of a restoration. That event, as Stubbe recognized, could never be averted if the people as a whole desired it; but it might be prevented if it were merely the aim of a conspiratorial minority.[4] Moreover, Stubbe's platform offered scope for the exercise of the right of suffrage by all at an early date. Its extraordinary senate was to be perpetual, just as Milton's would have been; and it is not unlikely, in fact, that the poet borrowed some of the notions in *The Readie & Easie Way* from Stubbe. But the latter, contrary to Milton's republican constitution, placed the legislative power in a successively elected popular assembly, and provided for periodic investigations of the senate lest that body grow dangerous.

It was, however, too late for such schemes, whatever their merit. The leading anti-royalist politicians who might have tried to effect them were

---

[1] *A letter to an officer of the army concerning a select senate*, 59–60.
[2] *Ibid.*, 60–2.
[3] *Ibid.*, 62–3.
[4] *Ibid.*, 65, 67 (mispaged).

completely divided. The unrest and uncertainty of the time opened the way to a restoration as the means by which stable government could be re-established. The substantial economic elements in the City of London and elsewhere were ready for Charles II. His coming, it was well-understood from all signs, would result in no white terror, in no undoing of the extensive property changes which the revolution had accomplished. As for the people, they were, perhaps, not actively in favour of a restoration. But they were not against it, and could accept it with acclaim when it occurred. The republicans were hopelessly isolated and outnumbered. They had lost their chance long before. Sixteen hundred and forty-nine was the moment when the free commonwealth should have begun to take shape; in 1659, their opportunity had passed. The period of Cromwell's despotism had bred a growing distaste for the revolution which could not be overcome by attractive visions of a republican government. Years of strife and of religious enthusiasm yearning towards a promised land which was never reached and lay always over the horizon, generated at last a widespread fatigue against which republican zeal was powerless. Thus the heyday of the republicans was brief— a few short months during 1659, while the restoration cast its lengthening shadow. Thenceforth, though republicanism lived on,[1] it survived primarily as an element merged in the thought of the Whigs, its principles helping to inspire the followers of Shaftesbury and those who, by placing the crown under strict Parliamentary control, would reduce the King of England to the impotent status of a Duke of Venice.

[1] Details in Z. Fink, *op. Cit.*, Chs. V–VII.

163

XIII

THOMAS HOBBES

Few thinkers have given sharper offence to the prejudices of their critics than has Hobbes. Assailed in his own time by a host of writers,[1] his ideas evoked an antagonism which has followed him until the present and resulted in obscuring the true nature of his greatness. No one who read him, of course, could fail to perceive the marvellous power of his mind. But too often, his supremacy has been held to consist in an unmatched ability at playing the devil's advocate. Even to-day, some of his commentators feel the same urgency to refute him as did many of his contemporaries. They seek eagerly for contradictions in his argument, and in their anxiety to expose his errors, ascribe notions to him that a disinterested scrutiny of his work fails to disclose. Of this order are the accusations that he equated might with right, or that his political theory is totalitarian.[2]

Despite the continuing animosity which has been felt for Hobbes's ideas, in recent years, nevertheless, a new estimate and a new understanding of his achievement have been steadily emerging. The reasons for this are no part of my subject, though they would themselves form an interesting episode in the intellectual history of the first half of the twentieth century. Partly, perhaps, they have to do with the realization by the generation which experienced the first world war and the rise

---

[1] The widespread discussion of Hobbes's thought in the seventeenth century, till now a neglected episode in the history of English political philosophy, is treated in the recent study by John Bowle, *Hobbes and his critics*, London, 1951. Mr. Bowle exaggerates the importance of Hobbes's critics. Very few of them, I think, understood what the philosopher was getting at.

[2] See, e.g., C. E. Vaughan, *Studies in the history of political philosophy*, 2 vols., Manchester, 1925, I, Ch. 2; B. Landry, *Hobbes*, Paris, 1930; J. Vialatoux, *La cité de Hobbes*, Paris and Lyon, 1935; J. W. Gough, *The social contract*, Oxford, 1936, Ch. VIII; W. T. Jones, *Masters of political thought*, London, 1947, Ch. 4. On Hobbes's supposed totalitarianism, see the excellent remarks of R. Capitant, 'Hobbes et l'état totalitaire', *Philosophie du droit et de sociologie juridique*, Nos. 1–2, 1936. A full and annotated bibliography of modern works on Hobbes will be found in Z. Lubienski, *Die Grundlagen des ethisch-politischen Systems von Hobbes*, Munich, 1932, 275–88.

of fascism that the fabric of human society is more fragile, and the brutishness of the state of nature less distant, than had formerly been imagined.[1] However that may be, one indication of the changing attitude towards Hobbes lies in the description nowadays of the *Leviathan* as 'a work of gigantic stature',[2] 'the greatest, perhaps the sole, masterpiece of political philosophy in the English language'.[3] Another, and more important indication lies in the characterization of Hobbes, so contrary to traditional evaluations, as, in basic respects, the philosopher of liberalism,[4] the thinker who 'with a clarity never previously and never subsequently attained, made the "right of nature", i.e. the justified claims of the individual, the basis of political philosophy'.[5] Such a judgement may at first sight appear surprising. But it will be less so, even apart from any consideration of Hobbes's text, when it is remembered how strong a connection existed between him and the philosophic radicals, or utilitarians, of the nineteenth century. The latter were the van of the liberal and middle-class reform movement of their time; hence it is significant that they should have been so much under Hobbes's influence, even while differing from him in their preference for popular government. Bentham and James Mill, it has been said, lived in his shadow all their intellectual lives.[6] One of the group, Sir William Molesworth, published the first complete edition of Hobbes's works and dedicated it to his fellow-radical, the politician and historian, George Grote.[7] And if we wish to see at a glance how much the reforming aims of the utilitarians could find justification in Hobbes's theories, we need only read Grote's essay defending the philosopher against his detractors.[8]

With Hobbes, as later with the utilitarians, it was in political philosophy that his accomplishment was greatest and his influence most widely felt. This was as it should be; for despite his absorption in other

[1] See the remarks of R. G. Collingwood, *The new Leviathan*, Oxford, 1942, Preface, iv.

[2] *Ibid.*, iv.

[3] M. Oakeshott, Introduction to Hobbes's *Leviathan*, *Blackwell's political texts*, Oxford, 1946, viii.

[4] Cf., e.g., F. Tönnies, *Thomas Hobbes Leben und Lehre*, 3rd enlarged ed., Stuttgart, 1925, 222; L. Strauss, 'Quelques remarques sur la science politique de Hobbes', *Recherches philosophiques*, II, 1932–3, 609–10; M. Oakeshott, *op. cit.*, lvii.

[5] L. Strauss, *The political philosophy of Hobbes*, 156.

[6] J. Plamenatz, *The English utilitarians*, Oxford, 1949, 2. The link between Hobbes and the utilitarians is discussed in *ibid.*, 10–15; and see also the remarks of T. Parsons, *The structure of social action*, New York, 1937, 89–94.

[7] Except as otherwise stated, I cite from this edition of Molesworth's, 16 vols., London, 1839–45. Citations are *E.W.* when the reference is to Hobbes's English works, *L.W.* when the reference is to his Latin works.

[8] 'Notice of Sir William Molesworth's edition of the works of Hobbes', *The minor works of George Grote*, ed. A. Bain, London, 1873.

branches of philosophical study and his outstanding place in the history of materialism, it was political knowledge which he regarded as the crown of wisdom. Like Bacon, he held that 'The end of knowledge is power', and the end and scope of philosophy 'the commodity of human life'.[1] Hence, he declared that 'not he that hath skill in geometry, or any other science speculative, but only he that understandeth what conduceth to the good and government of the people, is called a wise man'.[2] There is, in consequence of this attitude, a pragmatic intention permeating all of his work, which alone can account for the amount of attention he bestowed on political problems. His admiring friend and biographer, John Aubrey, remarked that Hobbes's interest in the conflict between crown and Parliament was so great that 'for ten yeares together his thoughts were much, or almost altogether, unhinged from the mathematiques';[3] and it is significant that though in Hobbes's tripartite division of philosophy, the theory of the state forms the third and concluding section, in order of writing it was treated first, and at much greater length, than the earlier sections dealing, respectively, with body in general and man as a particular kind of body.[4] In comparison with *The Elements of Law*, the *De Cive*, and the *Leviathan*, the bulk of the *De Corpore* and *De Homine* is not great; and if the former is a composition of the highest order, the latter seems sketchy and inadequate to its subject.

The strong interest which, as I have tried to show, politics had for Hobbes, did not first express itself during the controversies raging just before 1640, presaging the civil war soon to come. It had already been given voice previously in his career, though at that time in connection with the study of history rather than philosophy. In 1629, he put forth as his earliest published work a translation of Thucydides, believing the Greek writer's masterpiece to be a perfect fulfillment of history's function, which he conceived as the instruction of men, and especially of great personages, in the prudent management of affairs.[5] It is not unlikely, though it is, of course, only conjecture, that Thucydides's memorable analysis of the terrible effects of the Corcyran revolution and his description of the type of revolutionary man were important in impressing upon Hobbes's mind the conviction that rebellion is the most dreadful of political evils. Whether this was so or not, by the time his

[1] *De corpore*, 1655, *E.W.*, I, 7; cf. Bacon, *Novum organum*, I, aphorism 81.

[2] *The elements of law* (circulated in MS. from 1640, first printed in 1650), ed. F. Tönnies, Cambridge, 1928, 140; cf. *De cive*, 1642, Preface, *E.W.*, II, xiv.

[3] *Op. cit.*, I, 333.

[4] Cf. *De cive*, Preface, *E.W.*, II, xix–xx.

[5] Thucydides, *History*, trans. Thomas Hobbes, *E.W.*, VIII, Dedicatory epistle, iv–v, To the reader, vii. Hobbes's interest in history and Thucydides is discussed by L. Strauss, *The political philosophy of Hobbes*, Ch. VI. R. Schlatter, 'Thomas Hobbes and Thucydides', *Journal of the history of ideas*, VI, 3, adds little to Strauss's analysis.

translation appeared, he had turned his attention away from history to philosophy, henceforth the principal mode for the expression of his ideas. This shift followed upon the familiar incident, related by Aubrey,[1] of how, in 1628, at the age of forty, Hobbes came by chance upon Euclid's *Elements* and was thereafter drawn into the great movement of thought called the new philosophy, which was associated with such names as Bacon, Galileo, and Descartes. The aim of this movement, whose ideas were developed in close connection with the physical sciences, was the explanation of nature in terms of motion by means of the application of mathematics. For Hobbes, this encounter was decisive. In his youth, while a student at Oxford, he had been taught the Aristotelian philosophy of the schools, but tells us that he abandoned its doctrines in disgust when he discerned that wise men derided them as vain and empty.[2] It was after this that he began to read classical poets and historians and to project his translation of Thucydides.[3] So when his appetite for philosophical inquiry revived, it was because he saw in the new philosophy a way of proceeding free from the logomachies of a decadent scholasticism and capable of arriving at exact truth.

It was under the influence, then, of the scientific movement of the seventeenth century that Hobbes became a philosopher. Three consequences, broadly speaking, ensued from this fact: he was led to regard mathematics as the model upon which philosophical inquiry must form itself;[4] he was led to seek for mechanical principles as the universal explanation of phenomena;[5] and he was led to a thoroughgoing materialism which made body, or matter, the subject of philosophy, for 'that which is not Body', he said, 'is no part of the Universe: And because the Universe is All, that which is no part of it, is Nothing. . .'.[6] In this repertoire of ideas, political theory was assigned its place. Like natural philosophy, its subject, the commonwealth, is body, with this peculiarity, however, that it is artificial body, something not existing by nature but made by the wills of men. The commonwealth needed to be understood, therefore, in relation to its cause, the disposition of human beings.[7] Now reasoning in philosophy, Hobbes declared, is exclusively in terms of cause and effect.[8] This he called, after Galileo, the resolutive-composi-

---

[1] *Op. cit.*, I, 332.

[2] *Vita Tho. Hobbes, L. W.*, I, xiii.

[3] *Ibid., L.W.*, I, xiii–xiv.

[4] Cf., e.g., *The elements of law*, Epistle dedicatory, xvii, 50–1.

[5] *De corpore, E.W.*, I, 69–70, where Hobbes calls motion the universal cause. On this subject see the valuable study of F. Brandt, *Thomas Hobbes' mechanical conception of nature*, Copenhagen, 1928.

[6] *De corpore, E.W.*, I, 10; *Leviathan*, 1651 (I cite from the reprint of the edition of 1651, Oxford, 1943), 524.

[7] *De corpore., E.W.* I, 11.

[8] *Ibid., E.W.*, I, 3.

tive method. According to it, one could begin either with a phenomenon which is an effect, and by resolving it into its components, find out its causes, or with a cause, and by composition, or deduction, demonstrate its effects.[1] As applied to human society, this method presented the alternatives of commencing with the commonwealth and demonstrating it by rational argument to be an effect consequent on the nature of man, or with the nature of man as a cause which is shown to result in the commonwealth as an effect. Hobbes's way in his political writings was the latter,[2] but either way is possible, since both man and the commonwealth are equally given as objects of investigation.

What relationship is there, we may ask, between Hobbes's adoption of the standpoint of the new philosophy and the innovative and untraditional character of his political thought? We know that in his own view, the two were connected, for he compares himself to such great inaugurators as Copernicus, Galileo, and Harvey, and coolly lays claim to be the founder of politics as a science.[3] Not long ago, however, convincing grounds were advanced by Professor Strauss for believing that Hobbes's conception of the antithesis between unjust vanity and just fear of death, which is of great importance in his moral theory, antedated and was quite independent of his interest in the new philosophy.[4] From this, Professor Strauss has concluded that the new philosophy did not affect Hobbes's argument, but only his method of reasoning and presentation; and he has contended also that the employment of this method was a detriment because it led Hobbes to renounce discussion as to the end of the state and as to standards, or, at least, to discuss these questions in an inadequate manner.[5]

Now I do not think Hobbes did, in fact, fail to discuss these questions, and quite adequately, too. But as to the relation between his politics and his mechanical-materialist standpoint, there is, of course, a respect in which we could consider them to be wholly unconnected, as he himself, in a sense, admits when he tells us that the principles of politics can be derived independently and without reference to the behaviour of body, or matter, in general.[6] This is merely evidence that

---

[1] Ibid., E.W., I, Ch. 6, 'Of method'; cf. E. Cassirer, Die Philosophie der Aufklärung, Tübingen, 1932, 341–2, and L. Strauss, The political philosophy of Hobbes, 151. It should be pointed out that, by cause, Hobbes did not mean a fact which is experimentally proved to stand in a necessary connection with another fact. He meant, rather, a plausible and hypothetical explanation of a phenomenon, found out by reasoning, and not incompatible with common experience; cf. De corpore, E.W., I, 6, and F. Brandt, op. cit., 194–201.

[2] De cive, Preface to the reader, E.W., II, xiv.

[3] De corpore, Epistle dedicatory, E.W., I, viii–ix.

[4] The political philosophy of Hobbes, xv, 27–8, 112; cf. also Ch. II.

[5] Ibid., 112, 136–8, 151–4.

[6] De corpore, E.W., I, 73–4.

all the positivistic efforts, of which that of Hobbes is the first great example, to found a science of man on the strict model of the natural sciences, are based upon a delusion. If there is one thing which the development of the sciences of man over the past half-century has shown, it is that human action is a level on which the procedural notions and the generalizations of the natural sciences, physical and biological, have either a very limited applicability, or none at all.

Yet it seems perverse to disregard Hobbes's own view of his work and not to recognize how profound a bearing for him the new philosophy had, for it was the latter, in its emphatically sceptical and naturalistic implications, which helped him, I think, to pose and to deal with the ethical-political problem in the specifically modern way. When one proceeds from the state to the nature of man, or from the nature of man to the state, one goes from the empirically-given to the empirically-given, and the problem of norms is then presented in the most difficult manner, since norms must, in consequence, be sought in the given, i.e. 'ought' must be derived from 'is'. The problem of norms is not a difficult one —indeed, it is merely avoided—when it is referred, as medieval ethics and politics did, to a transcendent and divine order of reason or will where the ultimate origin and basis of standards are thought to repose. In that case, an eternal, transcendentally fixed point of reference for norms is believed to exist, and when disagreements arise, it is imagined that the latter concern merely the application of these norms, themselves known, essentially, once and for all, to the conduct of earthly life. It was in just this fashion that medieval political thought conceived of natural law and granted it primacy over positive law. But what if all belief in a transcendent order is rejected, as Hobbes rejected it, and the steely arguments of a naturalistic scepticism employed to demonstrate that the notion of such an order is an error? In that case, the traditional foundation of ethics has been disintegrated, the reassuring illusion of a cosmic and divine basis for moral valuations dispelled, and man, now left solitary in a universe that is literally God-forsaken, is hurled back upon himself, to seek in his human nature and in the natural order for the norms of his social existence.

This is the situation in which thought increasingly found itself after the seventeenth century, and it is the situation with which Hobbes coped, the first thinker fully and clearly to do so. And out of his effort, he evolved, in systematic fashion, another type of normative order totally different from that postulated by medieval thought. For now that order is man himself, the claims and needs of whose human nature are alone to furnish the standard for moral valuations. The implications of this position are far-reaching, though I do not mean to suggest that Hobbes saw them all. In the first place, with recourse to human nature as the exclusive basis for norms, the whole emphasis in politics

169

shifts from duties to rights. The foundation-propositions of traditional political discourse assert man's duty; Hobbes's assert man's right. Human beings, in virtue of the needs of their nature, have an original claim or right, and its fulfillment Hobbes considers to be the sole justification of the commonwealth.[1] In the second place, the relationship between the ideal and the actual is placed in a new focus. To the transcendentally oriented medieval ethic, an impassable gulf separated the actual from the ideal in this world. Man was conceived as a fallen being, and though it was his duty to live by the standards which the Church proclaimed in the name of God, as a sinner he could do so only infrequently, by great effort of will, and with many lapses. But when, as for Hobbes, man is the source from which norms are derived, the gulf between the ideal and the actual is, in effect, eradicated, because the ideal itself is evolved from the nature and capacities of man. And so, while it requires effort, of course, as well as the instruction of reason, to live as one ought, this effort can be crowned with success, and the ideal is attainable. In the third place, the life of society now receives an unprecedented validation. To medieval political thought, even as softened and moderated by Aquinas under the influence of Aristotle's *Politics*, the life of society with its pain and coercion is the sign of man's fall from grace. To Hobbes, it is an immeasurable advance. Outside it is the slime of the state of nature; within it man has the world to gain and the possibility of realizing his ideals. Finally, in working out an ethic and politics based on man, Hobbes created an individualistic type of thought which had always to come back to the needs of human nature that make peaceful social life possible. This meant, as we shall see, that despite Hobbes's absolutist predilections, a basis was suggested for the judgement of rulers by their subjects. For if men have a prepolitical right or claim which it is the commonwealth's business to secure, then the implication is, however unwillingly faced, that a commonwealth which habitually fails to fulfill this claim, may be rejected.

I have somewhat anticipated the argument in the preceding paragraph because it seemed important to stress the impulse which the new philosophy furnished to Hobbes's denial of a transcendent normative order. Now we must consider his doctrine of human nature which is the formal starting-point of his political theory. The analysis begins with the passions, and its subject at the outset is typical man, or man in general, the existence of multitudes of men being for the moment disregarded. It is when the analysis descends from this abstractness to take into account the myriads of individuals behaving in accordance with the description of typical man that the political problem is faced in all its starkness, and the question answered as to how peace, justice, and virtue are to be evolved out of the passions and actions of individual persons. How does

[1] Cf. the remarks of A. P. d'Entrèves, *Natural law*, London, 1951, 59–60.

Hobbes draw man? First of all, he is a creature of activity who must always be doing and can have no final end, no *summum bonum*, at which he can rest.[1] This is in no sense a normative statement. Hobbes intends it in a purely descriptive sense, for he means to make clear that a true account must recognize that man aims always at definite objectives which, when reached, become starting-points for new activity. Then, secondly, the things to which man gives the names 'good' and 'evil' refer to the objects of his activity. What a man wants, he calls 'good'; what he fears or is displeasing to him, he calls 'evil'. Good and evil, therefore, are not absolutes, known simply in themselves, and they have meaning only with reference to the ends of activity.[2] Yet a believer in the method of Euclid cannot acquiesce in ethical subjectivity, and as he shows us later, Hobbes will find an objective norm for good and evil. This will still retain a relative character because it will be formulated exclusively in terms of what is good and evil for man; but it will overcome subjectivity in being shown as what reason requires from all men if they are to achieve the thing they all evidently desire, namely, self-preservation, the prerequisite to any striving whatever.

Hobbes anatomizes the passions in a masterly way.[3] Each of them is treated with relation to man's success or lack of success in achieving his ends in the race which is life. So, e.g., to see those behind us in the race is glory, to see those ahead is humility; to see one falling behind whom we would not is pity, to see one going ahead whom we would not is indignation; continually to outgo the next before us is felicity, continually to be overtaken is misery; and the forsaking of the course is death.[4] The description is in a decidedly egotistic vain, but I do not think Hobbes intends us to make, as yet, any moral judgement on the situation. Typical man cannot help but refer all things to his own self, for his is a consciousness in which the knowledge of the existence of other selves, and what must follow from this fact, has not struck home. Hobbes is giving us what he thinks is a description of man as such, premoral man. The nature of the case will be altered as soon as all the consequences are drawn from the fact that there are many men. Nor even when these consequences become plain does Hobbes think that man ceases to make reference to his own single welfare. This sort of reference is simply a datum, and, as such, not to be exorcised. What will be new is the recognition of reason that a man must permit his fellows to secure their welfare if he is to secure his own, and that to secure self-preservation, welfare's *sine qua non*, he must refrain from certain ends. A moral judgment on passion's egotism, therefore, is possible only when reason

---

[1] *The elements of law*, 22–3; *Leviathan*, 75.
[2] *The elements of law*, 22; *Leviathan*, 41.
[3] *The elements of law*, Ch. 9; *Leviathan*, Ch. 6; *De homine*, 1657, *L.W.*, II, Ch. XII.
[4] *The elements of law*, 36–7.

has made clear what man in the pursuit of his welfare must refrain from. And any such judgement cannot condemn a man's reference to his own good. It can only condemn a formulation of good which is unreasonable because it fails to take into account the good of others. From this it follows that reason does not and cannot strive to obliterate passion's making a man's own self the sole point of reference. What it does, rather, is teach that the welfare of one self is dependent on the welfare of other selves; or, put another way, reason does not extinguish passion, it instructs it.

The passions thus play a role of prime importance in Hobbes's philosophy. And however terrible may be his account of the effects of the passions' free-rein in the state of nature, what is notable is his naturalistic attitude with regard to them. He does not, of course, remain indifferent to the immoral consequences of passion rampant. But at the same time, he accepts the passions, denying that they are sinful in themselves or that they prove man to be wicked by nature,[1] and condemns them only in so far as they remain uninstructed. It is because of this, no doubt, that he rejects the Aristotelian doctrine of virtue as consisting in the mean.[2] For him, virtue is not opposed to passion, but built upon it. Hence, he says that the origin of just actions is in the passions,[3] and, in a significant statement, declares that the way to reduce politics to the infallibility of reason is 'first to put such principles down for a foundation, as passion not mistrusting, may not seek to displace . . .'.[4]

When the discussion turns from man as such to the state of nature, where allowance must be made for the coexistence of many men, then we are brought face to face with the political problem. The state of nature is the hypothetical alternative to the commonwealth and sovereignty.[5] It is a condition, therefore, in which human beings in pursuit of their ends are subject to no power or authority beside what they can casually impose upon one another. Whether such a condition ever possessed an historical existence is of no importance to Hobbes. He does tell us, it is true, that the ancient Germans and other primitives were without government,[6] and he finds direct analogies to the state of nature both in civil war and in the relations of sovereign states to one another.[7] The point is, however, that Hobbes intends his description of the state

---

[1] *De cive*, Preface to the reader, *E.W.*, II, xvi; *Leviathan*, 97, 223–4.

[2] *The elements of law*, 73.

[3] *Ibid.*, 64.

[4] *Ibid.*, Epistle dedicatory, xii.

[5] Cf., e.g., the following passage: 'Let us return again to the state of nature, and consider men *as if* but even now sprung out of the earth, and suddenly, like mushrooms, come to full maturity, without all kind of engagement to each other.' (*De cive, E.W.*, II, 108–9; italics mine.)

[6] *The elements of law*, 56; *Leviathan*, 97.

[7] *Leviathan*, 97–8, 141; *De cive, E.W.*, II, 141, 169.

of nature to be a plausible account of what life would be like in the absence of a coercive political order.

Since real human beings are merely individual versions of typical man, their association in a state of nature could not produce any happy consequences. A situation is displayed to us of unending and oppressive fear. There is no property, for nothing is anyone's with certainty, nor any arts, letters, sciences, or the comforts of life. An unremitting war of all against all takes place, and every man goes in terror of his life.[1] In such circumstances, the notions of justice and injustice have no place, every man having a right to everything, because everything is, in a literal sense, as much his as it is anyone else's.[2]

And now, in this very anarchy, Hobbes discovers the beginning of all right, and on this conception builds the route of escape. Each man desires what is good for himself, and shuns what is evil, and on this account shuns the chief of all evils, death; 'and this he doth', says Hobbes,

'by a certain impulsion of nature, no less than that whereby a stone moves downward. It is therefore neither absurd nor reprehensible, neither against the dictates of true reason, for a man to use all his endeavours to preserve and defend his body and the members thereof from death and sorrows. But that which is not contrary to right reason ... [is] done justly, and with right. Neither by the word right is anything else signified, than that liberty which every man hath to make use of his natural faculties according to right reason. Therefore the first foundation of natural right is this, that every man, as much as in him lies endeavour to protect his life and members.'[3]

In other words, man has an original right which is prior to all social arrangements. This right is not superimposed by Hobbes, for he has deduced it from the presupposition of all man's activities and passions, the desire to live. This is his natural right; and when man's reason shows him that however free he is in the state of nature to secure his right as he pleases, he still remains insecure, and that only by agreeing with other men not to do as he pleases can his right be made effective, then the avenue of egress from anarchy to the commonwealth and civilization has been pointed out.

Reason, in revealing the way of escape from the state of nature, has special affinity, it is evident, with the passions of desire for life and fear of death. And the foundation of Hobbes's moral theory, as Professor Strauss has shown,[4] is in the conception of the antithesis between the passions connected with vanity and those connected with fear of death.

[1] *The elements of law*, Ch. 14; *De cive, E.W.*, II, Ch. I; *Leviathan*, Ch. 13.
[2] *Leviathan*, 98–9.
[3] *De cive, E.W.*, II, 8–9.
[4] *The political philosophy of Hobbes*, 28.

For vanity leads to pride, to over-estimation of one's self, to arrogance towards one's fellows, and so to war; while fear of death makes for peace and living quietly together.[1]

> *Times there be when fear is well;*
> *Yea, it must continually*
> *Watch within the soul enthroned.*
> *Needful too straits to teach humility.*
> *Who of those that never nursed*
> *Healthy dread within the heart,*
> *Be they men or peoples, shall*
> *Show to Justice reverence?*

These lines spoken by the Furies in Aeschylus's *Eumenides* well express the importance which Hobbes ascribed to fear. Yet if we are to understand his position rightly, we must bear in mind that though he sees in the fear of death an educative factor resulting in the subordination of vanity and pride, he does not make this fear the leading principle either in the genesis of the commonwealth or in its maintenance after it has come into being. It is reason, not fear, that impels men to create the commonwealth and to subject themselves to the sovereign power. Fear is reason's substratum, a passion which shuns the effects which must follow upon the dissolution of the commonwealth; yet not it, but reason only can create political society.[2] And that is why Hobbes will have man obey the laws not from fear of punishment, but because they are the means which the sovereign power has laid down to maintain peace, and why, too, he calls that man unjust who obeys only out of fear.[3]

One thing more must be remarked about the fear of death, and that is that it is only the negative side of man's striving, the positive side being a desire for life and the goods of life. Physical survival is the minimum, the first of all goods,[4] to secure which men enter into the commonwealth. But political society is also for 'commodious' and 'contented living',[5] for industry, and for the arts and sciences, all of which are lacking in the state of nature.[6] Moreover, these latter, we are told, men desire by nature as much as they do life itself.[7] This being so, I do not think we are unjustified in interpreting self-preservation in an expanded sense as meaning not only life, but those other goods man needs in virtue of his humanity. Thus interpreted, the right of self-preservation, which

---

[1] *Leviathan*, 98.
[2] Cf. A. Levi, *La filosofia di Tommaso Hobbes*, Milan, 1929, 375–6.
[3] *De cive*, *E.W.*, II, 33; cf. Z. Lubienski, *op. cit.*, 110–15.
[4] *De homine*, *L.W.*, II, 98.
[5] *Leviathan*, 98, 131.
[6] *Ibid.*, 96–7.
[7] *De homine*, *L.W.*, II, 99.

Hobbes considered the primal human claim, entails a fatal contradiction that undermines all of his subsequent emphasis on obedience. For may not men be freed from obligation not only when the security of their lives is no longer guaranteed by the sovereign power to which they owe obedience, but also when that power has acted to create insuperable obstacles to contentment and happiness, i.e. to the fulfillment of self-preservation in an expanded sense? Hobbes, to be sure, might not be willing to grant this, yet between his notions of natural right and absolute sovereignty there is, as we shall see, a contradiction which he never succeeded in resolving.

Having discerned in self-preservation the foundation of right, Hobbes goes on to evolve the norm which all must accept if this right is to be realized. Now if it is a fact that all men want to preserve themselves, it is equally a fact that they frequently err as to the means that conduce towards this end. A distinction can thus be made between real and apparent good, according to whether that which man wills does or does not really lead towards his desired end.[1] Only reason can show which means do, in fact, conduce to that at which all men aim, and such means alone will be real goods. Reason, therefore, which 'is no less of the nature of man than passion, and is the same in all men, because all men agree in the will to be directed . . . to that which they desire to attain',[2] is called by Hobbes the law of nature; and the precepts of reason are the norm to which men must conform in order to achieve their end, self-preservation.[3] So '. . . the law of nature . . . is the dictate of right reason conversant about those things . . . to be done or omitted for the constant preservation of life and members . . .'.[4] Yet to call reason the law of nature is to employ a metaphor, and a misleading one at that. For the precepts of reason are advisive, not compulsive, and there is nothing externally obligatory about them. Consequently, they are not really law at all, but rather 'Theoremes concerning what conduceth to conservation . . . wheras Law properly is the word of him that by right hath command over others'.[5] Hence, the 'force of the . . . law of nature, is no more than the force of the reasons inducing thereunto',[6] and the breach of the law of nature consists in 'false reasoning . . .'.[7]

That we here find Hobbes speaking, as earlier political thinkers did, of the law of nature, must not divert us from realizing that, in his hands, the concept has been absolutely emptied of its traditional meaning. It is important to see how this is so. In the Middle Ages, and right down

[1] *De cive, E.W.*, II, 10.
[2] *The elements of law*, 58.
[3] Cf. A. Levi, *op. cit.*, 264.
[4] *De cive, E.W.*, II, 16; cf. *The elements of law*, 58; *Leviathan*, 99.
[5] *Leviathan*, 122–3.
[6] *The elements of law*, 63.
[7] *De cive, E.W.*, II, 16 n.

175

to Richard Hooker at the end of the sixteenth century, natural law was thought of as embodying ethical rules which were prior to and above the enactments of earthly communities. Knowledge of these rules was implanted in men's minds by God,[1] and there was no question that they were really law, since their origin lay in that divine order where the ultimate binding force of all law was to be found.[2] Accordingly, natural law was allowed primacy over the commands of earthly rulers, such commands being acknowledged as law only in so far as they were not thought incompatible with natural law.[3] Owing to this primacy, it was never doubted that formal law, in the sense of a ruler's command, may be material 'unlaw', and that formal 'unlaw' may be material law.[4] But the question is, what are the dicta of natural law, and how can we make any sense out of them? From the scientific standpoint, there are three reasons, at least, why the answer to this question presents insuperable obstacles. In the first place, natural law originates in a transcendental realm about which we can have no knowledge. In the second place, men have differed, and do differ, about the principles which God is alleged to have implanted in them as rational creatures. In the third place, even when we are presented with rules which are described as dicta of natural law, they turn out to be meaningless without a positive legal order to define their operation.[5] We are told, for example, by St. Thomas Aquinas that the prohibition of theft is an express first principle of the natural law.[6] It seems obvious, however—apart from other objections which could be made to the statement—that such a prohibition is devoid of sense until a positive legal order has defined property. Thus, it is impossible for the supposed rules of natural law to possess intelligibility in the absence of the definitions commanded by particular communities.

Now Hobbes was fully aware of the difficulties connected with the traditional notion of natural law, and he notes the many contradictions on the matter among philosophers, remarking that of all laws, it has become the most obscure.[7] In employing the notion, therefore, he had to free it from the ambiguities in which it was encumbered. He could not derive its dicta from the divine order because, on his principles, knowledge of such an order is unobtainable. This is why God and revelation

[1] Cf. St. Thomas Aquinas, '. . . natural law is nothing else than the participation of rational creatures in the eternal law', *Summa theologica*, Prima sec., qu. 91, 2; and see Hooker's whole discussion in *The laws of ecclesiastical polity*, I, 8.

[2] St. Thomas Aquinas, *op. cit.*, Prima sec., qu. 93, 3; cf. M. de Wulf, *History of mediaeval philosophy*, 3rd. ed., trans. P. Coffey, London, 1909, 341.

[3] St. Thomas Aquinas, *op. cit.*, Prima sec., qu. 95, 2.

[4] I take this formulation from O. von Gierke, *The development of political theory*, trans. B. Freyd, New York, 1939, 306.

[5] On this point, see the discussion of Hans Kelsen, *General theory of law and the state*, Cambridge, 1946, Appendix, 'Natural-law doctrine and legal positivism'.

[6] *Op. cit.*, Prima sec., qu. 94, 4.

[7] *The elements of law*, 57; *De cive, E.W.*, II, 14–15; *Leviathan*, 212.

are rigorously excluded by him from the scope of philosophy: as subjects assumed to be either ingenerable, immaterial, or known by faith, they have no place in a study which uses reason exclusively, deals with body, and proceeds by the method of cause and effect.[1] Nor could he admit that the formulae of natural law are meaningful in the absence of a positive legal order to provide the appropriate definitions. Hence, he declares that, though theft, murder, and adultery are forbidden by the law of nature, it remains for the civil law to determine by its commands what actions are to be called theft, what called adultery, and what murder.[2] So when he speaks of the law of nature, he evades the difficulties which had beset the idea in two ways: by denying that it is a law at all, and by deriving its precepts, not from the realm of a divine reason, but quite autonomously, from the rationally instructed strivings of human beings for self-preservation. After he has done this, he does endeavour, it is true, to equate his law of nature with the law of God.[3] But this, I think, is merely an inconsistent, and perhaps an insincere, obeisance to orthodoxy, for here, too, as he makes clear, civil law—the command of an earthly legislator—is required to give the law of God its meaning, and he transcribes the Decalogue thus: 'Thou shalt not refuse to give the honour defined by the laws, unto thy parents'; 'Thou shalt not kill the man, whom the laws forbid thee to kill'; 'Thou shalt avoid all copulation forbidden by the laws"; etc.[4]

In treating the law of nature in this way, Hobbes took a decisive step towards ridding political philosophy of an occult entity. No doubt, by the seventeenth century, important progress had already been made in detaching the idea of natural law from its traditional theological moorings and grounding it in certain autonomous rational principles. Grotius's remark that the injunctions of natural law would be the same even on the hypothesis that there is no God, is a familiar instance.[5] But for Grotius, the law of nature originates in God and is truly law.[6] Hobbes's position is far more radical, indeed, in basic respects, his ideas inhabit a different world. He was denying, in effect, the divine origin of moral valuations. He was saying that it is senseless to imagine law as existent outside and apart from particular communities. To him, the law of nature is not a pervasive principle of the universe expressing the rational constitution of a divine mind. It is only a name for the means which the calculating human intelligence finds efficacious to achieve its ends of preservation and contentment. He directs us, if we

[1] *De corpore, E.W.*, I, 10–11.
[2] *De cive, E.W.*, II, 85.
[3] *Ibid., E.W.*, II, 50–1.
[4] *Ibid., E.W.*, II, 189.
[5] *De jure belli ac pacis*, Prolegomena, sec. 11, Book I, x, 5.
[6] *Ibid.*, Prolegomena, sec. 12, Book I, x, 1–2.

wish to find moral standards, to seek them in the nature and capacities of man, not in the supposed dicta of a supernatural order. Later we shall see him attempt entirely to merge these standards in the civil law so as to buttress the position of the sovereign power. But he will be unsuccessful in this, for it contradicts his root conception of the foundation of politics upon right. At this point, however, it seems fair to say that Hobbes has introduced increased clarity into political discussion. His repudiation of the traditional law of nature may be condemned by those who deplore the secularized character which thought increasingly assumed from the seventeenth century onwards. Yet we need not be absolutists with Hobbes to agree with him that men create their moral universe themselves, and that the perfection of their humanity is the work of their own reason, for it is the essence of their situation that they must advance alone, there being no extra-human realm whose aid they can invoke.

These considerations having been made clear, we may go on to ask what it is that reason, or the law of nature, dictates; and the answer, in the most general sense, is that men should seek peace, so as to remove themselves from the danger and insecurity of the state of nature.[1] The specific inference from this is that they should relinquish their right to all things,[2] and that each man 'be contented with so much liberty against other men, as he would allow other men against himselfe'.[3] To accept this principle, Hobbes declares, is to obey the Golden Rule.[4] But, obviously, it is not enough for men to agree to surrender their right to all things; there must be a power to see that this rational resolution is habitually adhered to. Thence arises, as a further inference of reason, the necessity for the commonwealth, for one will to represent the wills of all and to possess the right of coercing and punishing any men who seek to violate the agreement reason initially leads them to make.[5] A commonwealth exists, therefore, only in virtue of each man's consent to submit his will to the will of one man or an assembly of men, and to let that will represent his person.[6] The ultimate cause of the commonwealth is the foresight of men, who, though they love liberty and dominion over others, realize that civil society is the sole means of preservation and a contented life.[7] Because the commonwealth is the rational creation of human beings, Hobbes regards it as an artifice, deliberately made and maintained, not as something begotten by man's uninstructed human nature. He rejects, therefore, the Aristotelian doctrine that man is naturally a political animal. In Hobbes's view, man creates and upholds

---

[1] *Leviathan*, 100.   [2] *De cive, E.W.*, II, 17.
[3] *Leviathan*, 100.   [4] *Ibid.*, 100.
[5] *De cive, E.W.*, II, Ch. V; *Leviathan*, Ch. 17.
[6] *Leviathan*, 126.   [7] *Ibid.*, 128.

his society as a work of reason; he makes himself a political animal by the rational discernment of the means required to secure his fundamental right.[1]

Hobbes now proceeds to show that the basis of the political order is in a contract. At the outset, he distinguishes, in accordance with their possible origins, two kinds of commonwealths, one institutive, the other indifferently characterized as despotic, as commonwealth by acquisition, and as patrimonial or natural government.[2] Institutive government is created by the mutual convenants of the consenting individuals to let their wills be represented by one man or an assembly of men who will bear their person and of whose actions they will thenceforth be the author; and in the *Leviathan*, Hobbes depicts in elaborate detail how this would be done.[3] His intention here is to make clear that even on the assumption of the origin of government in a primeval assembly, the erection of sovereignty could only result from the covenants men make with one another, so that the sovereign power itself would never be party to the covenant, and never be open, therefore, to the charge of violating it.[4] In effect, this was a reply to those sixteenth- and seventeenth-century theorists who justified rebellion by supposing a breach on the king's part of an original contract made between the crown and the people. Despotic government, the second sort of commonwealth, arises from the power men have over their children, or from conquest.[5] But here, too, Hobbes is careful to insist that there is a contract at its basis.[6]

'. . . Dominion is then acquired to the Victor [he declares] when the Vanquished, to avoyd the present stroke of death, covenanteth, either in expresse words, or by other sufficient signs of the Will, that so long as his life, and the liberty of his body is allowed him, the Victor shall have the use thereof, at his pleasure. . . . It is not therefore the Victory, that giveth the right of Dominion over the Vanquished, but his Covenant.'[7]

In this twofold division of commonwealths, Hobbes seems quite clearly

---

[1] *Ibid.*, 130–1; *De·cive, E.W.*, II, 66–8.

[2] *The elements of law*, 81–2; *De cive, E.W.*, II, 70–1; *Leviathan*, 132.

[3] *Leviathan*, Chs. 16–17; cf. F. Tönnies's discussion (*op. cit.*, 236–44, and n. 121–2 on pp. 302–6) of the interesting variations in Hobbes's account of institutive government.

[4] *Leviathan*, 134.

[5] *De cive, E.W.*, II, 108–9; *Leviathan*, 153.

[6] Since Hobbes insists in his three largest political works (see next note) that despotic government rests on covenant, I cannot agree with Professor Croom Robertson (*Hobbes*, Philadelphia, 1886, 147) that the philosopher's stress on this point is an oversight.

[7] *Leviathan*, 155–6; cf. *The elements of law*, 99; *De cive, E.W.*, II, 109–10; on child's covenant with parent, see, *apud alia, Leviathan*, 153.

to have regarded the second—government by conquest and by generation of children—as truest to the facts of history.[1] But just as earlier in
the case of the state of nature, so now, too, the question of historical
origins is irrelevant. However it may have originated, government rests
on contract—this is all Hobbes is concerned to argue. Contract, therefore, is a postulate of reason, and need never have occurred as a distinct
event. The emphasis here upon the contractual foundation of government is not inconsistent with Hobbes's general position, as has sometimes been erroneously contended.[2] It is, on the contrary, a strict deduction from his previous assertions. His theme has been that men make
and maintain government as the rational expression of their right to
preserve themselves. Government, in consequence, must always presuppose consent; and the hypothesis which corresponds to consent is that
of a covenant. For this reason, Hobbes insists upon the covenant in
despotic and institutive government alike; it is the correlate to his belief
that the political order is unthinkable except as something in which men
voluntarily acquiesce to secure life and contentment.

If the fulfillment of man's pre-political right entails the commonwealth, the latter, in turn, entails sovereignty, a supreme power to perform the actions required to maintain peace. For Hobbes, sovereignty
is a fact of political life. Wherever there is a body politic, there is also
sovereignty. Without it, he says, 'there will be a liberty for every man to
do what he hath a mind, or whatsoever shall seem right to himself,
which cannot stand with the preservation of mankind. And therefore in
all government whatsoever, there is a supreme power . . . somewhere
existent.'[3] Following out this idea, he maintained that civil wars are
always fought, not to limit sovereignty, but to determine who shall possess it.[4] Indeed, it cannot be limited, he pointed out, for '. . . whosoever
thinking Soveraign Power too great, will seek to make it lesse; must subject himselfe, to the Power, that can limit it; that is to say, to a greater'.[5]

The attributes which Hobbes lists as properly belonging to sovereignty
are as great as we can imagine them: the sovereign may not be removed
nor punished by his subjects; he is to be the sole judge of what conduces
to peace, and, therefore, of what doctrines and opinions are allowed to
be taught; he makes law, and thus determines the rules of property, of
good and evil, of lawful and unlawful actions; he rewards and punishes,
decides on war and peace, and commands the armed forces.[6] These, the

---

[1] *A dialogue of the common law*, 1681, *E.W.*, VI, 147, 150–1; *Leviathan*, 550–1 (this
appears only in the English ed. of *Leviathan*).
[2] J. Gough, *op. cit.*, 107, and J. Plamenatz, *op. cit.*, 13.
[3] *De cive, E.W.*, II, 145.
[4] *Ibid., E.W.*, II, 135.
[5] *Leviathan*, 160.
[6] *Ibid.*, 133–9.

chief powers of the sovereign, are the same in both institutive and despotic government,[1] and the sovereign is said to possess them by right, because as the representative of the consenting individuals, he has been invested with the latters' right to do everything needful for preservation.[2] Finally, they are indivisible, for if one of them is granted away to be exercised by someone other than the sovereign, the rest are deprived of all effect, and sovereignty itself ceases to be.[3]

The great difficulty with this list, as Hobbes himself admits, is that, in practice, sovereigns for the most part neither exercise, nor are acknowledged the right to exercise, so large a range of powers.[4] How, then, can it be said that wherever there is a commonwealth, there is also sovereignty? The difficulty vanishes, however, when we realize that Hobbes has been speaking of sovereignty in two distinct senses. One sense is purely descriptive: any political order does, in point of fact, presuppose a supreme power whose will makes law and against whose judgement there is no appeal other than to the private sword of civil war. The other sense is normative: if the supreme power is to be entirely effective in performing its function, it should be, and its subjects should admit it to be, vested with every attribute Hobbes has assigned it. These attributes are, in their totality, the logically necessary counter-concept to the state of nature.[5] They are deductions 'from the . . . need, and designes of men, in erecting of Commonwealths, and putting themselves under Monarchs, or Assemblies entrusted with power enough for their protection'.[6] They ought, therefore, to be conceded as the sovereign's rights; and it is the failure to admit this, Hobbes points out, that is one of the causes responsible for the dissolution of states.[7]

The outcome of Hobbes's discussion is the validation of any government as such. In each of the three forms of commonwealth—monarchy, aristocracy, and democracy—sovereignty, though differently located, is an inescapable fact; and, logically speaking, the attributes which belong to it are the same.[8] Men may unreasonably refuse to see this, or they may think the consequences of political life, with the sovereignty it necessitates, to be harsh. Yet these latter are as nothing compared with the calamities of civil war and 'that dissolute condition of masterlesse men, without subjection to Lawes, and a coercive Power to tye their hands from rapine and revenge . . .'.[9] And so, of the three forms of government, which is best ought not to be disputed, we are told, but we ought to maintain and prefer that government under which it is our fortune to live.[10]

By this iron reasoning, Hobbes brought the modern doctrine of sove-

---

[1] *Ibid.*, 153, 156–7; *De cive, E.W.*, II, 121–2.   [2] *Leviathan*, 133.
[3] *Ibid.*, 139.   [4] *Ibid.*, 160.   [5] Cf. F. Tönnies, *op. cit.*, 231.
[6] *Leviathan*, 157.   [7] *Ibid.*, 247–8.   [8] *Ibid.*, 142–3.
[9] *Ibid.*, 141.   [10] *Ibid.*, 429.

reignty into the full light of day. It had been first enunciated in the sixteenth century by Bodin, who formulated it as 'the supreme power over
citizens and subjects unrestrained by laws'.[1] But Bodin's discussion had
been inconsistent and equivocal, for he held that the sovereign, though
not subject to positive law, is certainly bound by the law of nature, and
the latter, to Bodin, was really and literally law.[2] Hobbes swept away
all such hesitations. From the legal standpoint, the sovereign is not
bound by anything; not by positive law, since the latter originates in his
will; and not by the law of nature, since, on Hobbes's demonstration, it
is not law at all, but merely a precept of reason.

The proclamation of the unlimitedness of the sovereign is, of course,
absolutism, and is one of the things which has aroused such animosity
against Hobbes. We must not think, however, that this absolutism is
unequivocally maintained, for as I have been suggesting, and must now
show in detail, it is incompatible with his construction of political
philosophy on the foundation of an original human right. The appropriate point at which to commence our examination of this matter is
Hobbes's discussion of the relation between natural law and civil law.
We recall that, among other attributes, Hobbes gives to the sovereign
the power to make law, i.e. to establish rules 'by which every man may
know what may be called his, what another's, what just, what unjust,
what honest, what dishonest, what good, what evil . . .'.[3] He thinks of
law exclusively as a command, and finds its basis not, as was traditionally thought, in reason, but in will.[4] Accordingly, he sees the basis of
obedience to law, not in its content, but in the fact that it is commanded.
This provides the criterion by which he distinguishes counsel from command: in counsel, the cause of obedience is the thing advised, i.e. the
content; in command, the cause of obedience is the will of the commander.[5] With this positivistic conception of law, he quite logically
denied any legal standing to the law of nature, characterising the latter
simply as 'Conclusions, or Theoremes concerning what conduceth to
. . . conservation . . .'.[6]

Now the problem raised by Hobbes's formulation of the civil law is
this: if the identity of law lies solely in its form as a command, and if it
lays down the rules to be accepted as fixing the just and the unjust, good

---

[1] 'Summa in cives ac subditos legibusque soluta potestas', *De republica sex libri*,
I, 8.

[2] Cf. G. H. Sabine, *op. cit.*, 407–11, J. Laird, *Hobbes*, London, 1934, 73, and J. W.
Allen, *Political thought in the sixteenth century*, 422. This is only one of Bodin's inconsistencies. There are others, as, e.g., his denial that the sovereign has a right òver
subjects' property.

[3] *De cive, E.W.*, II, 77; cf. *Leviathan*, 137.

[4] *De cive, E.W.*, II, 185; *Leviathan*, 203.

[5] *De cive, E.W.*, II, 183.

[6] See above, 175.

and evil, have we any ground remaining upon which the law itself can be judged? We do not mean a legal ground, for Hobbes has convinced us that such there cannot be. We mean a moral ground. Does the law of nature—i.e. the rational precepts leading to preservation—give us such a ground? Or are we to acquiesce in the horrid conclusion that *ius* is merely *iussum*, and morality equal to legality? This is the question on which Hobbes runs into difficulties. He wishes to persuade us that the law of nature finds its realization in political society as such. But we are left asking why the reason which impelled men to consent to the commonwealth as the way of fulfilling their claim to life and contentment, should not continue, after the commonwealth is constituted, to judge whether the latter is effective in serving its purpose.

Such a conclusion Hobbes strives with might and main to avoid. He goes about it, first, by denying the possibility of a right reason separate from the reason of the sovereign power. Once the commonwealth is in existence, the advocate of certainty and demonstrable truth is ready to turn traitor to his philosophy by allowing reason to be wholly conventional: whatever the sovereign calls reasonable should be accepted as such. So he says that he would consent to the opinion that quarrels should be decided by right reason 'if there were any such thing to be found or known *in rerum natura.* . . . But . . . seeing right reason is not existent, the reason of some man, or men, must supply the place thereof; and that man, or men, is he or they, that have the sovereign power. . . .'[1] Next, Hobbes endeavours to merge the law of nature completely in the civil law. The two contain each other, he says, and are of equal extent in every commonwealth,[2] with the result that 'It is not possible to command aught by the civil law, contrary to the laws of nature'.[3] Even the conflicting laws of different states, he insists, are all equal to the law of nature.[4]

I do not see, however, why we need accept these assertions. Indeed, on Hobbes's own showing, we need not. The question is not whether there is a right reason *in rerum natura*, for nothing at stake in the argument requires us to think there is. Yet since it is right reason which causes men in the state of nature to give up some of their rights so as to secure preservation, right reason cannot be merely conventional. Its task was to discover the real means towards peace and the satisfaction of the needs of life, and it solved this task by deducing the necessity for the state and for sovereignty. If this was a true solution, then right reason could not be a mere convention; and as it was separate from the sovereign power

---

[1] *The elements of law*, 150; cf. *De cive, E.W.*, II, 268–9; *Leviathan*, 33; *A dialogue of the common law, E.W.*, VI, 22, 121–2.
[2] *Leviathan*, 205.
[3] *De cive, E.W.*, II, 190, margin.
[4] *De homine, L.W.*, II, 116–17.

which it creates, there is no justification why the sovereign's judgement should always be taken for right reason after the state is in being. Hobbes himself inadvertently admits this. He tells us expressly that no man is bound to obey a command which 'frustrates the End for which ... Soveraignty was ordained ...'.[1] But whose reason is to decide this? Clearly, it can be decided only by the subject's reason. In making this concession, Hobbes opened an irreparable, yet inevitable, gap in his argument that the sovereign's reason should always be accounted right reason.

There is a similar weakness in his effort to have the civil law and the law of nature identical. This amounts to saying that every law should be regarded as rational and good. But the philosopher obviously felt doubts, as is proved by his numerous statements informing us that the sovereign is subject to the law of nature and must not act against it. How could he have supposed the possibility of a conflict between the sovereign and the law of nature, if he had remained true to his assertion that the civil law and natural law never contradict each other? Yet he declares that the sovereign 'has ... no other bounds, but such as are set out by the ... Law of Nature';[2] that 'All Punishments of Innocent subjects ... are against the Law of Nature';[3] that to 'Equity ... as being a Precept of the Law of Nature, a Soveraign is as much subject, as any of the meanest of his people';[4] and that sovereigns 'may diverse ways transgress against the ... laws of nature, as by cruelty, iniquity, contumely, and other like vices ...'.[5]

It is evident that Hobbes's emphasis on obedience contains serious inconsistencies. And we can see how this emphasis is further qualified in his discussion of the liberty of the subject and the obligation of the sovereign. In general, he says, the subject's liberty consists in two things: first, in the right to do that which could not have been surrendered in any covenant; second, in the right to do whatever the law does not forbid.[6] It is the rights in the first category which interest us here, for they contain some important concessions. Thus, in the nature of the case, a subject need not obey a command to kill, wound, or maim himself; he may also refuse to endanger his life by service in war; and in the event that many men should unjustly unite to resist the sovereign, they have a right, civil war being begun, to continue their resistance in order to preserve themselves.[7] This list shows that subjects, in Hobbes's view, retain significant original liberties in civil society. They have other liberties as well. To one I have already drawn attention; I mean the statement of Hobbes that obedience may be withheld if a command frustrates the end for which sovereignty was ordained.[8] This, of course,

---

[1] *Leviathan*, 167. [2] *Ibid.*, 173. [3] *Ibid.*, 244.
[4] *Ibid.*, 265. [5] *De cive*, E.W., II, 101. [6] *Leviathan*, 167–8.
[7] *Ibid.*, 168. [8] See above.

can only be decided when the subject exercises a liberty of private judgement. Again, subjects need not obey the sovereign power when it has lost its ability to protect them.[1] It is on this ground that Hobbes, in the final chapter of the English version of the *Leviathan*, justified, by implication, the transfer of allegiance from the Stuart dynasty to the revolutionary government erected by Cromwell. But at what point in the complicated contest of a civil war is an old sovereign overthrown and a new one in a position to afford protection? Here, also, is a matter which only the individual's private judgement can determine.

So far as concerns the sovereign's obligations to subjects, legally there are none. Yet the sovereign has a duty which is expressed in the maxim, *salus populi suprema lex*. And by safety is meant not bare preservation, Hobbes says, but 'happiness' and all the 'contentments of life', for these, too, are among the ends at which men aim in consenting to government.[2] He declares that sovereigns should yield obedience to right reason,[3] thereby assuming what he had previously denied, namely, that the sovereign's reason and right reason might differ. He goes on to advise sovereigns to administer justice equally, to impose fair taxes, to provide charity, encourage labour, make good laws, and not more laws than are needful. Legally, no doubt, sovereigns need do none of these things. But if they omit to do them, Hobbes points out, they will lose their power, since 'Negligent government', he says, is punished with 'Rebellion . . . For seeing Punishments are consequent to the breach of Lawes; Naturall Punishments are naturally consequent to the breach of the Lawes of Nature; and therefore follow them as their naturall, not arbitrary effects.'[4] Hence, owing to rebellion, the long-run result of misgovernment, there is, indeed, a real obligation of rulers to their subjects. It is true, of course, that Hobbes is usually ready to place the main responsibility for rebellion on subjects and to treat civil war as a manifestation of the irrational side of human nature.[5] On this account, he commits some dreadful sophisms, as when he says that 'Doctrine repugnant to Peace, can no more be True, than Peace and Concord can be against the Law of Nature'.[6] Did he really have no idea of the extent to which rulers have despised and suppressed truth in the interest of upholding their power? Nevertheless, for Hobbes it remains emphatically the case that the sovereign exists for the people's sake, and not the other way around.[7] Because of this, he was compelled to admit that the sovereign had a moral obligation, the obligation to act rationally. '. . . he,

---

[1] *Leviathan*, 170.
[2] *De cive, E.W.*, II, 167; *Leviathan*, 258.
[3] *De cive, E.W.*, II, 166.
[4] *Leviathan*, 284.
[5] *Ibid.*, 141.
[6] *Ibid.*, 137.
[7] *A dialogue of the common law, E.W.*, VI, 13.

who being placed in authority,' he declares, 'shall use his power other-wise than to the safety of the people, will act against the reasons of peace, that is to say, against the laws of nature.'[1]

The foregoing considerations reveal the existence of a deep cleavage running through Hobbes's thought. This cleavage is nothing trivial. It lies, rather, at the very heart of his political philosophy, and arises from the conflict between two fundamentally opposed tendencies: the stress on natural right, and the desire to validate any government as such. The former is liberalism, the latter absolutism. Between the two, it is the stress on natural right which is unquestionably stronger, for it is that concept on which his theory rests. Even against his will, therefore, Hobbes has forged a revolutionary weapon. If he defended absolutism, it was only on the ground that absolutism is in the general interest; and should this be denied, as his own thought gives us a basis for doing, absolutism disappears, and in its place is substituted the liberal system for which the philosopher's nineteenth-century utilitarian disciples con-tended. It is, then, quite accurate to call Hobbes 'a radical in the service of reaction',[2] and to hold that his ideas contain 'the germs of the con-stitutionalism he combated';[3] indeed, I should say they contain more than the germs. He has affirmed that men, in virtue of their humanity and apart from every social circumstance, possess a natural right which it is the commonwealth's duty to fulfill. This right involves more than a claim to bare preservation; it is a right also, as we have seen, to 'con-tentment', to 'commodious living', even to 'happiness',[4] for government is instituted so that men may, as far as their human condition permits, 'live delightfully'.[5] This being the case, we are irresistibly brought to conclude that men will be rationally and morally justified when they reject a commonwealth in which the fulfillment of their right has become an impossibility.

It must not, however, be imagined that Hobbes believed it the commonwealth's responsibility to make its subjects happy. Such a doc-trine was far from his mind, its appearance as a force being reserved for a later day in the history of political thought. In Hobbes's view, men are to seek their contentment and happiness for themselves. But the commonwealth is not to impose obstacles to this quest. It has, we may say, a negative duty, the duty of not interfering. This is the meaning of Hobbes's admonition to rulers to make no more laws than are needful.[6]

---

[1] *De cive, E.W.*, II, 166–7.

[2] J. Tulloch, *Rational theology and Christian philosophy in England in the seven-teenth century*, 2 vols., Edinburgh and London, 1872, II, 26.

[3] A. E. Taylor, *Thomas Hobbes*, London, 1908, 92. Professor Taylor goes on to remark on the community of spirit between Hobbes and Locke.

[4] See above, 174, 185.

[5] *De cive, E.W.*, II, 167.

[6] *Leviathan*, 268.

If our analysis has been correct, then it should be evident that, in the most important respects, Hobbes's thought is no mutation, no sport of nature or monstrous birth without a counterpart in its time. The case is just the reverse. No less than Lilburne, Milton, and Harrington, Hobbes is a man of the English revolution and the age it ushered in.[1] The proclamation of natural right expressed the European consciousness as it emerged, at last, from feudalism and became bourgeois, anti-clerical, and revolutionary.[2] For a century and a half, and more, natural right was to be one of the great watchwords inspiring men to recreate society in a new image. It is by this theme that Hobbes is joined to the revolution with which, at first sight, he may seem to have so little in common. A proponent of absolutism, his doctrine, none the less, is an equalizing one. It enforces, as his utilitarian defender, Grote, pointed out, 'a like claim on the part of every subject to partake in the common benefit'.[3] Even his occasional remarks on economic subjects carry the distinct flavour of the order for which the revolution won full freedom of operation. We observe this in his praise of thrift and labour, in his suggestion that the surplus poor be transported to colonies, and in his advocacy of laws for the encouragement of manufactures, agriculture, fishing, and merchant shipping.[4]

Running back beyond Hobbes's synthesis of ideas is a tradition of social thought that is very ancient, always taxed with unorthodoxy or tainted with heresy, and ever the view of a sceptical minority. It is the tradition which is based on the avowed or implicit denial that there exists any cosmic support for ethical judgements and the good life. At its beginning stand the Greek sophists, rejecting the notion that the state exists by nature; and after them, Epicurus, showing how justice is but the result of a compact of men to refrain from hurting one another; then Carneades, the famous opponent of the Stoics, affirming that God could not have given one identical law to all men; later still, Epicurus's great disciple, the poet, Lucretius, who depicts men as the creators of their civilization and morality from savage and animal origins; and not so far from Hobbes's own time, the excommunicated, anti-papal nominalist, Marsilio of Padua, pronouncing that command is the criterion of law.[5]

---

[1] I think, however, that Lips is wrong in ascribing to Hobbes a special sympathy for the revolutionary government (J. Lips, *Die Stellung des Thomas Hobbes zu den politischen Parteien der grossen englischen Revolution*, Leipzig, 1927).

[2] Cf. B. Croce, *The philosophy of Giambattista Vico*, trans. R. G. Collingwood, London, 1913, 75–6, and G. De Ruggiero, *The history of European liberalism*, trans. R. G. Collingwood, Oxford, 1927, 24.

[3] G. Grote, *op. cit.*, 64.

[4] *De cive, E.W.*, II, 166–7; *Leviathan*, 267.

[5] For the sophists, see, of course, Plato's *Dialogues, passim*; on Epicurus: the fragments cited in C. Bailey, *The Greek atomists and Epicurus*, Oxford, 1928, 511–12;

With Hobbes, this tradition reaches its fruition, and then issues forth to form a powerful constituent in the thought of the age that is coming into being. Nowhere more clearly than in his writings is there incorporated the reorientation of values which the seventeenth century was hastening on. We see this, at the very outset, when he takes it for granted that death is the worst of evils. How far a remove from this to the vanished Christian hope in a world to come! Only when the life of man in the natural order is assigned supreme and exclusive value can it be imagined that death is the thing most to be avoided. We see it also in the negation of every form of transcendancy. The orthodox status of natural law is set aside, the possibility of divine knowledge denied, and there remains only the autonomous human being, finding the norms of social life alone. Then, too, the political order is deprived of its sacrosanct character. It ceases to be the repository of that divine charisma which St. Paul impressed upon Christians in his admonition that 'the powers that be are ordained of God'. A cold-eyed disenchantment takes the place of the religious awe with which rulers were wont to be regarded. Now the state is man's creation, and its sole justification is its utility. When a state is unable to fulfill man's needs, it has lost its only *raison d'être*. This reorientation of values is expressed, lastly, in Hobbes's conception of society. Social life is exhibited as composed of individuals separate from one another as Epicurus's atoms, pursuing their private and personal ends. Society is not an organism; it is a mathematical aggregate exactly equal to the sum of its parts. It is assumed that self-interest is the spring of behaviour, and that altruism is a concealed and illusionary form of egoism. But it is also assumed that the human atoms, so far as they pursue their egoistic ends rationally, will spell out a social good.

So we see that the rationalizations and the tone of life, as they were to be for many a long year, are palpably present in Hobbes's outlook. The poet, Abraham Cowley, spoke truth when he called him the 'great Columbus of the golden lands of new philosophies'.[1] Hobbes is one of the heroes of thought, dauntless in the task of reconstruction, as the last renderings of the political philosophy of the medieval world lost their power to command assent.

on Carneades: Cicero, *De re publica*, III, xi; on Lucretius: the great account of human origins in *De rerum natura*, Book V; on Marsilio: the texts cited in G. de Lagarde, *La naissance de l'esprit laïque au déclin du moyen age*: II, *Marsile de Padoue*, Saint-Paul-Trois-Chateaux, 1934, Ch. X, part II; the parallels between Marsilio and Hobbes are striking and deserve investigation.

[1] 'To Mr. Hobbes.'

XIV

THE ROYALISTS
AND SIR ROBERT FILMER

ALTHOUGH much has been written about the importance in the seventeenth century of the theory of the divine right of kings, I cannot find that it played a conspicuous role in the doctrines advanced by English royalist writers either before or during the revolutionary decades. According to Dr. Figgis, the divine-right theory of royal power meant not only that monarchy is ordained by God, that its hereditary right is indefeasible, and that, by the law of God, it may not be resisted; entailed as well was the view that kings are legally unlimited and that positive law is solely the product of their will.[1] Now this last article was upheld by scarcely any royalist theorist. Before 1640, we may find much fulsome rhetoric in adulation of kingship, and much talk of nonresistance: the well-known sermons of Roger Manwaring are an example.[2] But James I seems to have been the only writer to state unequivocally that the king alone, and without the consent of Parliament, can make law.[3] This claim, however, was advanced by James in a purely speculative manner, and he never urged it, and even repudiated it, in his dealings with his Parliaments.[4] After 1640, the same position was maintained by but a single royalist thinker, Sir Robert Filmer. In doing so, moreover, Filmer placed himself well outside the main body of royalist publicists. For the latter, while they certainly agreed that the king was, in some sense, above positive law, were also clear that he could not make law without the concurrence of his Parliament. Indeed,

---

[1] J. N. Figgis, *op. cit.*, 5–6.

[2] *Religion and allegiance*, 1627.

[3] *The trew law of free monarchies*, 1598, *The political works of James I*, ed. C. H. McIlwain, Cambridge, 1918, 62. Miss Judson suggests that the clergyman, William Dickinson, in a sermon entitled *The kings right*, 1619, also ascribed law-making power to the king (*op. cit.*, 213–14). From her citations, however, I am not sure that this is what Dickinson meant.

[4] *A speach to the lords and commons of the Parliament at Whitehall, Political works*; cf. J. W. Allen, *English political thought*, 5–6.

it was just this which appeared to some of them the chief advantage and special glory of the English monarchy.

If the majority of royalist writers had asserted that the king could make law of his sole will, or that the privileges of Parliament were merely a concession which the king could at any time revoke, they would have been unequivocally adopting the doctrine of sovereignty. But they made no such assertion, and we must be careful to read them accurately on this point. They may say that there must be some power above law in every government and that, in a monarchy, such a supremacy is the king's. They may even characterize the king as absolute. But almost always they go on to explain that in England, the king's supremacy or his absoluteness does not exclude the right of Parliament to share in the making of law. On this subject, the statement drawn up by Charles I's advisers in reply to Parliament's Nineteen Propositions (1642), is characteristic. 'Nothing . . . is more (indeed) proper for the High Court of Parliament,' wrote Culpepper and Falkland, 'then the making of Laws, which not only ought there to be transacted, but can be transacted nowhere else. . . .'[1]

In thus denying that the royalists were claiming for the king a power to make law, I do not mean to overlook the aggressive measures taken by Charles I and his ministers before 1640. It is necessary, however, to understand clearly what these measures amounted to. No doubt, the Laudian attempt to suppress Puritanism and impose a strict religious uniformity was disturbing to Commons. No doubt, too, the king's endeavour after 1629 to rule without summoning Parliament, and his exaction of forced loans and ship-money, aroused justifiable anxiety. But these, and much else which Charles undertook to do, had their basis in the legal position of the crown and were no more than his Tudor predecessors had done before him. Supremacy over the Church had been vested in the crown ever since the Reformation. It had always lain with the king whether or not to summon Parliament. Moreover, the ship-money case is significant as showing that the judges were not upholding an unlimited power on the king's part to impose what taxes he pleased without Parliamentary consent. Such a power was expressly denied.[2] What was held lawful was the king's power to exact an extraordinary tax for purposes of national defence when, in his judgement,

[1] J. Rushworth, *op. cit.*, V, 729. It is Clarendon who tells us that Culpepper and Falkland drafted the king's answer (*The life of Edward earl of Clarendon . . . by himself*, Oxford, 1847, 953; this edition of the *Life* is bound together and paginated continuously with the *History*, Oxford, 1843). Clarendon took exception to the statement because it went on to speak of the king as one of the estates of the realm rather than as above them all (*Life*, 953; cf. B. H. G. Wormald, *op. cit.*, 12), but he agreed, of course, that the king made law with the consent of the Houses.

[2] See the argument of Justice Berkley in *State trials*, ed. T. B. Howell, 21 vols., London, 1816, III, 1090.

the kingdom was in danger.[1] The obvious reply, of course, is that the kingdom was not in danger. But this, as we shall see, was a question which, under the king's prerogative, he alone had, legally, power to decide.

Was there, then, no real danger of a royal despotism in the decade before the Long Parliament met? The answer, I think, is that there was. But such a danger lay in prospect not because the crown was claiming new powers, but because the existing constitution had ceased to correspond to reality. After its long apprenticeship during the sixteenth and early seventeenth centuries, Parliament, and Commons especially, had achieved maturity,[2] and could no longer be expected to remain in its traditional subordination to the king. It was absurd that the royal prerogative should enable the king to disregard Parliament's will, exclude the Houses from considering crucial questions of policy, and carry out measures which they opposed. Despite all the limitations which that age placed upon the franchise, Commons was representative in a sense that the crown was not. Together with the Lords, it spoke for the bulk of the economically dominant class in the country. That the king should act against Parliament's wishes, that he should summon and dismiss Parliament as he willed—this was despotic. Inevitably, Charles's effort to rule without Parliament and to raise extra-Parliamentary forms of revenue called forth alarm and opposition. It seems probable that the king's continued enforcement of policies which Parliament condemned would only have led to further repression and, eventually, even to the virtual nullification of those rights and privileges which Parliament had come to possess.

In 1640, however, matters had not gone nearly so far as this, and the issue was not the survival of Parliament. Nor was it a theory of monarchy which ascribed legally unlimited power to the king. It was whether supremacy in the determination of public policy should remain where, legally and traditionally, it had always been, in the king.[3] Already before 1640, by its encroachments on the king's powers, Parliament had been threatening this supremacy. Now the effect of the Long Parliament's demands was to deprive the king of it altogether. Nothing less than a declaration of Parliamentary sovereignty is embodied in the resolution which the Houses passed in March 1642, 'That when the Lords and Commons in Parliament . . . shall declare what the Law of the Land is, to have this not only questioned and controverted, but contradicted, and

---

[1] Cf., e.g., *ibid.*, III, 1096–7, and see the remarks of J. W. Allen, *English political thought*, 18–19.

[2] Cf. W. Notestein, *The winning of the initiative by the House of Commons, Proceedings of the British Academy*, XI, 1925, and J. E. Neale, *The Elizabethan House of Commons*, London, 1949.

[3] Cf. J. W. Allen, *English political thought*, 375–6.

a Command that it should not be obeyed, is a high Breach of the Privilege of Parliament'.[1] And in this same month, by their ordinance on the militia, the Houses did actually and unconstitutionally assume legislative power to themselves.[2]

Under these circumstances, the standpoint which the royalist writers took up was a defensive one. Not by the utterance of new claims, but by the reaffirmation of the king's legal position in England—this was how they met the innovative measures of the Long Parliament. There is, accordingly, little that is new in royalist doctrine after 1640.[3] Right through the previous decades, in reply to the growing attempts at resistance of the exercise of the king's supremacy, the details of the royalist position had been elaborated. Now these were marshalled and restated to comprise the royalist argument in the controversy that broke forth after the Long Parliament's assembling. There were a few able writers who performed this task, notably Dudley Digges and Henry Ferne, both of whom have already been mentioned in another connection.[4] But neither of these, even, was of much significance, and the only thinker of real importance to appear on the royalist side was Sir Robert Filmer.

We can proceed more easily to grasp the peculiarities of Filmer's position if, by way of comparison, we first note more fully than we have done so far the character of the ordinary royalist argument both before and during the revolution. This argument was, as I have suggested, in the main legal, not philosophical; that is to say, its ground was more a conception of the king's position in England than a philosophical theory of kingship or the state. Prior to 1640, its clearest formulation, probably, was in the opinions advanced by the law-officers when upholding the king's right to do some particular act whose exercise had been legally questioned. The notions that were there expressed formed the core of the royalist standpoint, being far more characteristic of the latter than were the ornate utterances of such clerical ideologues as Roger Manwaring.[5] Between these notions and the views put forth in

---

[1] *Lords journals*, IV, 450; cf. also Parliament's declaration of 29th May 1642 (J. Rushworth, *op. cit.*, V, 551–2), which Professor McIlwain calls a formal assertion of sovereignty (*The high court of Parliament and its supremacy*, New Haven, 1910, 352).

[2] C. H. Firth has pointed out that the first ordinance of the Houses was passed in August 1641, but that, though unconstitutional, it attracted little attention because of its unimportant subject-matter. It was the militia ordinance, passed 5th March 1642, which precipitated the issue of how Parliament could legislate without the king (*Acts and ordinances of the Interregnum*, ed. C. H. Firth and R. S. Rait, 3 vols., London, 1911, III, xiii–xv).

[3] Cf. F. D. Wormuth, *The royal prerogative 1603–1649*, Ithaca, 1939, 119.

[4] See above, 73–74.

[5] Cf. K. Feiling, *A history of the Tory party 1640–1714*, Oxford, 1924, 31–2.

the writings of the royalist critics of the Long Parliament, the continuity, as already observed, was marked.

In the ordinary royalist argument, the principal conception was that of the king's prerogative. Prerogative signified various things: the king's special privileges in the common-law courts, his particular rights as chief feudal lord, and his rights as head of the state.[1] Only the last category concerns us here. As head of the state, the king legally controlled provinces of government in which he had sole decision, exercising his powers therein by his own authority simply.[2] Though these provinces did not extend to the making of law, they did encompass such matters as the control of foreign policy, the making of war and peace, pardoning of felons, supremacy over the Church, and exercise of jurisdiction in various conciliar courts like the Star Chamber. They also included an undefined right to do whatever seemed necessary for the general welfare. Some of the powers in the prerogative had belonged to the crown anciently, others had been annexed during the sixteenth century when the Tudors established their strong monarchy on the ruins of the feudal nobility and took jurisdiction over the Church by throwing off the papal supremacy. It was the king's right to control these several areas of government that gave substance to his position as head of the state. It was in respect of their 'high prerogatives', as Sir Roger Twysden observed, that '. . . kings with us have ever beene . . . justly named monarchs'.[3]

Now when the royal law-officers spoke of these powers that fell within the king's prerogative, they frequently characterized them as absolute. Particularly the king's power to act in the general welfare was called absolute. As this idea occurs in each of the three great constitutional cases that arose between 1603 and 1640, we can form a tolerably clear idea of what was meant by it.[4] By the king's absolute power, the law-officers of the crown intended to indicate that, when exercising his right as head of the state, and especially his right to do what was needful for the general welfare, the king was not bound by law. The judges, it must be observed, took care to segregate the sphere of the king's absolute from that of his ordinary power. Thus in Bate's case (1606), Chief Baron Fleming pointed out that in questions pertaining to the disposi-

---

[1] I have taken this classification from Miss Judson, *op. cit.*, 23.

[2] Cf. J. R. Tanner, *Constitutional documents of the reign of James I*, Cambridge, 1930, 5.

[3] *Certaine considerations upon the government of England*, ed. J. M. Kemble, *Camden society*, London, 1849, 21. Twysden's remark on p. 94 shows that his work was written some time after 1648.

[4] Bate's case, 1606: *State trials*, II, 389 (Chief Baron Fleming), *ibid.*, II, 383, 384 (Baron Clarke); the five knights' case, 1627: *State trials*, III, 37 (Attorney-general Heath); the ship-money case, 1637: *State trials*, III, 1083–4 (Justice Crawley), *ibid.*, III, 1098–9 (Justice Berkley).

tion of private property, the king was always bound by law as administered in the common-law courts.[1] But just because the king was supreme, there had to be a realm, it was held, in which his supremacy could be freely exercised. This was the realm of his absolute power, and here he was not tied to law.

What the ordinary royalist position at most asserted, therefore, was not that the king could make law, but that, being supreme, he could, in certain matters, break law. Thus, in 1627, in the five knights' case, the attorney-general, after expressly denying that the king may do whatever he pleases, went on to argue that, as head of the commonwealth and by his *'absoluta potestas'*, the king may, for the commonwealth's good, imprison without showing cause.[2] Similarly, in the ship-money case, the judges upheld the right of the king, as part of his supremacy, to exact a tax for national defence in time of danger without consent of Parliament.[3] If the king may not determine questions of *salus reipublicae*, said Justice Berkley, then 'I do not understand how [he] may be said to have the majestical right and power of a free monarch'.[4]

Of course, the royal law-officers asserted that the king always used his absolute power for the common good.[5] Yet this is just what Parliament had come to deny. The leaders of Commons were increasingly doubtful that the king was employing his position in the general interest, and they feared lest the doctrine of prerogative be made the cover for measures which would render Parliament superfluous altogether; hence Parliament's growing encroachments on the prerogative and the objections as to the legality of its exercise. In this situation of sharpening disagreement, the royalist argument was in an embarrassed condition, for while it insisted on the king's supremacy, it did not ascribe to the king a power of making law. How could the king be supreme when legislation, the highest act of sovereignty, was not in his sole will? In the sixteenth century, this question had not yet arisen. Parliament was then still widely conceived of in its medieval sense as a judicial body declaring law, rather than in its modern sense as a legislative body making law.[6] Moreover, the supremacy of the Tudors did not need to encompass the legislative power to be effective. The interests of Parliament were, on the whole, those of the crown, and it usually did the monarch's bidding willingly. With an extensive prerogative and an obedient Parliament, Henry VIII and Elizabeth exercised a supremacy which was real enough. By the early seventeenth century, all this was changed. Now that the

[1] *State trials*, II, 389.
[2] *Ibid.*, III, 37, 44–5.
[3] *Ibid.*, III, 1086–7, 1096–7.
[4] *Ibid.*, III, 1099.
[5] Cf., e.g., *ibid.*, III, 45–6.
[6] On this whole subject, see the well-known work of Professor McIlwain, *op. cit.*

interests of the crown and the classes represented in Parliament had diverged, the king's supremacy became a problematical thing. In the face of Parliamentary encroachments on his position, his prerogative could not assure his supremacy unless it encompassed the power to make law. This, however, was a claim which the legal doctrine of the royalists made it impossible to advance on the king's behalf.

Thus the royalist argument after 1640 was imprisoned in a cul-de-sac. It asserted that the king was supreme and that Parliament had, therefore, no legal right to rebel against him. But it would not recognize that, since Parliament opposed the king, the latter's supremacy, his right to determine public policy, were of no avail, indeed, were meaningless, without legislative power. The royalists were certainly on sound ground when they met Parliament's innovations of 1642 by the denial that the Houses could make law without the king's personal assent.[1] But their position was clearly untenable when they insisted on a royal supremacy which, they yet acknowledged, could not legislate. Such an argument might be adequate to refute the newly hatched claim of the Houses; it was quite insufficient to maintain the king's position in the circumstance of fundamental disagreement in the state.

Throughout the revolution the royalists failed to resolve this contradiction. So, for example, we find both Dudley Digges and Henry Ferne distinguishing the area of the king's absolute power from that in which he is limited by law and required to act with consent of Parliament.[2] Much the same conception was expressed by the great Anglican casuist, Robert Sanderson, in his Oxford lectures on conscience (1646), mentioned in an earlier chapter.[3] Sanderson recognized, as Digges and Ferne did not,[4] that law-making is the principal act of sovereignty, and he expressly declared that the king, as supreme, alone has the right of legislation. But what this means, he explained, is that no bill or order of the Houses may become law unless established by the royal assent and authority. He then went on inconsistently to deny that the king's acts can oblige to obedience without the consent of Parliament.[5] How, then, could the king be said to have legislative power? Clearly, Sanderson, despite his terminology, was still thinking in the traditional royalist manner of a king really supreme but not making law. And such, too, is

---

[1] Cf. the king's reply of 26th March 1642 concerning the militia ordinance: '. . . we are extreamly unsatisfied what an ordinance is; but well satisfied, that without our consent it is nothing, not binding . . . . we must declare to all the World, that we are not satisfied with, nor shall ever allow our Subjects to be bound by your printed Votes . . . or that under pretence of declaring what the Law of the Land is, you shall without us make a new Law . . .' (J. Rushworth, *op. cit.*, V, 540).

[2] D. Digges, *op. cit.*, 64, 118; H. Ferne, *Conscience satisfied*, 1643, 13–21.

[3] See above, 74.

[4] Cf. M. Judson, *op. cit.*, 392.

[5] *Lectures on conscience and human law*, the seventh prelection, *passim*.

the notion of other royalist writers. Peter Heylyn, Laud's former chaplain, on the authority of Bodin, calls the king of England an absolute monarch. Yet in listing the king's powers, he says nothing of law-making, and speaks only of interpreting and dispensing from law. He admits, also, that the Lords and Commons possess the right to assent to legislation.[1] Robert Sheringham, a fellow of Gonville and Caius College, Cambridge, likewise describes the king as absolute, but observes that in many cases the king may only act with the concurrence of the Houses.[2] This, there seems little doubt, was the common royalist understanding of the king's position.[3]

As Sir Robert Filmer alone seems to have broken clearly and conclusively with this point of view, we have in this fact one reason for his importance. About fifty-two years of age when the Long Parliament assembled, Filmer had doubtless been stimulated by the ship-money case and other constitutional controversies to think through the issues involved in the claims of the crown. These issues were also discussed, it is likely, in the cultivated circle of Kentish gentlemen of which he was a member and which included some personalities of wide reading and real intellectual distinction.[4] How isolated he must have been in his opinions, however, is shown by the fact that they were not even shared by his closest friends, the antiquarian, Sir Roger Twysden, and the high-churchman, Peter Heylyn, both royalists.[5] Under the influence chiefly, it would appear, of Bodin,[6] Filmer was led to accept the doctrine of sovereignty and to see in the king of England an absolute monarch whose will makes law. This is the conception which he expressed first in *Patriarcha*, his earliest political writing, composed no later than 1642,[7] though not published until 1680, and thereafter in all his other works until his death in 1653.

For purposes of analysis, Filmer's ideas fall rather easily into three

[1] *The stumbling-block of disobedience*, 1658, 233, 253, 267–74. This is signed only with the initials, P. H., but is ascribed to Heylyn by Wood, *Athenae Oxonienses*, III, 562.

[2] *The kings supremacy asserted*, 1660, 21, 34, 73.

[3] For other instances, cf. John Digby, earl of Bristol, *An apologie*, 1647, Robert Grose, *Royalty and loyalty*, 1647, Edward Bagshaw, *The rights of the crown of England*, 1660.

[4] For these and other details of Filmer's life mentioned in this paragraph, see P. Laslett, 'Sir Robert Filmer: the man versus the Whig myth', *The William and Mary quarterly*, 3rd series, V, 4, and the same writer's introduction to Filmer's *Works*.

[5] For Heylyn, see the preceding page. Twysden's views are contained in his *Certaine considerations upon the government of England*, written some time after 1648 and first published by the Camden Society in 1849.

[6] Filmer refers to Bodin as 'the great modern politician' (*The anarchy of a limited ... monarchy*, 1648, *Works*, 304). He published a selection from Bodin's *De republica* under the title, *The necessity of the absolute power of all kings: and in particular of the king of England*, 1648, reprinted in his *Works*.

[7] *Patriarcha, Works*, 95.

categories: first, his conception of the king's position; second, his criticism of the doctrine of popular sovereignty; third, his patriarchal theory of the state. We may proceed with these in order.

On the matter of the king's position, Filmer was unequivocal. He accepted as axiomatic the theory which defines law as a command of the sovereign power.[1] Law is will, he pointed out, and signified his agreement with Hobbes's version of the attributes which pertain to sovereignty.[2] It followed, therefore, that in a government which is properly called monarchy, the will of the king alone makes law.[3] Filmer was at great pains to emphasize this point. Against both his fellow-royalist, Henry Ferne, and the Parliamentarian writer, Philip Hunton, he denied that there could be any such thing as a limited monarchy.[4] If the king is really supreme, he asked, how can he be limited by law? It is a mere contradiction to speak of a supremacy which is limited. Either the king possesses legislative power or he is no king at all.[5]

All this might serve well as a commentary on the meaning of political supremacy; it did not, however, throw much light on the actual position of the king of England. Did the king of England, in fact, make law? This, the location of legislative power, Filmer saw, was really the constitutional issue which was at stake in the revolution.[6] His answer was in the affirmative, and, by citing precedents, he sought to prove this in *The Freeholder's Grand Inquest* (1648), his sole writing devoted exclusively to the English constitution. He was not, I think, very happy in this enterprise, for his contention that the king legislated without consent of the estates of the realm ran counter to history. Perhaps he had been misled by Bodin's view of the English monarchy.[7] He would have been on firmer ground if, like Hobbes, he had spoken of what the king (and in Hobbes's opinion, any sovereign power) ought logically to have the right to do, rather than of what the king had, in fact, done. As proof of his belief that the English king made law, Filmer pointed out that statutes were cast in the form of royal commands.[8] But in explaining statutes, he expressed their character by the formula, 'the King ordains,

---

[1] *Ibid., Works*, 106.

[2] *Observations upon Aristotles politiques*, 1652, *Works*, 228; *Observations concerning the originall of government*, 1652, *Works*, 239.

[3] *Patriarcha, Works*, 93.

[4] *Anarchy, Works*, 279. Hunton was the author of a capable Parliamentarian work, *A treatise of monarchy*, 1643.

[5] *Anarchy, Works*, 281–3, 284.

[6] *The freeholder's grand inquest*, 1648, *Works*, 158. This composition has been commonly attributed to Sir Robert Holborne, but Mr. Laslett has shown that it is Filmer's (*Works*, 128).

[7] Cf. Bodin's remarks in the extracts from his *De republica* which Filmer printed under the title, *The necessity of the absolute power of all kings*, *Works*, 319–20.

[8] *The freeholder's grand inquest*, *Works*, 158–61.

the Lords advise, the Commons consent'.[1] What did he think this consent signified? This is a question which he ignored, though it is the crux of the whole subject. Yet if the consent of the Commons was really required, then it is impossible to understand how the king could ordain without it.

When we turn to Filmer's criticism of the doctrine of popular sovereignty, we see him at his keenest. Like almost every other political thinker of the time, he was much concerned to provide government with some durable moral foundation, and it seemed to him that no such foundation could possibly exist were the belief, so widespread in the later 1640s, really true that men are born free and that a lawful government is one only to which they voluntarily consent to subject themselves. Against this belief Filmer directed a variety of arguments which enabled him to show quite easily that it was open to every sort of objection. He pointed out that there is no proof that all the people of the world had ever assembled at some time in the past in order to consent to government. Nor is there proof that a majority had ever done so. If a majority had thus assembled, it could not have consented for those who were absent without robbing the latter of their natural freedom. Indeed, majority-rule and representative government at any time are nothing but thin legal fictions which absolutely contradict the supposition of a natural freedom in every man. On such a supposition there can be no rightful subjection at all. Parents would have no right to command their children nor masters their servants. The various kingdoms and other political divisions in the world would be illicit, for they do not exist by nature and they were certainly not created by popular consent. Moreover, men could withdraw obedience whenever they pleased, any petty company, any family, might establish its own kingdom, and no generation would be bound by the political order under which its predecessors lived.[2] Let it but be imagined, Filmer said, 'that the people were ever but once free from subjection by nature, and it will prove a mere impossibility ever lawfully to introduce any kind of government whatsoever, without apparent wrong to a multitude of people'.[3]

As far as they went, these criticisms were unanswerable. The social contract was a myth: the contract had never been made, it never could have been made. There never was a government in the world that rested on the universal consent of its subjects; to say so was a clear distortion of the facts. But these and Filmer's other arguments really miss the point of the doctrine of popular sovereignty. For the latter's significance, as we can see in retrospect, did not lie in its unhistorical notions con-

[1] *Ibid., Works,* 158.
[2] *Patriarcha, Works,* 81–2; *Observations upon Aristotles politiques, Works,* 223–5; *Anarchy, Works,* 285–7; *Directions for obedience,* 1652, *Works,* 231.
[3] *Anarchy, Works,* 287.

cerning the origin of government. In reality, the doctrine was not a rendering of the past at all; it was a call for the reshaping of the future. By invoking a natural and pristine freedom, it was enabled to cast aside all the accretions of history, all inherited ranks and chartered privileges, all thrones and altars, and to appeal to a higher standard than these: the appeal was now to man and to what man could claim in virtue of his mere humanity. If the existing order could not provide the measure of freedom which man, simply as man, had the right to demand, then a new order must be created to do so. Thus the myth of a natural freedom propelled society forward, opening the way to the more democratic polities which resulted from the European revolutions of the seventeenth and eighteenth centuries.

Filmer, of course, could not have known anything of this, and to him popular sovereignty was only a principle of anarchy destructively at work in social life. The political order, he held, needed a firmer basis upon which to rest than the fancy of a subjection which might be withdrawn whenever men had a mind to do so. It required a doctrine of obligation which would be both morally irreproachable and historically in accord with the facts. As fulfilling these qualifications, he advanced his patriarchal theory of the state, the idea by which he is best known and which we must note as the final aspect of his political thought.

The patriarchal theory represented Filmer's effort to derive all political obligation from the obedience which children owe their parents and, ultimately, from the obedience which the descendants of Adam owed the latter as their father and first ancestor. Like the doctrine of popular sovereignty, the patriarchal theory also sought to gain the sanction of nature for its assertions.[1] In this effort, however, it had a decided advantage over its rival, for to the seventeenth-century mind, nothing could seem more natural than the extensive control which the father exercised, both by law and custom, over his wife and children and over his household of dependents and servants. Paternal authority being the natural thing, how, in the face of this fact, could it be said that men are born free? The truth is just the reverse: men are born in subjection to their fathers.

This was the circumstance to which Filmer could point and which he insisted had always been the case. For proof, he referred his readers to Scripture, which was not only the most sacred of books, but also, as he was at pains to emphasize, the most ancient.[2] It is, he declared, because people foolishly take their information from the heathen Greek and Roman writers rather than from Scripture, that they have succumbed to the error that men are born free.[3] Scripture, however, tells a different

---

[1] Cf. J. N. Figgis, *op. cit.*, 149.
[2] *Observations upon Aristotles politiques, Works*, 187.
[3] *Ibid.*, 188, 203–4; *Anarchy, Works*, 278.

story. It tells how God created Adam as the first man and gave him entire dominion over all creatures. Adam, therefore, was a monarch, and the first government in the world was monarchical. The whole basis of obedience to superiors is contained, accordingly, in God's commandment, 'Honour thy father'. Thus from the very beginning, men have been tied in subjection to their fathers, and monarchy, as the specific form of paternal power ordained by God, alone possesses divine right.[1]

With these conceptions as premises, Filmer went on to contend that the right of Adam, the first king and father, can only be exercised by kings, and that all monarchs are to be regarded either as heirs of Adam or as usurpers of such heirs, but, in any case, as exercising the paternal power originally established by God.[2] His reasoning was fanciful, and his conclusions far-fetched, to say the least. It required a fine stretch of the imagination to assume a link between Adam I and Charles I. All the same, with this argument, Filmer achieved his object. He vindicated monarchy and gave government a moral basis by connecting it directly with the unlimited power conferred by God upon Adam.[3] Granted such a connection, resistance to kings must always be sin, for to resist them is to resist God's commandment of obedience to fathers.

Such, in brief, was Filmer's patriarchal theory. It was the most ambitious effort by any royalist writer in this period to evolve a theory of the state and to invest monarchy with the sanction of religion and nature alike. It was also the only royalist conception which deserves, in any strict sense, to be called a theory of the divine right of kings. As an argument against the right of the living rashly to alter the political order inherited from the dead, Filmer's patriarchalism inevitably suggests a comparison with the thought of Edmund Burke. Though Burke was far Filmer's superior as a thinker, the two men have more than a little in common. Both exalted prescription and tradition, and warned against the innovating temper which sought to disrupt historical continuity in the name of natural rights. Both emphasized the importance of unreasoning sentiment and natural loyalty as the chief ties keeping men in obedience to superiors and the social order together. Filmer's *Patriarcha* and Burke's *Reflections on the Revolution in France* (1790) were, each in its own way, admonitions that the accumulated wisdom of generations is preferable to the inconsiderate counsels of one day. And finally, both Filmer and Burke, it is just to add, were decidedly obscurantist when they invoked the past as a bar against the struggle of the living to realize new possibilities latent in social life. Filmer's history, with its tale of Adam's absolute monarchy and of kings as Adam's heirs, is a piece of

---

[1] *Anarchy, Works*, 289; cf. *Patriarcha, Works*, 57; *Observations upon Aristotles politiques, Works*, 187.

[2] *Anarchy, Works*, 288–9.

[3] Cf. J. W. Allen, 'Sir Robert Filmer' in *loc cit.*, 45.

mystification; it is just as much of a myth as the social contract, and even more far-fetched; while Burke, with his exaltation of the state as 'the mysterious incorporation of the human race', and his celebration of 'eternal society, linking the lower with the higher natures, connecting the visible and the invisible world'[1], only imposes an occult entity upon his readers which evokes awe at the same time as it defies analysis. The social-contract theory, at least, suffered from none of these faults. It brought the state and society into the clear light of day for study and examination; it understood, even if but dimly and in a highly simplified way, what Filmer and, with less justification, Burke did not: that society is at every point the work of man, and that institutions at any time are a human creation, existing for human purposes, and to be altered in accordance with human intention.

Important as Filmer was among royalist writers, his work attracted little attention in his own time, and he became famous only after he had been dead thirty years. With the publication of *Patriarcha* in 1680 as a royalist weapon in new controversies, he acquired a posthumous renown that grew even greater when he was singled out for attack in the first of Locke's essays on civil government. But by this time, so far as political philosophy is concerned, the royalist cause had been lost. It had been lost in the years between 1640 and 1660, and no amount of talk later could nullify this defeat. It is an interesting fact that by 1648, when Filmer's first political writings began to appear, the quantity of royalist literature had markedly decreased; in the 1650s, it was a mere trickle. This is a testimony to the weakness which overtook the royalist cause. The king had been vanquished in the civil war, and the claims made on his behalf by the royalists had become dead issues compared with the new questions that were interesting political thinkers. Alongside the important writings of the Levellers, Winstanley, Hobbes, and the republicans, royalist doctrine was trivial. By the end of the 1640s belief in non-resistance had been fatally undermined and monarchy deprived of its aura. All the doctrines which were anathema in the royalist creed had come into wide acceptance. Popular sovereignty, as Filmer himself conceded, was regarded as an axiom in politics.[2]

Thus royalism, it seems not unfair to say, had ceased to be of much importance as a theoretical force. In 1660, the king was restored as a result of the divisions on the revolutionary side, not because of the strength of royalist beliefs. The Presbyterians, who were the most influential agents in bringing about the recall of Charles II, were themselves exponents of the very ideas attacked by the royalist writers in the early 1640s. Despite the restoration, therefore, it is not a mistake, I think, to regard the revolutionaries as the victors and the royalists as the

[1] *Reflections on the revolution in France*, Oxford, 1878, 39, 114.
[2] *Observations upon Aristotles politiques, Works*, 226.

vanquished. This is true not only because much of the important work of the Long Parliament—the abolition of the king's conciliar jurisdiction and the rest—survived, not to be undone after 1660. It is true also, and above all, because the ideas of the revolution triumphantly lived on, working with undiminished force, subverting the old order in Europe. They were the basis of English Whiggism and the revolution of 1688; transmitted to later generations, they helped to inspire the great struggles in France and other countries against the *ancien régime*; they are written imperishably into the document in which the American colonies declared their independence. They live yet, a weapon in the hands of all who strive to-day for a freedom commensurate with the promise and the possibilities of the second half of the twentieth century.

INDEX

Adams, John, 125
Aeschylus, 174
Agrarian law, proposed by John Lilburne, 18; by the author of *Tyranipocrit*, 60; by James Harrington, 138–9; by William Sprigge, 156; by the author of *Chaos*, 157; opposed by Cicero, Livy, Machiavelli, 139
An agreement of the free people of England (1649), 36
An agreement of the people (1647), 36
Agreement of the people, circumstances of its origin, 13; what it was, 13–14; conception of influenced by John Lilburne, 14–16; intended as a social contract, 14–17; the third *Agreement of the people*, 36–40; called for in 1659, 42
An alarum to the headquarters (1647), 35
Alsted, Johann, 96
Anabaptists of Munster, 57, 97
Andrewes, Lancelot, 73
Aquinas, St. Thomas, 170, 176
Archer, John, 96
Aristotle, 151, 170, 172
The armies duty (1659), 155
Ascham, Anthony, 64–7, 75
Aspinwall, William, 99, 101
Aubrey, John, 166

Bacon, Francis, 3, 54, 166
Bagshaw, Edward, 196
The banner of truth displayed (1656), 98
Baxter, Richard, 143
Bentham, Jeremy, 165
Berkley, Justice, 193, 194
Biddle, John, 158
Bodin, Jean, 182, 196, 197
Boehme, Jacob, 46
Bradshaw, William, 79, 116
Bristol, John Digby, earl of, 196
Browne, Sir Thomas, 4
Buchanan, George, 148
Burke, Edmund, 200–1

Calvin, John, 72, 74
Canne, John, 80, 83, 96, 98
Carneades, 187
Carre, Thomas, 72
Cases: ship-money case, 190, 193, 194; Bate's case, 193–4; five knight's case, 194
Certain quaeres presented by way of petition (1649), 98
Chamberlen, Peter, 99, 100
Chaos (1659), 157
Church-levellers (1649), 26
Cicero, 139
Clarendon, Edward Hyde, earl of, 93, 145, 147, 190
Clarke, Baron, 193
Clarkson, Laurence, 31–2
A commonwealth and commonwealthsmen, asserted (1659), 155
Contract, doctrine of, in Henry Parker, 5; in Samuel Rutherford, 5–6; in John Lilburne, 9; in Richard Overton, 24; in John Milton, 110; in Henry Stubbe, 161; in Thomas Hobbes, 179–80; involved in the *Agreement of the people*, 15–16; invoked by defenders of a right of resistance, Ch. VI, *passim*; influences Sir Henry Vane the younger, 154
Convocation of 1606, 73, 74
Cook, John, 79, 149
Copernicus, Nicolas, 168
Covenant, idea of, 14
Cowley, Abraham, 188
Crawley, Justice, 193
Cromwell, Oliver, and the Levellers, 7, 41; opposes the *Agreement of the people*, 17; and Gerrard Winstanley, 55; his reluctance to break with the monarchy, 62; on the right of resistance, 78, 95; his defence of the protectorate, 88; and Machiavelli, 94; denounced by the Fifth-monarchy men, 98–9; criticizes the Fifth-monarchy

For Product Safety Concerns and Information please contact our EU
representative GPSR@taylorandfrancis.com
Taylor & Francis Verlag GmbH, Kaufingerstraße 24, 80331 München, Germany